GREAT WESTERN RAILWAY OF CANADA

GREAT WESTERN RAILWAY OF CANADA

Southern Ontario's Pioneer Railway

DAVID R.P. GUAY

DUNDURN
TORONTO

Editor: Cheryl Hawley
Design: Laura Boyle
Cover Design: Laura Boyle
Cover Image: Ian Cameron Collection, Elgin County Archives
Printer: Webcom

Library and Archives Canada Cataloguing in Publication

Guay, David R. P., 1954-, author
Great Western Railway of Canada : Southern Ontario's pioneer railway / David R.P. Guay.

Includes bibliographical references and index. Issued in print and electronic formats.

ISBN 978-1-4597-3282-7 (paperback).--ISBN 978-1-4597-3284-1 (pdf).-- ISBN 978-1-4597-3283-4 (epub)

1. Great Western Railway Company (Canada)--History. 2. Railroads-- Ontario--History. I. Title.

HE2810.G74G93 2016 385.09713 C2015-905598-9
C2015-905599-7

1 2 3 4 5 19 18 17 16 15

We acknowledge the support of the **Canada Council for the Arts** and the **Ontario Arts Council** for our publishing program. We also acknowledge the financial support of the **Government of Canada** through the **Canada Book Fund** and **Livres Canada Books**, and the **Government of Ontario** through the **Ontario Book Publishing Tax Credit** and the **Ontario Media Development Corporation**.

Printed and bound in Canada.

VISIT US AT
Dundurn.com | @dundurnpress | Facebook.com/dundurnpress |Pinterest.com/dundurnpress

Dundurn
3 Church Street, Suite 500
Toronto, Ontario, Canada
M5E 1M2

CONTENTS

ACKNOWLEDGEMENTS

The author wishes to thank the following persons/organizations for their assistance in bringing this book to a successful conclusion:

Don McQueen (whose careful review of the manuscript resulted in comments that substantially improved its quality)

Carl Riff (whose meticulous review of contemporary newspapers added significantly to the chapters regarding construction and accidents)

Richard McQuade

Andrew Merrilees (deceased)

Ted Rafuse

OurOntario.ca Community Newspaper Collection

Denis Hoffman

Goad fire insurance maps were kindly provided by:

Theresa Regnier, Archives and Research Collections Centre, University of Western Ontario, London, Ontario

Windsor Community Museum, Windsor, Ontario

Photographs were kindly provided by:

Canadian National Photo Archives (accessed via Marcia Mordfield of the Canada Museum of Science and Technology, Ottawa, Ontario)

Cathy Roy, Niagara Falls Public Library

G.L. Smith

Joan Magee

Joseph P. Day (deceased)

John Speller

Malgasia Myc, Claude T. Stoner Collection, Bentley Historical Library, University of Michigan, Ann Arbor, Michigan

Hamilton Public Library

Dana W. Ashdown

Patricia Lawton, Archives of Ontario, Toronto, Ontario

Great Lakes Marine Collection, Wisconsin Marine Historical Society, Milwaukee Public Library, Milwaukee, Wisconsin

Robert Graham, Historic Ships of the Great Lakes, Bowling Green State University, Bowling Green, Ohio

Marlo Broad, Thunder Bay National Marine Sanctuary Database, Alpena Public Library, Alpena, Michigan

G.W. Hilton

Stanford University Press

Burton Historical Collection, Detroit Public Library

Toronto Public Library

David Rumsey Map Collection

Buffalo Historical Society

Library and Archives Canada, Ottawa, Ontario

Randy Goss, Delaware Public Archive, Dover, Delaware

Loutit District Library Collection, Grand Haven, Michigan

William Cunningham, City Archives, Grand Rapids, Michigan

Southwestern Ontario Digital Archive, University of Windsor, Windsor, Ontario

Clinton Northern Railway, St. Johns, Michigan

Cindy Sinko, Stratford-Perth Archives, Stratford, Ontario

Gina Coady, Elgin County Archives, St. Thomas, Ontario

Karolee Tobey, Grand Rapids Public Library

Christine Riggle, Baker Historical Collection, Harvard Business School, Boston, Massachusetts

The author also wishes to thank David Henderson at Railfare DC books and Cheryl Hawley at Dundurn Press for transforming computer files and a collection of photographs and digital scans into a finished product of which we all can be proud. Dede Johnston, word processor extraordinaire, did a masterful job in preparing the manuscript in its entirety for subsequent production into the finished product, a feat for which I am truly grateful.

In this book, pounds sterling (£) are expressed as British units. Since Canada did not have the dollar as a form of currency until 1858, all dollars are expressed as United States units up to and including the year 1857, while Canadian units are used from the year 1858 and thereafter. Unless otherwise specified, all municipalities associated with the Great Western Railway are in the province of Ontario while those associated with the Detroit and Milwaukee/Detroit, Grand Haven, and Milwaukee railways are in the state of Michigan.

INTRODUCTION

The arrival of the railway as a practical and relatively inexpensive mode of transportation was the nineteenth-century technological equivalent of the computer and the Internet in the last quarter of the twentieth century. However, at least early on, it turned out to be a double-edged sword. The way that people lived and worked, their interactions with the world around them, and their economic base were transformed forever. Although steam transportation on water revolutionized the maritime industry, its effect was not nearly as transforming as that of the railway industry, at least on a national basis. However, the demands of railways placed unforeseen burdens on the rudimentary engineering of the time. Every year demands upon engineering and materials increased, as trains became heavier and faster. This, in turn, quickly exposed the absence of the scientific method in the design and maintenance of structures, roadbed, and equipment and the crudeness of materials. When early trains failed, they often did so in a spectacular fashion. The Great Western Railway of Canada as a pioneer railway had more than its share of spectacular failures. However, the vast majority were caused by a combination of failures of physical plant, as described above, and profound human error by workers and managers alike.

Human behaviour and morality were profoundly different in the Victorian era compared with today. These differences should be understood so that the reader can judge North American railway practices in the 1840s to 1880s using accepted norms of the period. Judging our ancestors using the norms of today is unfair. However, it should be stressed that this should not be used to excuse egregious behaviours, a few of which will be exposed in this book.

THE LANDSCAPE IN VICTORIAN CANADA

Railway promoters who were also parliamentarians were compelled by the politics of the day to at least put on the appearance of great concern for the public welfare while engaged in the very act of seeking to enrich themselves. They would always present themselves as lawmakers having the development of Canadian resources and expansion of the nation's wealth at heart.

To understand the large and important role that legislators assumed as personal beneficiaries in the original promotion of railways, it is only necessary to examine the lists of incorporators of the first railways.

The seventy-six promoters of the London and Gore Railroad Company, chartered in 1834, were headed by Allan N. MacNab and comprised a large contingent of politicians at all levels of government. This line ultimately became the Great Western Railway, the subject of this book, and was headed by MacNab as president. Although an obscure name today, in his time MacNab was a conspicuous individual — member of Parliament for many years, speaker of that body, knighted, becoming the equivalent of prime minister in 1854, and raised to a baronetcy in 1856. His was a commanding presence to be sure. As further evidence of his importance in pre-Confederation Canada, his daughters married into British titled aristocracy.

The Great Western was not unique in this regard. The directorate of the Grand Trunk Railway was a "who's who" of some of Canada's most illustrious individuals. These included John Ross, member and speaker of the Legislative Council, solicitor general of Upper Canada, and stockholder in the Grand Trunk. He became the road's president through the all-powerful influence of the English contractors controlling the stock (Peto, Brassey, Jackson, and Betts) and remained so until 1862. Francis Hincks, Grand Trunk incorporator and promoter, became inspector general (analogous to finance minister), the equivalent of prime minister, and was knighted. In fact, of the nine Canadian directors, four were cabinet ministers and eight of nine were, in truth, nominees of the all-powerful English contractors. Most of these individuals were also stockholders.

Politicians, whether or not they were also railway officials, would not hesitate to use their political clout to assist "their" railways. For example, in 1852 MacNab attempted to press legislation banning all railway competition of the Great Western in southern Ontario west of Toronto. He failed because, by that time, Grand Trunk forces had become dominant in the legislature. Francis Hincks materially assisted the Grand Trunk by shepherding successful passage of the Guarantee Act in 1849 and then, in 1851, modifying the act to limit its application to trunk lines like the Grand Trunk (see chapter 1).

Lines were granted government loans and in some cases paid off neither interest nor principal. Between November 1852 and June 1855 the Canadian government loaned the Great Western a total of £770,000 ($3.75 million U.S.). In 1868–69 Finance Minister Rose accused the Great Western of using $1.225 million in a totally illegal way — to construct a railway in the United States (i.e., the Detroit and Milwaukee Railway). He further asserted that fully $4 million was eventually used to complete the road, build other lines, and run a cross-lake steamship service from Grand Haven, Michigan, to Milwaukee, Wisconsin. In contrast to the Grand Trunk, almost all of the government loans were paid back by the Great Western.

From 1853 through 1858 the Grand Trunk benefitted from the "relief" granted it by the Canadian government as it lay "destitute," to the tune of £3.115 million ($15.17 million U.S.), fourfold that of the Great Western. Relief was in the form of guaranteed provincial (Canada) debentures under the Guarantee Act. Despite this "cash infusion," the financial position of the Grand Trunk worsened and the interest and principal of these loans were forgiven. And, in another half century, the Grand Trunk would again appear before the government asking for "relief"! The only difference would be the amount requested, which would be astronomical.

Even bribery was an accepted method for influencing decisions. Isaac Buchanan, wealthy Hamilton merchant and legislator, assumed control of the Woodstock and Lake Erie Railway (a component of the planned Great Western competitor known as the Great Southern Railway) by issuing a $100,000 bribe to obtain the removal of three opposing directors of the company. Mr. Buchanan then sought to gain control of the other component of the Great Southern (i.e., Amherstburg and St. Thomas Railway) by another $100,000 bribe. At this time, he also approached the Great Western and sought to force it to buy the Great Southern at an exorbitant price. Fortunately, he was caught and a select committee of the legislature investigated the incident. Although it thoroughly castigated Buchanan, other cases of corruption were not exposed in the committee's report despite clear proof being disclosed in the evidence itself and in legislative debates.

In an era rife with bitter competition between individuals and firms for privileges, power, subsidies, and traffic, railway companies had "sturdy representatives in Parliament" (i.e., lobbyists who were politicians) who sought to cripple or destroy their opponents. If one line was felt to be unduly favoured with government loans, grants, subsidies, mail contracts, or favourable legislation, aggrieved parties sounded the battle cry. The same politics were noted at the provincial and municipal government levels. At these two levels, competing companies used every available means, whether honourable or ethical or otherwise, to deny letters of incorporation or grants-in-aid.

The two most bitter foes in the 1850s through 1870s were the Grand Trunk Railway Company of Canada and the Great Western Railway Company of Canada, as will be discussed in chapter 2.

Early organizers of Canadian railways had an astonishing record of extracting money from municipalities in the form of bylaws providing bonuses. From the town of Port Hope (population 3,000), a bonus of $740,000 was obtained. The towns of Niagara, Brockville, and Cobourg, with respective populations of only 2,500; 4,000; and 4,000, were influenced to give corresponding bonuses of $280,000; $400,000; and $500,000. The cities of Ottawa and London, each having a population of below 10,000, were coerced into providing bonuses of $200,000 and $375,000, respectively. Brantford, with a population of not more than 6,000, handed over $500,000. These are just a few examples of small and poor municipalities being corrupted or compelled to mortgage future generations to line the pockets of railway contractors and owners. Even on the smaller scale seen in Canada, the moniker of "robber baron" could readily be applied. However, the railway contractors and owners were not the sole perpetrators of these legal, though unethical, methods. All bylaws involving the granting of municipal bonuses had to be approved ("made legitimate") by the governor-in-council as required under the Railway Loan Act. It is difficult to fathom how a responsible individual could allow municipalities to beggar themselves in the "railway lottery" process. There was even one village allowed by the governor-in-council to provide a bonus to the extent of $300 per town resident!

SAMUEL ZIMMERMAN: "ONE BOLD OPERATOR"

Samuel Zimmerman was a true Canadian enigma. Described as "one bold operator," his occupations included railway contractor, financier, manipulator, showman, philanthropist, and scamp (i.e., scoundrel). He lived life on a grand scale and was able to balance the cut-throat tactics of business and extravagant hospitality. As a railway contractor, he routinely subcontracted the work and never took pride in a job well done, unlike the great civil engineering firms of the period, such as Grand Trunk builders Peto, Brassey, Jackson, and Betts. There were few his equal in "railway morality" — the unsavoury ethics characterizing transportation politics of the era. Unfortunately, the Great Western Railway would interact frequently with Zimmerman, much to the detriment of the railway.

Zimmerman was involved with the Great Western Railway from early in its existence. His sale of the remaining block of his land holdings in Clifton (Niagara Falls, Canada) to a partnership that included Roswell Gardiner Benedict was to pay dividends that he could scarcely believe years later. Benedict, being the same age as Zimmerman, arrived in Canada about 1847, after employment as a civil engineer on several U.S. railways in New York and Ohio. The two met during the Welland Canal project. Benedict's appointment as assistant to the chief engineer of the Great Western Railway resulted in Zimmerman's firm securing lucrative contracts for building the eastern section of the road. Later, when Benedict became the chief engineer, he certified the shoddy work of Zimmerman's firm, approved dubious claims for cost overruns, and arranged early work completion bonuses on work completed considerably late! The Benedict-Zimmerman collaboration was a synergistic one that was to have a substantial negative impact on the Great Western Railway for years to come.

The Great Western, having witnessed firsthand the Zimmerman business "technique," tried to distance itself from further dealings with him. The company certainly tried to shy away from him. When the railway proposed the Hamilton-to-Toronto extension, the British home office awarded the contract to the British firm of George Whythes (which had already successfully built large portions of two major British railways). Zimmerman may have lost the contract but he was not to be totally denied. Before legislative approval of the extension could be secured, Zimmerman's political "friends" had obtained for him a £10,000 "fee" along with a commitment that his firm would be contracted when the Komoka-to-Sarnia extension came due.

In 1855, the Great Western realized that traffic was overwhelming the single track line and began arrangements to double-track the entire line. Apparently resigned to the inevitable, the railway enlisted the aid of Zimmerman's firm. His price for securing the necessary legislative approval to double-track the line was the contract itself. By supreme irony, the act that made its way through the legislature with Zimmerman's "stamp of approval" was to indirectly lead to his premature death on a frigid late afternoon in March 1857.

In this act was a clause which freed the Great Western from compliance with other legislation mandating that all trains come to a full and complete stop before crossing all drawbridges. This latter legislation had been passed in response to the disaster in Norwalk, Connecticut, several years prior when a passenger train plunged into open water due to a drawbridge being open, causing forty-six deaths. As will be detailed in chapter 6, had the train on which Zimmerman was a passenger on March 12, 1857, come to a full stop before proceeding over the bridge, it is quite likely that the Desjardins Bridge disaster claiming the lives of Zimmerman and fifty-nine others would never have occurred.

The final chapter in the Zimmerman railway saga would also haunt the Great Western for years, through the creation of a competitor across southern Ontario known as the Canada Southern Railway, this railway lasting well beyond the Great Western itself. Zimmerman, anxious to expand commercial development in the Niagara region where he was an extensive landholder, had acquired two local businesses: the Erie and Ontario Railway and the Niagara Harbour and Docks Company. The former was one of the earliest railways in Upper Canada, originally being a horse-powered portage railway around Niagara Falls. The latter was established below Queenston (i.e., north of the falls). As early as 1853, Zimmerman had attempted to entice the Great Western to purchase these assets. Had the Great Western done so, Zimmerman would have amassed a great deal of money on heavy construction contracts in the Falls area. If the railway refused to buy, Zimmerman threatened to include the Erie and Ontario right-of-way as the initial section of a railway built south of the Great Western main line, providing a substantially shorter route between Detroit and Buffalo, New York. It would also tap the regional traffic that the Great Western desired.

Zimmerman "convinced" then-managing director of the Great Western, Charles John Brydges, of the benefits of purchasing the Zimmerman assets, subject to board approval. The battle surrounding this issue forever soured the relationship between Brydges and Sir Allan MacNab, resulting in MacNab's eventual dismissal from the board. Fortunately, MacNab's counsel to disapprove prevailed. He happened to know that the purchase and selling prices for the dock company were £9,000 ($43,830 U.S.) and £179,000 ($871,730 U.S.), respectively. Further, he believed that whether or not the Great Western purchased Zimmerman's companies, there would be a southern competitor built sooner or later. This view persuaded the board. The Brydges agreement was abrogated and the Zimmerman offer was refused.

As expected, Zimmerman began to promote the threatened new independent southern route. Two projected railways would constitute the major portion of the road: the Woodstock and Lake Erie Railway and Harbour

Company and the Amherstburg and St. Thomas Railway. By 1857 the contract for the former was already in hand and his associates formed the majority of the board. The latter line was somewhat of a problem as both the Great Western and Zimmerman had oversubscribed the capital. Citing irregularities in the conduct of the Great Western, Zimmerman held a parallel organizational meeting in an Amherstburg hotel on August 7, 1856. At precisely the same time, the Great Western group held their meeting in the Amherstburg town hall! Two boards and two presidents. Although Zimmerman was to play no role in it, the Canada Southern Railway was destined to play a major role in rail transportation in southern Ontario.

Given the unsatisfactory nature of the work performed by Zimmerman's firm, it might be reasonable to assume that his company would have to compensate the railway or make extensive and expensive repairs and even lose money on the contract. In fact, the opposite occurred. Why? The work had been done "according to contract" — that is, in a manner to meet legally the minimum standards of performance set out, but also according to a contract mutually agreed upon in advance by the engineer and the contractor, approved by a board of directors composed partly of inexperienced local and/or non-local businessmen and usually also including some of the contractor's "friends." According to contract the contractor, on the approval of the engineer, imposed additional unforeseen charges pushing costs well above initial estimates. According to contract the contractor was paid when his work was completed. If not, he would refuse to turn over the tracks, locomotives, and rolling stock until he was paid. Frequently, railway companies would start operations without funds since the money raised by municipalities would go to the contractor. In addition, contractors frequently were paid in a combination of company bonds (50 percent) and cash (50 percent). It should be remembered that the process just described applied to the majority of contractors of early Canadian railways, not just to Samuel Zimmerman.

* * *

Even with only the brief background presented herein, the reader should come away with the sense that pioneer railway travel in the 1850s through 1870s was in a somewhat chaotic state. It was somewhat akin to the Wild West. These early years were the era of link-and-pin couplers, hand brakes, no effective means of communication between stations, wood fuel, and no signalling equipment. It was an era of a virtual absence of governmental oversight over the railways, even with respect to safety. And it was an era with a broad lack of financial oversight by government and the companies themselves.

However, slowly but surely things got better. Link-and-pin couplers would be replaced by safer couplers. Hand brakes would give way to air brakes, and the telegraph and signals would improve communication dramatically, improving safety as well. Government would step in and begin to regulate critical aspects of railway life, introducing inspectors and the Board of Railway Commissioners. And, although the Great Western would start out "with wobbly knees," things would improve for the Great Western as well.

CHAPTER 1

EARLY YEARS

January 9, 1834, was an historic day upon which a select committee of the Legislative Assembly of Upper Canada enthusiastically recommended approval of a petition under consideration. This petition called for the granting of a charter to construct a railway from the town of London to the head of Lake Ontario. Supporters of the petition included many progressive and influential citizens of London, Hamilton, and all points between, including Allan Napier MacNab, Edward Allen Talbot, Colin C. Ferrie, James Belle Ewart, James Hamilton, Mahlon Burwell, James Ingersoll, George J. Goodhue, and Jasper T. Gilkison. In fact, seventy-six sponsors affixed their names to the petition, including one man who was member of Parliament for the London district and chairperson of the select committee that approved the petition: Mahlon Burwell!

The result was the incorporation of the London and Gore Railroad Company on March 6, 1834, "for the purpose of constructing a single or double track wooden or iron railway or way commencing at the town of London and extending to the harbour in Burlington Bay at the head of Lake Ontario … and also the navigable waters of the Thames River [Ed. note: up to Chatham] and Lake Huron." The inclusion of a clause authorizing the use "of steam or the power of animals, or any mechanical or other power" indicated that railways were still in their infancy at this time and that steam locomotives had yet to prove their superiority. Naturally, the railway was allowed to cross any watercourse or road, provided that the watercourse or road was restored to its original state, and usefulness was not impaired. This was especially emphasized for the Grand and Thames Rivers. As will be seen in the next chapter, the successor Great Western Railway did not always behave in this prescribed manner. Capital stock was established at £100,000 ($487,000 U.S.) with a proviso that it could be increased to £200,000 ($975,000 U.S.) in the event of extending the works to the Thames River or Lake Huron. Construction was to be commenced within two years of passage of the act and was to be completed between London and Burlington Bay within ten years and from London to the Thames River and Lake Huron within twelve years of passage of the act (Upper Canada Statutes, 4 William IV, chapter 29, assent date March 6, 1834).

Promoters of the new company immediately set to work, with the *Montreal Gazette* (May 3, 1834) reporting:

> We perceive by the True Patriot that the first meeting of the friends of the London and Gore Railroad was held in London on Monday, April 7 [1834]; and we rejoice to find that stock on the amount of four or five hundred shares [£10,000–12,500] was taken up before the meeting adjourned.... When it is considered that every landholder within ten miles of the intended road must be greatly benefitted by its completion, and that the produce of the finest and most fertile country in America must in a few years be of little value, unless some such improvement is effected, we are not at all surprised to hear that the farmers are coming forward to take up stock....

Unfortunately, the promoters found themselves unable to attract necessary capital, despite a modest objective of £100,000. Despite a lack of capital, enthusiasm continued unabated. In 1836 Elisha Johnson, civil engineer, was engaged to conduct a preliminary survey of the route and report to the directors.

In his "Report of the Engineer upon the Preliminary Surveys for the London and Gore Rail Road," dated 1836, Johnson gushed with some of the most eloquent prose ever to grace the pages of an engineer's report. He not only assured the directors that the proposed route was remarkably straight and level, with no serious physical barriers to overcome, but predicted that "the rude features of an unfrequented wilderness" would be transformed "as if by enchantment" into a "diversified and profitable cultivation ... with thickening throngs of active, useful, and intelligent families."

The eloquent engineer concluded his report with a plea that the directors pursue what he considered their divine mission:

> The Creator of the world has stretched out between Canada and the United States the most magnificent series of internal waters that anywhere adorn His footstool. From these waters he has, for ages, sent forth his dews, and his rains to clothe the vast interior with lavish fertility.... Can you doubt or hesitate as to the task assigned you? Were the richest bounties of the physical world designed to go forever unimproved and unenjoyed by him to whom dominion is given over all the world?

A variety of newspapers extolled the merits of the proposed route, as did travellers and visitors to Upper

Canada. One of the most famous examples of the latter, Anna Jameson, considered this railway

> One of the grandest and most useful undertakings in the world — in this world I mean. The want of a line of road, of an accessible market for agricultural produce, keeps this magnificent country poor and ignorant. Here all grain, all fruits which flourish in the south of Europe might be cultivated with success — the finest wheat and rice, and hemp and tobacco.... If there were but a railroad ... there is no calculating the advantages that must arise from it.

The pressing need was for money, not enthusiasm. For this reason, the company approached the government for financial assistance. In 1837, with the aggressive support of Allan MacNab, and convinced that the colony, as a whole, would benefit from its construction, the legislature approved a loan of £200,000 ($975,000 U.S.) (Upper Canadian Statutes, 7 William IV, chapter 61, assent date March 4, 1837).

The money was never received nor was any attempt made to begin construction. The unsettled political and economic conditions in Upper Canada occasioned by the Rebellion of 1837 and the financial crisis (panic) of that year, combined with a continued interest in canals, brought any progress on the railway to an abrupt stop. With neither public nor private funds available, promoters of the London and Gore, and other railways in the colony, had no choice but to temporarily abandon the project. In the near term, prospects for the railway were bleak indeed. However, the dreams of those behind it lingered on.

In 1845 the London and Gore Railroad Company was revived with the incorporation of the Great Western Rail Road Company, which had an extended route (from some point on the Niagara River through Hamilton and London to Point Edward at the foot of Lake Huron and to the Detroit River). This was done in order to avoid a lapse in the act of 1834. Capital stock was increased to £1.5 million ($7.31 million U.S.) maximum. Construction had to begin within four years of passage of this act and had to be completed within twenty years of the passage (Province of Canada Statutes, 8 Victoria, chapter 86, assent date March 29, 1845).

The reasons for the reinvigorated enthusiasm and more ambitious plan embodied in the 1845 act was closely related to significant developments in Britain and the U.S. during this period.

The changing trade policy of the mother country between 1846 and 1849 had profound effects upon railway development in Canada West (Ontario). Colonial produce, formerly sheltered by Britain's preferential tariff structure, became exposed to the competition of foreign traders as Britain removed the tariff structure. In addition, exports from the U.S. Midwest, which had used the St. Lawrence route in order to gain freer access to British markets, would now enjoy equal treatment even if exports left from U.S. ports on the east coast. Bitter resentment boiled up in Canada, especially among Montreal merchants and St. Lawrence shipping interests, due to the major disaster of the loss of British preferential tariffs. This resentment culminated in the famous "Annexation Manifesto." However, farmers in Canada West continued to be prosperous as they increasingly looked southward, rather than overseas, for trading opportunities.

Charles B. Stuart, chief engineer of the Great Western, produced a report on September 1, 1847, which dealt with the final location of the main line and final specifications for everything from roadbed to bridges and buildings. He indicated that of the entire distance between the Suspension Bridge and Windsor of 228 miles, over 217 miles was perfectly straight. He was pleased to state that he knew of "no other case in this country or elsewhere comparable with this, and it is doubtful whether another location of the same extent can be found on the Continent, so well adapted to the attainment of high velocity, and great economy of transportation."

Stuart felt that there was no doubt that, although it would cost £1,218,520 ($5.93 million U.S.) to build, the Great Western would prove a profitable investment for its promoters. Everywhere along the line, roadbed property was being provided free of charge while municipalities had promised sites for depots and freight sheds. However, municipalities were providing next to nothing in terms of financial support. For example, in 1845 Hamilton's municipal council voted to provide £25 ($122 U.S.) in funds upon receiving the company's request for aid. Using Stuart's estimate of £4,332 ($21,100 U.S.) per mile, this £25 would finance the construction of thirty feet of track!

On October 23, 1847, the time had arrived for turning of the first sod in London, Ontario. In the words of the *Globe* (October 27, 1847):

> Daylight broke on the eventful morning in all the splendor of an October day in Canada.... From a very early hour the streets of London gave evidence of a holiday. The shops were decked out in their best style ... and innumerable wagons filled with the hardy lords of the soil, and their merry families, poured into the town.

Per Talman in 1948:

> On that day, something less than ninety-nine years ago, Colonel Talbot turned the first sod which represented the beginning of construction of the Great Western. The fact that the survey was changed and that the railway did not go over the place he marked does not detract from the importance of the occasion. Talbot turned sod in a vacant lot on Richmond Street where the Hyman tannery stands today and, of course, the Great Western came through on the present line of the C.N.R. When he turned the sod, Talbot is reported to have said "I slept on this spot fifty-five years ago when my best friend was a porcupine. What a change has occurred since! Now I see different beings around me, no porcupines with bristles but in their place a company of half-civilized gentlemen." Talbot possibly was slightly under the influence of alcohol at the time for his speech. No reporter recorded what the half-civilized bystanders thought of Talbot's remarks.
>
> — J.J. Talman, *Western Ontario Historical Notes* 6(1) (March 1948), 3

A public dinner followed, at which sixteen toasts were made.

As 1848 came to an end, there must have been many who doubted whether the dream first conceived in 1833 would ever be fulfilled. Fortunately, the fortunes of the Great Western (and several other railways in Ontario) would improve markedly in 1849. In April 1849 Francis Hincks, inspector general, introduced the Guarantee Act into the Legislature of the Province of Canada. This measure clearly stated that there was a need for government assistance to allow the construction of railways in rural areas where capital was scarce. The assistance took the form of a guarantee of interest at 6 percent on not more than 50 percent of the bonded debt of railways over seventy-five miles long, after the completion of at least one half of their mileage. Obviously, Sir Allan MacNab temporarily abandoned his role as leader of the opposition to help shepherd the bill to pass unanimously (Province of Canada Statutes, 12 Victoria, chapter 29, assent date May 30, 1849). Although the Guarantee Act could not benefit a railway until it had completed at least half of its mileage and could not benefit lines less than seventy-five miles long, it was an all-important first step in the long story of government guarantees and subsidies for Canadian railways. Its usefulness was further restricted in 1851 by Hincks's decision to restrict the act to lines forming part of the province's trunk system, in an attempt to help his Grand Trunk Railway (Province of Canada Statutes, 14 & 15 Victoria, chapter 73, assent date August 30, 1851). Luckily, the Great Western was considered to be the western extension of the trunk line in 1851, and thus it continued to receive aid under this act (Province of Canada Statutes, 14 & 15 Victoria, chapter 74, assent date August 30, 1851).

In 1849 an act was passed that repealed the act of 1846 and placed Canadian and British Great Western Railway shareholders on an equal footing (Province of Canada Statutes, 12 Victoria, chapter 156, assent date May 30, 1849).

Of more immediate value to the Great Western was a bill introduced in 1850, which allowed municipalities to subscribe to the stock of railway companies (Province of Canada Statutes, 13 & 14 Victoria, chapter 129, assent date July 23, 1850). Earlier apathy gave way to exuberant largesse on the part of municipalities. The counties of Oxford and Middlesex and municipalities of Galt and London each purchased £25,000 ($121,750 U.S.) stock subscriptions, while Hamilton purchased £50,000 ($243,500 U.S.) in stock.

Railway fever seems to have infected the entire province. Commercial distress had disappeared and new confidence and initiative were rising to the fore. The struggle for responsible government had been fought and won, constitutional strife no longer dominated the country, and Canada was on the fast track to becoming an independent nation. In the 1850s, in the words of Sir Allan MacNab, railways became the politics of Canadians. By the end of the 1850s Canada was far different from what it had been in 1850. By 1860 Canada had shed its pioneer status and had become a full-fledged member of the great world of commerce and finance.

Contemporary newspapers revealed this radical new enthusiasm for railways:

> Railroads! Railroads! The Canadian world is at last thoroughly alive on the subject of Railroads. Every newspaper teems with the proceedings of public meetings, with discussions as to the best routes, urgent appeals to capitalists to lend their aid …

> and confident predictions as to the advantages to be reaped from them. Opposition seems to have died away, and there seems to be an unanimous desire to build the roads, some way or other; the prospect that something effectual will at last be done seems really good.
>
> — *Globe*, November 26, 1850

Referring specifically to the Great Western, the *Canada Directory* gushed that it would

> pass through the finest portion of the Province, and when completed must necessarily be the great highway for the travel, and for the transport of a large portion of the produce of the North Western States of the American Union, as well as of Western Canada.
>
> — Lovell's *Canada Directory* for 1850–1851

This sudden and complete change in attitude regarding railway construction was, in great measure, due to deliberate promotion by its advocates — the MacNabs, Buchanans, and Galts in Parliament, and Keefers outside of Parliament:

> Old Winter is once more upon us, and … our rivers are sealed fountains, and an embargo, which no human power can remove is laid on all our ports.… The animation of business is suspended, the life blood of commerce is curdled and stagnant.… On land, the heavy stage labors through mingled frost and mud.… Far away to the South is heard the daily scream of the steam whistle — but from Canada there is no escape: blockaded and imprisoned by Ice and Apathy, we have at least ample time for reflection; or if there be comfort in Philosophy may we not profitably consider the PHILOSOPHY OF RAILROADS.
>
> — T.C. Keefer, *Philosophy of Railroads* (Montreal: John Lovell, 1850)

The eloquent Keefer, a famous civil engineer, assured Canadians that the resources of Canada were on a par with American states in which railways had been built:

> There is a greater amount of unemployed capital amongst our agricultural and trading population than is generally supposed; and of fixed capital and absolute wealth, there is more than sufficient … to warrant the construction of all the roads proposed. A very considerable class of the stockholders in New England roads are farmers, with investments from £50 to £500.
>
> — Keefer, *Philosophy of Railroads*

Keefer warned Canadians of the consequences if the "chilling influence of popular apathy, ignorance, and incredulity" continued. Without a doubt, such promotional literature played a significant role in generating railway fever in the 1850s.

This railway mania proved to be a mixed blessing to the Great Western, for with it appeared the possibility of a competitor in the guise of the Niagara and Detroit Rivers Railroad Company. This line was also planned to run through southwestern Ontario to unite New York and Michigan railroads. As such, it posed a serious threat to Great Western aspirations. When its promoters petitioned Parliament for a widening of its powers in 1850, Great Western interests vigorously opposed the bill. It was eventually defeated by only one vote! Hincks made it clear to the directors of the Great Western that its rival would receive its charter at the next session of Parliament unless it began construction. Spurred on by this warning, but still without its finances fully in order, the Great Western looked south to the United States. Directors of the Great Western were hoping that American enthusiasm for their project would be translated into dollars.

They were not disappointed! Their plea for funds coincided with the abolition, by the New York state legislature, of canal tolls charged on freight transported by railroads. This was expected to result in a tremendous increase in freight traffic along the New York chain of railways. New York Central and Michigan Central interests united in support of the Great Western, "the only link wanting in the most profitable chain of roads that have ever been constructed." Erastus Corning, president of the Utica and Schenectady Railroad and soon to be the first president of the New York Central, persuaded the New York state legislature to allow New York railroads to subscribe to Great Western stock. Several lines immediately subscribed for substantial amounts, Corning's road alone subscribing $200,000.

On May 5, 1851, Great Western officials met with interested American businessmen in Niagara Falls. John M. Forbes opened the meeting with a blunt pronouncement that the time had come to complete the Great Western, provided that U.S. interests lend their aid to the tune of $1 million. Expressing the hope that the New York roads and Michigan Central would furnish $800,000 to $850,000 of the $1 million goal, he reminded the stockholders of these lines that "the large amount of already-invested capital to be materially benefitted by its construction calls loudly upon the rest of the links in this great chain to render their aid in making up the balance necessary for its early completion."

In March 1851 the *Detroit Free Press* had published "An Appeal to the Citizens of Michigan," urging them to take action on behalf of the Great Western. Concerned about the potential devastating effects of railways being built south of Lake Erie, the writer warned:

> Unless we move ourselves … we may rest assured that in less than three years Michigan will be far behind all of her sister states of the West as to facilities for trade and commerce. It is well known that thousands upon thousands are prevented from even visiting us in the summer season by reasons of fear of crossing Lake Erie, while in the winter we see no one who is not compelled by absolute necessity to come here. We have complained of the travel and emigration passing by us, but the past is nothing to what the future will be.… The rich and fertile lands of the northern portion of our state will remain an uncultivated wilderness, while the surrounding states will flourish like a garden.

This gloomy prophecy was contrasted with the benefits to be derived by the speedy completion of the Great Western, whose

> effect upon the state would be almost magical.... We shall have no winter to close up our navigation. No seasons where we cannot reach our great market — no time where we are shut out from our intercourse with New York.... The tide of emigration which has so long passed by us, will pass through our state. Under such a stimulus we may expect our population to double in the next ten years.

On September 17–19, 1851, a Railroad Celebration was held in Boston. A special committee was appointed with the mayor and eight aldermen, and the president and thirteen fellow members of the Common Council. This committee reported:

> in their opinion, the time has come when the Great Western Railway of Canada may be completed, provided that the parties who are interested on the American side, will lend them aid by a subscription of stock to the amount of one million dollars.

This pronouncement appeared to be a virtual carbon copy of Forbes' May 5 comment. The consistency in the message should not be lost by the reader.

These appeals brought a favourable response from American capitalists in Detroit and elsewhere and, within a year, private subscriptions totalled over £210,000 ($1 million U.S.). Together with the $800,000-plus in aid from interested U.S. roads, the longstanding financial woes of the Great Western were finally over. For their assistance, three Americans were admitted as directors: Erastus Corning, John Forbes, and John W. Brooks (the latter being superintendent of the Michigan Central).

It was time to build a railway!

CHAPTER 2

CONSTRUCTION AND OPERATIONS

Work on the section between London and Hamilton began in early 1851. By May, fifteen hundred to two thousand men were at work. Parties involved felt that trains would be running by December 1, 1852, an extremely optimistic prediction, indeed.

Westward from Paris, Ontario, most of the construction work was performed by an American company, Ferrell and Van Voorhis. The contract for the eastern portion was given to Farewell and Company, in which the dominating figure was Samuel Zimmerman. Zimmerman, from Pennsylvania, had come to Canada "having no capital but his own energy and farsightedness," and gained construction experience during construction of the Welland Canal. Aggressive, unscrupulous, and, ultimately, notoriously wealthy, Zimmerman was the subject of controversy among his contemporaries and later writers (see Introduction). The contractors' interest in the railway was sustained by the $800,000 in stock that they held as partial payment for their services. The actual work was done by local subcontractors and transient labourers. The latter frequently went on strike for higher wages and resorted to violence to prevent non-strikers ("scabs") from working. As early as February 1851 a petition from Hamiltonians to the government reported that

> already many of the men engaged on the work have twice left their employment on a demand for higher wages, and armed with bludgeons and threats of violence have drawn off and effectually prevented the peaceable and industrious laborers from earning a livelihood for themselves and their families.

The petition requested that the government send troops to maintain order. The government recognized the problems in Hamilton and did remedy the situation with additional troops. However, problems arose and/or continued elsewhere. On April 10, 1851, the editor of the *Dundas Warden* indicated the deep concern of a small community subjected to unruly labour thugs.

> We deeply regret to state that our peaceful town has again been the scene of strife. Some further difficulty having arisen between the contractors and laborers on the Great Western, a portion of the latter came into town yesterday, armed with bludgeons, and drove off those employed on the works hereabouts. Two or three of the overseers were brutally maltreated and abused. We have no knowledge of the grounds of difficulty between the employers and employed … but this we must say, that the frequent repetition of scenes of violence is positively disgraceful.

Within a week, the municipal council of Paris would forward another petition for military protection to the government.

There is no reason to believe that labour strife was more serious on the Great Western than on other railway or canal projects of the era. No doubt, feuds among the many Irish immigrants were partially responsible. Workers took advantage of the difficulty the company had securing labourers. The boom period, with its extensive railway building, not only caused wages to soar but made it very difficult to obtain the quantity and quality of men needed. There is evidence that some of the supervisory personnel ruled with an iron fist and tried to take advantage of the immigrant workers. Regardless of who was at fault and to what extent, labour strife certainly delayed construction, increased costs, and left an unpleasant legacy in many southwestern Ontario communities.

By the end of 1852 progress, as measured by grading alone, had occurred on only a few very small and detached portions of the line. This was despite the request by company officials that the contractors start much earlier in the year (as early as February). The Hamilton-to-Twenty-Mile-Creek section had only been lightly graded and the procrastination of the contractors assured that it would be May 1853 at the earliest before rails could be laid.

Grading on the section from the Detroit River to one hundred miles east had also commenced. The original plan to build pile trestles over fourteen miles of the wet prairie west of Chatham was slow in its initiation. As engineers re-examined this plan they decided to modify it substantially. Instead of temporizing with pile trestles, the area was permanently graded using fill removed adjacent to the line and/or by hauling beach sand from nearby lakes.

Grading and masonry work on the eastern division, both east and west of St. Catharines, were problematic. Temporary grade and wooden pile trestles were to be used at Ten and Twelve Mile creeks. West of Hamilton there were more problems: the gorge of the Desjardins Canal, the ascending grade out of Dundas, and a deep quicksand deposit near Copetown. Costs skyrocketed due to the massive amount of overburden that had to be moved or excavated, by the huge and continuous earth slides in the deep cuts, and by the number/depth of wooden piles necessary to protect the foot of the slopes. In section 11, the sinking of an embankment into a deep morass or subterranean lake, not unlike muskeg, forced adoption of a new tactic. An extensive platform of coniferous trees and bushes, interwoven with earth so as to prevent the loss of ballast by its own displacement, proved the solution.

The area around London had but two cuttings with which to contend. West of London work proceeded around the clock.

Copetown was the most problematic site on the entire main line. The quicksand swallowed everything placed in it, and was so deep that a twenty-foot-long rod did not reach bedrock. Work was frustrating. After excavation of the roadbed to a depth of five or six feet during the day, the excavation would be reversed overnight by the weight of the adjoining banks. By the next morning it was as if nothing had been excavated the previous day!

This area led to the first major delay in the construction schedule for 1853. Roadbed was graded and rail was laid in a westerly direction from the edge of the quicksand. On Saturday May 14, 1853, with approximately 2.5 miles of line laid from Copetown westward, the first impromptu excursion was held. The directors and significant others arrived by carriage along the Governor's Road to attend. The excursion train was locomotive #4, *Niagara*. Participants rode in the tender. Several round trips were made over the line and all proceeded to celebrate with food, drink, speeches, and toasts. Rails would be laid to Fairchild Creek and then Harrisburg, a full seven miles, by the end of the week.

July 1853 saw work progressing at full speed, in some locations around the clock, and Sunday alone brought rest. Tracks had been laid out of Hamilton, along the waterfront, for one mile, intersecting the Desjardins Canal. The plan had been to bridge the canal on its old route but, after the expenditures of many hours and a large sum of money, a bridge of permanent structure proved elusive. The canal was described as a "bottomless pit." Engineers and officers decided to cut a new channel for the canal through the heights and built a beautiful suspension bridge for carriage traffic across this new gorge. The old channel was to be eventually filled to create a solid roadbed.

The route now wound around and started its ascent of the Niagara Escarpment toward Dundas. At Dundas, a gorge approximately six to seven hundred feet long and one hundred feet deep had to be crossed. A masonry culvert costing $70,000 was built to convey water, large embankments were filled, and a bridge was erected over the Flamboro Road. July 1853 saw rails laid thirteen miles to the edge of the Grand River, at which point another excursion was run to Harrisburg followed by dinner at the Sawmill Hotel.

In July 1853 a branch line from the Great Western main line to a wharf on Lake Ontario (named Port Ontario) was under construction. This branch, less than one mile in length, was built to allow contractors to land locomotives, rolling stock, rails, and other materials close to the jobsite. This became the site of the Ontario depot, renamed Winona in 1867. Vessels with a draft of up to ten feet could dock at the wharf. July 25 saw the arrival of the steamer *Traveller* at 1030 hours. The locomotive *Middlesex* (#7) and its tender were off-loaded. Track was laid on the wharf, and the locomotive with tender was pulled up the gradient, using rope and tackle, in less than six hours. The steamer *Ontario* then arrived with a load of rails.

As construction proceeded west after crossing the Grand River, few problems were encountered in this straight stretch. By September 1853 a bridge had been built across Cedar Creek and Mill Street. It comprised five massive stone abutments, each reaching beyond the ordinary high-water mark, which were topped with five timber bents. It was originally planned to construct the entire bridge of stone. However, its massive size and the lack of stone in the area caused a change in plans.

Tuesday, November 1, 1853, was a day for celebration. The Great Western was opening the section between Hamilton and Niagara Falls (Ontario). A train with five cars waited at the Hamilton station. Local dignitaries boarded and the train proceeded east over the section from Hamilton to Ontario (Winona), which had been laid with a new compound rail developed locally. A stop was made at St. Catharines before proceeding over the Welland Canal and up the escarpment. Four miles from the falls, in a deep cut, the locomotive derailed and hit the embankment, becoming submerged in gravel and clay and breaking the centre driver pin. A few passengers detrained and began walking the remaining four miles. Once they arrived at the station, another train was quickly dispatched to bring in the remaining passengers. All marched down to the Clifton House, owned by the contractor Samuel Zimmerman, to partake in a sumptuous feast, with drink, speeches, and toasts. During celebrations a track crew was busy repairing the line for the return trip. In fact, a new track had been laid around the wrecked locomotive.

* * *

The following are examples of shipping manifests for Great Western-contracted vessels during the construction phase of the main line (month/day/year):

From Cape Vincent, two locomotives (12/22/1852)

From Cape Vincent, two locomotives (*Hamilton* and *Middlesex*)(7/22/1853)

From Cape Vincent, two locomotives and tenders (12/9/1853)

From Cape Vincent, one locomotive and tender, three firepans, four pilots, eight castings, three smokestacks, 65 pairs of trucks (12/12/1853)

From Montreal, two locomotives and tenders, one hundred fifty tons of coal, sixty tons of axles, thirty-eight tons of pig iron, one hundred barrels of resin, ten tons of iron pipe (10/11/1854)

From Montreal (three ships): ship number one = two locomotives, one hundred twenty tons of pig iron; ship number two = two locomotives, one hundred ninety-four tons of pig iron, two hundred twenty-six kegs of blasting powder; ship number three = two locomotives, two boilers, three tenders, seventeen pairs of wheels and axles, twenty cases of machinery, eight chimneys, six rods, eight buffers, forty-two pairs of wheels and axles, sixty-five tons of pig iron (all on 6/19/1855)

An example of a manifest of a vessel contracted to transport materiel from Hamilton to drop-off points near the western construction zone is that of the schooner *London* on December 3, 1853: three hundred fifty tons of rails, fifty-nine kegs of spikes, and one ton of furniture to Chatham.

In late December 1853 three Great Western locomotives were on the dock at Cape Vincent, New York (southeastern end of Lake Ontario). Winter had arrived and most ships were in winter quarters. However, the locomotives were needed for the winter construction season. The steamer *Magnet* was contracted to cross the lake, secure the locomotives, and bring them to the wharf at Port Ontario. In January 1854 the railway chartered the steamer *Princess Royal* to transport locomotives from Rochester to Burlington Beach at the canal. Four locomotives were delivered this way, with the last one arriving in late March.

The Great Western shops and yard in Hamilton were erected on reclaimed land in Burlington Bay, at its western end. Excavated material from railway construction was used for reclamation, pushing the new shore some seven hundred feet into the bay, creating forty new acres of land. All major buildings were built using solid stone. The locomotive shop was mammoth in size, being three-storeys tall and having twelve tracks exiting from a turntable and running one hundred fifty yards into twelve work bays. Each work bay could hold two locomotives. The ground floor had ponderous lathes to turn crankpins or driving wheels, as well as planing machines, drill presses, and cylinder-boring machines. The second floor had rows of lathes and woodworking machines. At the back was the

Canada Science and Technology Museum.

A bird's-eye view of the Hamilton yard facilities of the Great Western, with the photograph being taken from atop a grain elevator. The depot is evident in the left side of the photograph. The presence of dual rails indicative of dual-gauge trackage should be noted. This allowed simultaneous use of broad-gauge (five-foot six-inch gauge) and standard-gauge (four-foot eight-and-a-half-inch gauge) motive power and rolling stock. It also allows one to roughly date this photograph to the period between late 1866 and June 1873.

Stratford-Perth Archives, Stratford, Ontario.

Great Western erecting shops, Hamilton, circa 1862. Note, from left to right, the A-frame for heavy lifting, three newly built or newly outshopped broad-gauge locomotives (4-4-0s or 2-6-0s), two sets of driving wheels, and a handsome, open-ended passenger car in this staged photo shoot with shop personnel.

Ian Cameron Collection, Elgin County Archives.

Great Western station, St. Thomas, circa 1890s. View of the north side, looking southeast. The station was located opposite the north end of Station Street. The photographer was likely located on top of a rail car.

blacksmith shop with twenty-six smithy fires and a huge steam forging hammer. A stationary sixty-horsepower steam engine provided power for all machines in the locomotive and car departments via a complex system of pulleys and belts. To the west of the locomotive shop were the car shops housed in a wood frame building three hundred feet long by fifty feet wide.

Although construction of the Great Western did not require major physical barriers to be overcome, costs continued to climb, as did the concern/anxiety of shareholders and directors. At first their solution was dismissal of the chief engineer, whose estimates proved displeasing. When Charles Stuart was replaced by Roswell Benedict in 1851, the latter assured the directors that Stuart's

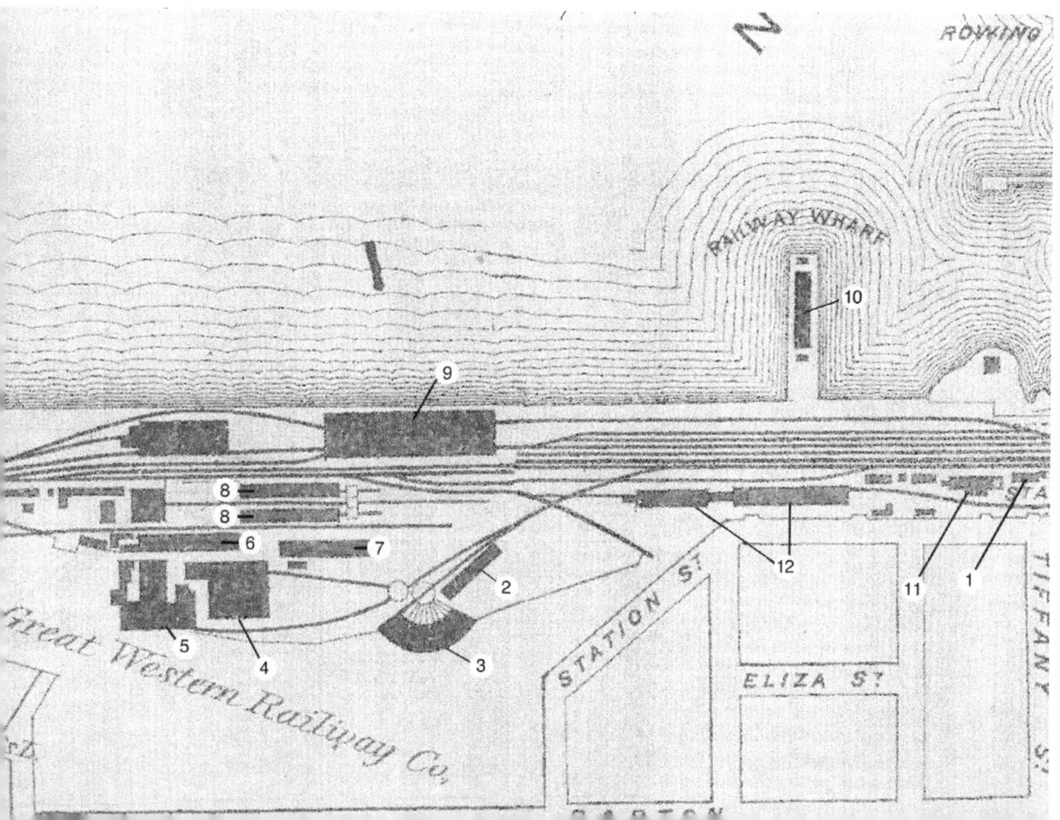

Plan of 1879 Hamilton, Ontario, Great Western Railway facilities: 1 = passenger station (stone); 2 = coal shed (wood); 3 = roundhouse (stone); 4 = locomotive shop (stone); 5 = two attached foundries (one brick, one stone); 6 = moulding shop/carpentry shop (latter stone); 7 = erecting shop/blacksmith and machine shop (both stone); 8 = car shops (wood); 9 = freight shed (stone); 10 = grain elevator (wood); 11 = baggage/freight/express building; 12 = coal sheds (not GWR-owned). Identities of other buildings cannot be verified.

From *The 1879 New Topographical Atlas of the Province of Ontario* (Burland Desbarats Lithography Co., Montreal, PQ).

estimates were reasonably accurate. By September 1852 Benedict reported that costs would exceed Stuart's estimates by as much as £286,000 ($1.393 million U.S.). Benedict was shown the door. The next chief engineer, J.T. Clark, had an estimate £336,000 ($1.636 million U.S.) higher than that of Benedict and £621,000 ($3.024 million U.S.) higher than that of Stuart. Of course, this was not an issue unique to the Great Western. Most early railways found that original estimates fell far short of the actual costs. In any case, George L. Reid had become chief engineer by 1854. Apparently, the shareholders and directors came to the conclusion that frequent dismissals of chief engineers would not solve their financial problems, since Reid maintained his position until at least 1870.

In actual fact the unexpected costs of construction, although partly the result of unrealistic estimates or unjustified charges by contractors for "unforeseen conditions," were largely the result of increasing costs of land, labour, and materials; exceptionally cold winters; and unforeseen physical barriers. The section immediately west of Hamilton presented a number of engineering problems: bridging of a marsh, a wide cutting, a stream diversion, deepening of the Desjardins Canal, construction of a bridge over the canal, another long bridge over a ravine, heavy embankments and formidable stretches of retaining wall. The decision to build across the marsh through which the Desjardins Canal passed proved exceptionally costly. Although an easier route from Dundas to Hamilton existed,

> all of this trouble was brought about by a desire ... to please two Canadian Directors, Sir Allan MacNab and Dr. Hamilton. MacNab wanted the line near or through Dundurn, which he then owned, and Dr. Hamilton owned the Fisher property at Dundas. He thought that by running the line along the mountain side he could open up building stone quarries.

In spite of such self-imposed engineering problems, the Great Western was truly fortunate that its route through southwestern Ontario presented few major physical barriers. There remained, however, the problems of crossing the rivers at both ends of the main line. The Detroit River was the lesser of the two problems. Although consideration was given to both a tunnel and a bridge, engineering and economic factors caused both to be abandoned in favour of a ferry service between Windsor and Detroit, as detailed in chapter 5. Unfortunately, until

Stratford-Perth Archive, Stratford, Ontario.

Great Western Railway Hamilton Works, circa 1862.

Canada Science and Technology Museum.

An engraving of a Great Western passenger train proceeding from the U.S. to the Canadian side of the Niagara River gorge over Roebling's historic Suspension Bridge. The American and Canadian (Horseshoe) falls can be seen in the background.

Canada Science and Technology Museum.

A magnificent view of the Suspension Bridge over the Niagara River gorge. The unidentified locomotive appears to be a Great Western 4-4-0. The photograph can be approximately dated by the absence of multiple (four) rails to accommodate multiple (three) gauges (i.e., four feet eight and a half inches, five feet six inches, and six feet), to 1871 or later. The colossal strength built into the bridge is echoed in the twin towers at each end.

railway cars could be ferried across the river year round, break-bulk shipping by ferries and sleighs resulted in delay, damage, and dissatisfaction. Ultimately, the issue would cause the Great Western to come dangerously close to losing the support of the American roads on which it was so dependent.

The Niagara barrier was more effectively overcome but not without an engineering feat that received worldwide acclaim. A suspension bridge was required by the circumstances at the building site. However, suspension bridges at that time had an alarming safety record of multiple collapses. After the failure of Charles Ellet Jr., John Roebling successfully built the world's first railway suspension bridge, a two-tiered, eight-hundred-seventy-foot-long, thousand-ton structure supported by four ten-

McCord Museum, Montreal, Quebec.

Roebling Suspension Bridge over the Niagara gorge, 1869. Note the interesting train-signal arrangements in the pre-semaphore era. The triple rails indicate that the line is open to locomotives and rolling stock of two gauges.

inch-diameter cables of wrought iron (each cable was comprised of 3,640 No. 9 wires), which would be used until 1897. Its replacement would be warranted only because of the heavier weights of locomotives, rolling stock, and car loadings of that era.

Promoters of the Great Western had confidently (recklessly?) predicted that trains would be running by December 1, 1852. However, one full year after this date, only the short section between Hamilton and Suspension Bridge (Niagara Falls) was, in fact, completed (the inaugural train ran on November 1 and regular service commenced on November 10). Not until December 15, 1853, did the inaugural train run from Suspension Bridge to London (with regular service commencing on December 21). This was followed on January 17, 1854, by the inaugural train from Suspension Bridge to Windsor (with regular service commencing on January 27).

The delay, however, in no way diminished the enthusiasm of the crowds turning out to welcome the first "iron horse" in southwestern Ontario. Dundas, Paris, Woodstock, Ingersoll, and London all made elaborate preparations that clearly demonstrated how well their citizens understood the importance of the completion of the railway. The *Globe* (December 19, 1853) described the reaction of the crowds along the line: "Joy and expectation lighted up every face. Each man appeared to feel that some great good had been conferred on him, and was now within his grasp."

The same author found it difficult to restrain himself from what might well be considered national pride:

> My English readers might well imagine from the heading that I had been on an excursion from Bath or Bristol to the Great Metropolis [London, U.K.]. But it is not so. We now possess in Canada, not only a London, but a Great Western Railway, which though not quite so broad [five feet six inches versus seven feet in gauge], is much longer than its English namesake.

Somewhat less impressed, however, was William Bowman, mechanical superintendent of the Great Western, who wrote in 1903:

> The weather was cold and raw, and the mud along the line was simply appalling.... We left Hamilton early in the afternoon, and it was near dusk when we arrived at London. The time was very slow, slow even for those days, owing to the condition of the roadbed; and it was my opinion at the time that it was a foolhardy notion to attempt the trip on such a roadbed. The rocking of the coaches was frightful, and I thought at times we would go into the mud in the ditch. We stopped at all stations along the line but it was difficult to leave the coaches, as there were no platforms as yet erected, and the mud was too deep to wade into.
>
> — *London Advertiser*, December 19, 1903

During the Suspension Bridge to Windsor inaugural service, two trains of twelve coaches each conveyed four hundred guests from New York State and three hundred guests from Hamilton and Toronto. Arriving at 1700 hours in Windsor (three hours late), a magnificent banquet was served in the Michigan Central freight shed in Detroit. Two thousand guests attended the latter celebration.

Dundurn National Historic Site.

A rare photograph depicting the British directors of the Great Western gathered outside of Dundurn Castle. The legend identifies some of those present. MacNab is just to the right of the two ladies in white. Also to be found are Isaac Buchanan (#4), C.J. Brydges, Great Western then later Grand Trunk manager (#14), and George Reid, engineer (#15). This photograph was taken before mid-1862.

Two days later a similar celebration occurred in Hamilton. An excursion from Detroit was given a twenty-one gun salute followed by a public procession. Sir Allan MacNab was confined to bed but a company of artillery, along with a large crowd, went to Dundurn to honour MacNab, who thanked them from his bedroom window. After arrival of another train with guests from Milwaukee and Detroit, all sat down to a sumptuous feast.

Despite the enthusiastic welcome to the "iron horse" in southwestern Ontario, the first year of operations on the Great Western would be a difficult one. As alluded to in William Bowman's reaction to the Hamilton-to-London inaugural trip, the railway was unfinished when opened to traffic. The line had been opened in an unballasted state with many deficiencies in the roadbed, including collapsed embankments, subsided fill, mud three feet deep in some cuttings, and a profile "like the side view of a sea-serpent." The quality of the work was truly abysmal, especially work performed by Zimmerman's crews. The cost of renovating and maintaining the roadbed would be enormous, as would the cost in broken-down locomotives and rolling stock. The most appalling feature of the first year, however, was the frequency of accidents on the line and the attendant fearful human cost, virtually all of which were due to either deficiencies in the roadbed due to poor workmanship and premature opening of the railway or errors on the part of railway employees. The reader is referred to chapter 6 for a complete discussion of these issues.

May 12, 1854, saw the groundbreaking ceremony for the Galt and Guelph Railway and was considered a holiday in the town of Preston. Stores were closed and throngs of people milled about. At 1400 hours a procession formed at Klotz's Hotel and proceeded to the site of the railway grounds, where Sheriff Grange addressed the crowd and then a quantity of earth was dug and tossed into a wheelbarrow. A cannon fired, the band played, more speeches were made, then all returned to the hotel for the usual celebration of food, drink, speeches, and toasts. This branch would not open for business until September 28, 1857.

The first non-roadbed-related infrastructure disaster occurred on Thursday July 30, 1854, when the St. George depot was destroyed by fire. The new locomotive *Jupiter* (#38) along with a number of cars were also lost. The locomotive had been expected in Galt, hauling a load of rails.

The Hamilton-to-Toronto branch was important in establishing that the Great Western was a "Trunk Line." By June 1855 grading had been completed from Hamilton to Port Credit (twenty-six miles), including widening the Great Western embankment around Hamilton Bay to accommodate double-tracking of the main line. Four cuttings required the removal of massive amounts of material. Cuttings on the west side of the Credit River, the east side of the Etobicoke River, and at the Mimico River required removal of four thousand cubic yards each, while the cutting through the Garrison Common at Toronto required removal of twenty-eight thousand cubic yards. Bridges were required at the old Desjardins Canal/gorge; Applegarths, Twelve Mile and Sixteen Mile creeks; and the Credit, Humber, and Etobicoke Rivers. Combination passenger/freight stations were built at Wellington Square (Burlington), Bronte, Oakville, and Port Credit. Water tanks and woodsheds were built at Bronte and Port Credit. At Toronto a permanent brick engine house and turntable and temporary passenger depot were located at Queens Wharf on eleven acres of Ordnance land adjoining the Old Fort. In fact, the first passenger depot in Toronto was a six-by-ten-foot ticket box adjacent to a small engine shed, between Brock and Front Streets. The Great Western had hoped to go east along the Esplanade to use the Northern Railway station, but this move was held up by Toronto City Council.

The grand celebration of the opening of the Hamilton-to-Toronto line took place on December 3, 1855. The celebration train, full to capacity, left Toronto at 0810 hours on its westward trip. All went well until the train slowed at Port Credit. A fence had been built across the right-of-way! A farmer, by the name of Cathew, had a dispute with the railway over the price paid for his land and the Railway Act and he wanted to make a point that he still owned his land. The locomotive obliterated the fence and the train proceeded to Hamilton, where a large crowd was waiting to greet their new visitors from Toronto. After speeches, Hamiltonians boarded the enlarged eastbound train, now ten cars long. With foresight, the conductor requested a constable to accompany the train. Leaving at 1045 hours, the train passed Wellington Square (Burlington) where a small crowd stood and a cannon was fired in salute. Farmer Cathew had been busy. Not only was the fence rebuilt, but now heavy stakes were driven into the middle of the roadbed. After stopping the train, the constable arrested Cathew and the fence and stakes were removed. The train arrived in Toronto at noon.

If the first year of operation brought about many self-inflicted problems and difficulties, it also brought traffic and financial success exceeding all expectations. In fact, *Scobie's Canadian Almanac* of 1854 reported that "the capabilities of the Great Western Railway are already strained in the endeavor to conduct the business which presses upon it from the West."

Passenger traffic was especially heavy, with up to 790 passengers being conveyed per train! The traffic in freight and livestock became of increasing importance as farmers of the American Midwest and Canada West came to realize the value of the new road. Bumper crops and tremendous British demand occasioned by the Crimean War were also significant factors in the rapidly increasing freight traffic. In response to this traffic growth, the

Great Western constructed the Komoka-to-Sarnia branch line, opening it for business on December 27, 1858. In retrospect, double-tracking of the main line would probably have been the wiser response. Table 2-1 illustrates the phenomenal early growth of traffic on the railway. With dividends of 8 percent (1855) and 8.5 percent (1856), branch-line construction proceeding, and rapidly increasing passenger and freight growth, the future looked quite bright despite a shaky first year.

In Toronto, city council finally relented, allowing the Great Western access to the station built by the Northern Railway of Canada in May 1853. The Great Western used the station from December 1855 until 1858. This station was a simple wooden structure that was located on the site of the current Toronto Union Station.

There were three locations on the Great Western that required pusher (helper) locomotives for all through-freight and express passenger trains and a large proportion of local trains:

- An incline starting half a mile east of St. Catharines and extending to within three miles of the Suspension Bridge (rise to the east = 261 feet in 7.5 miles or 0.66 percent). The series of gradients ranged from one foot in 156 feet (0.64 percent) to one foot in 135 feet (0.74 percent), with a level break at Thorold station. Pusher service was generally needed between St. Catharines and Suspension Bridge (11.25 miles).
- An incline starting at Hamilton station and extending to Copetown (10 miles) (rise to the west = 494 feet). The series of gradients ranged from one foot in 116 feet (0.82 percent) to one foot in ninety-four feet (1.06 percent). This incline was followed by a second one to the west of Harrisburg station (rise of 116 feet in 5,065 yards, or nearly three miles. average of one foot in 131 feet [0.76 percent]). Pusher services were needed over this second grade as far as Paris station, which was twenty-nine miles from Hamilton, especially with express passenger trains.
- There was a rise of 106 feet in two and a half miles (mean of one foot in 123 feet or 0.81 percent) to the west of London. At the summit, the grade was one foot in ninety-six feet (1.04 percent). Pusher services were needed up to the summit of the grade (4.25 miles). With westbound express passenger trains, pusher services were needed to Komoka (eleven miles). This grade passed through two of the deepest clay cuttings on the line, which were full of springs and quicksand, leading to high maintenance costs.

There were additional secondary class grades on the main line that did not require pusher services:

- Primarily between Paris and Princeton, with a rise to the west of sixty-five feet in 3,012 yards (average of one foot in 139 feet or 0.72 percent)
- East of Hamilton, rising one foot in 151 feet (0.66 percent) for three quarters of a mile.

The aggregate length of inclines on the main line requiring pusher services was twenty-three miles. However, pusher locomotives actually worked over forty to fifty miles in three separate sections. These would include eleven and a quarter miles for eastbound

Paris Museum and Historical Society, Paris, Ontario.

Joint Great Western/Buffalo and Lake Huron (GTR) station in Paris. The presence of three rails on the Great Western line date this photograph to the period of 1866 to 1871.

trains, thirty-three and a quarter miles (or forty miles for express passenger trains) for westbound trains. Pushers would return light so mileage would actually double, thus becoming an average of forty-five miles each way or nearly 20 percent of engine mileage of all main-line through trains! Table 2-2 provides elevation profile data for the Great Western main line and its affiliated railways.

The building of the railway had cost a great deal more than was expected. The first two hundred thirty-nine miles (Suspension Bridge to Windsor) had cost £2,705,264 ($13.175 million U.S.) up to April 30, 1854, and, by 1857, the cost of three hundred fifty miles, including the fifty miles of the Sarnia branch under construction and the seventeen miles of the Galt and Guelph branch, had cost an astounding £5,267,944 ($25.655 million U.S.).

The considerable costs of construction and maintenance of the Great Western can be explained by a number of factors. All rails, fasteners, and other materials had to be imported from Great Britain, being sent over in sailing ships to Montreal, where they were transferred to schooners and other small vessels capable of reaching ports on Lakes Ontario, Erie, and St. Clair and the Thames River. From these ports, they were hauled by oxen or horses over execrably bad roads to their final destination.

Grading and laying of tracks comprised the most laborious work, being performed with primitive equipment such as picks, shovels, and wheelbarrows. Most labourers and supervisory personnel originated from the British Isles.

Ties were of white oak, measured six inches by nine inches by nine inches, and were spaced thirty inches centre-to-centre. In the era before creosote and other wood preservatives, ties had a lifespan of approximately eight years. Buildings, bridges, and viaducts were virtually entirely of wooden construction when first built and constantly required renewal and were subject to damage by fire. In many cases, these fires originated from sparks emitted by locomotives fired with wood. Wooden bridges were gradually replaced by iron truss spans with stone abutments or were filled in as embankments, both methods being expensive improvements. In some cases, embankments were widened from fifteen feet to eighteen feet at the top due to the collapse of some of the earlier narrow embankments.

Iron rails used on the main line were of three types:

- Flange or T rail with fish joints (weighing sixty-five pounds/yard)
- U or bridge rail, fastened at the joints with wrought iron plates on which the ends of the rails rested, which

were spiked down to the ties and bolted together with bolts and nuts (weighing sixty-six pounds/yard)

- Light and heavy compound rail (weighing sixty-six and eighty pounds/yard, respectively). The two halves of these compound rails were riveted together and spiked directly to the ties.

On the main line, at the time of the railway opening for business, there were thirty-four miles of fished T rail, 156 miles of U rail, twenty-three and a half miles of light compound rail, and fifteen miles of heavy compound rail. The sidings (approximately eighteen miles) were laid with common T rail with cast-iron chairs at the joints (weighing sixty-two and a half pounds/yard). Like other railways of the era, the Great Western suffered severely from poor-quality rails. By the end of July 1860 the track composition had changed substantially so as to consist of 116 and 115 miles of fished T rails (weighing sixty-five pounds/yard) and U rails (sixty-six pounds/yard), respectively. Thus, over a span of six and a half years, all of the compound rails and forty-three miles of U rails had been replaced by fished T rails. The Hamilton-to-Toronto branch was laid with fished T rails throughout. Obviously, the Great Western had spent a great deal of money for rails while serving under quasi-experimental conditions as a pioneer Canadian railway.

Maintenance costs for locomotives and rolling stock were enormous, especially during the first winter of 1853–54. Owing to intense frosts, uneven track was the cause of many locomotive and rolling-stock breakdowns. The rough use of locomotives and rolling stock by contractors in building the road and in hurriedly ballasting it after it had opened for business led to frequent breakdowns as well. In the future, railways would demand that contractors provide their own locomotives and rolling stock during construction. As a result, motive power shortages were commonplace in the early days. For example, in July 1854, out of a total of thirty-four locomotives only twenty-six (not counting the eight locomotives assigned to ballast trains) were in working order.

At this time, locomotive cost per mile was one shilling and 3.5 pence, mileage was thirty-seven and a half miles per cord of wood (which increased by 1858 to forty-three and a half miles per cord), and locomotives averaged only a modest fifteen thousand miles annually. Rolling stock at this time comprised fifty passenger and 736 freight cars. Rough track and light construction of early rolling stock not only led to the need for heavy repairs but also rebuilding and strengthening of the original designs.

Weather contributed to high maintenance costs. The following extract from the directors' report of June 30, 1857, provided a synopsis of the severe preceding winter and its consequences:

> The locomotive expenses at a rate of one shilling and 7.5 pence per mile have been rendered heavy by the very severe winter weather during December and January. The breaking of wheels, tyres [tires], axles and various parts of the machinery, nearly all caused by the extreme cold have been of daily occurrence and far greater than during previous winters, the intense frost and quantity of snow on the ground prevented the engines from hauling their usual loads and caused extra consumption of

fuel, viz–26,893 cords of wood against 20,969 of the last half year, the price also was 8 pence per cord more.

Compounding the difficulties of the Great Western in the late 1850s was the rise of unexpectedly severe competition. In the mid-1850s, the Grand Trunk Railway was rapidly pushing its way from Montreal into Ontario, reaching St. Marys by November 1856. Construction continued on segments from St. Marys to Sarnia and Port Huron to Detroit (the latter as the affiliated Chicago, Detroit and Canada Grand Trunk Junction Railway), both segments being completed and opened by 1859.

The Great Western had to recognize the Grand Trunk for what it was: a vigorous competitor for the trade of southwestern Ontario and through traffic between Chicago/Detroit and the eastern seaboard of the U.S. The only aspect of this rivalry that could not be clearly seen in 1856–57 was how completely ruinous it would be, especially for the Great Western.

It was with a view to becoming part of the Canadian trunk line — while remaining a link in the American one — that the Great Western undertook the construction of a branch line between Hamilton and Toronto. Although the line was technically built by a separate company, the directors of this Hamilton and Toronto Railway Company were virtually all Great Western directors as well. Its acts of incorporation made it eligible for benefits under the Guarantee Act because, even though it was less than seventy-five miles long, it was considered fundamentally to be a part of the Great Western. Details regarding this and other affiliated lines are provided in chapter 3.

The Grand Trunk had originally intended to use the Great Western as its western section. Why it abandoned this proposed mutually beneficial strategy is a complicated question.

> Certainly there was little economic justification for constructing another through line west of Toronto. Negotiations for the amalgamation of the two companies failed, however, perhaps partly because of the influence of New York capital in the management of the Great Western … partly because the Grand Trunk directors had convinced themselves that they required their own independent connection with Detroit. The influence of Canadian contractors also may have been important.
>
> — W.T. Easterbrook and H.G.J. Aitken, *Canadian Economic History* (Toronto: 1958).

The Great Western's efforts to convince the government that the Grand Trunk was guilty of a breach of faith were to no avail.

Although the directors of the Great Western made many attempts to come to some sort of understanding with the directors of the Grand Trunk, the latter never showed any willingness to co-operate and adopted an aggressive attitude toward the Great Western that was maintained until amalgamation of the two lines in 1882.

By this time, it was clear that the Great Western would probably be challenged by rivals to the south. This was largely attributed to an unwise decision made by the Legislature of the Province of Canada regarding the five-foot-six-inch (or broad) gauge to be used by provincial railways. The American railways with which the Great Western would connect at both ends used a four-foot eight-and-a-half-inch (or standard) gauge (exception: Erie Railroad at the Niagara River used a gauge of six feet). It was natural that the Great Western should plan to use the same standard gauge and, indeed, all plans were drawn up with this in mind. Corning and Forbes had warned the company of the consequence of using a different gauge.

> It is certain that the New York Railroad Companies, who are authorized by law to subscribe to your stock, and who at best will require urging on our part to induce them to do so, will positively refuse their aid if you cut them off from the western connection they are seeking, by adopting a different gauge.
>
> — Letter to R.W. Harris, GWR president, dated June 26, 1851

In what proved to have a painfully negative impact on British North American railways and the Canadian economy, broad gauge was imposed upon the Province of Canada by selfish commercial interests and a provincial government duped by "glib talk." The Great Western Railway of Canada, which had developed all of its plans with the standard gauge in mind, was forced to scrap these when it was forced against its will by the government to abandon this gauge. In addition, for a line designed as a "bridge line" for east-west continental U.S. traffic between the two dominantly standard-gauged transition points of Detroit and Niagara Falls/Buffalo, forced use of the broad gauge was a recipe for potential disaster. The slow, uneconomical break-bulk transshipments necessitated by the change in gauge proved almost fatal to the Great Western. The bitterness engendered in its allied American railways would, in a few years, take the form of transfer of their traffic and financial support to the standard gauge Canada Southern in Ontario and the standard gauge Lake Shore and Michigan Southern Railway south of Lake Erie. In any case, the use of the broad gauge and eventual conversion to standard gauge led to economic pressures which severely weakened the Great Western and probably hastened amalgamation with the Grand Trunk.

* * *

GREAT WESTERN LABOUR POOL

When the Great Western commenced operations in the 1850s there was no pool of experienced railway workers in Ontario. The company had to either import a labour force or create one. It did both. Managers, superintendents, and foremen were recruited from U.K. railways as were skilled tradesmen such as engineers (engine drivers), fitters, boiler-makers, and other shop crafts. Central office clerks were also recruited from the U.K. as were several of the original stationmasters.

Innovation by the Great Western in locomotive and rolling stock development was due, in large part, to the importation, from the U.K., of gifted and skilled men such as Richard Eaton, Samuel Sharp, foreman Joe Marks, and many of the mechanics. This set the stage for numerous improvements and modifications in engine building and fuel economy.

Jobs requiring commercial skills or local knowledge without technical expertise — conductors, baggagemen, and freight clerks — were more often filled locally. Less-skilled manual workers and trainees for skilled jobs were also hired locally: brakemen, yardmen, engine cleaners/wipers, car repairers, switchmen, watchmen, porters, trackmen, shop helpers, and apprentices. Although the Great Western would look more locally during the 1860s and 1870s, it would still look to U.K. railways for some of its skilled mechanics. For example, in 1873 the London Board sent out five locomotive fitters from the North Eastern Railway and recruited a new assistant mechanical superintendent, John Ortton, from the London and South Western.

* * *

In addition to the antagonistic Grand Trunk, other problems began to surface in the late 1850s. The prosperity of the early 1850s was abruptly shattered in 1857 by a general commercial depression (panic). During the upswing in the business cycle, the Great Western had suffered from rapidly rising costs of construction and locomotives/rolling stock. In the succeeding depression, it suffered from a steady decline in freight and passenger traffic. As the depression deepened in the U.S., through-freight traffic almost ceased. The demand for North American wheat fell with the end of the Crimean War. A poor harvest, followed by an especially severe winter, further reduced traffic. The earnings of the company for the first half of four successive years illustrates the degree to which traffic declined: 1856 ($1,169,592), 1857 ($1,065,720), 1858 ($854,608), and 1859 ($725,904). Anxious shareholders, alarmed by falling prices, declining traffic, and widespread pessimism regarding investments, were pleasantly surprised by the 5.75 percent dividend paid in 1857. However, despite dramatic reductions in expenses, the dividend fell to 3.5 percent in 1858 and no dividend at all was paid in 1859. Although the depression was relatively short-lived, dividends would be very modest or non-existent during the remainder of the railway's independent existence.

The presence of railway management on different continents was a distinct disadvantage: directors and the majority (92 percent) of shareholders in England and management and the minority (8 percent) of shareholders in Canada. Obviously, the British directors and shareholders had no idea about the climatic and economic conditions in Canada or how business was conducted between Canada and the U.S. A great deal of angst may have been avoided had they been more in touch with these issues. For instance, they knew nothing about the possibility of a light, improperly ballasted track being practically raised out of the ground by a period of severely cold weather. Nor could they understand the North American practices of liberally issuing free passes for travel or payment of royalties to agents selling tickets (including Great Western employees who sold tickets on their own railway).

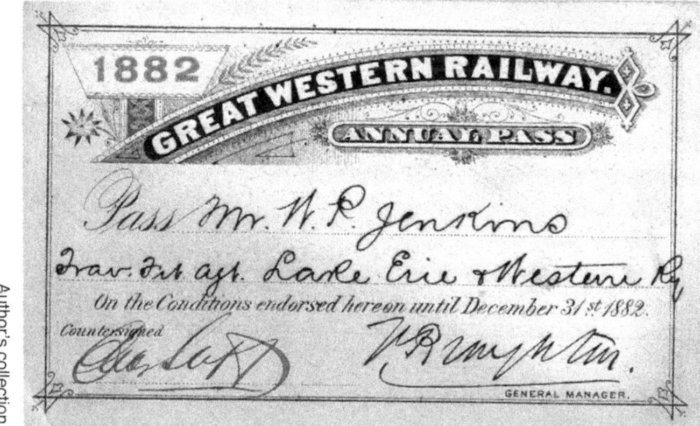

Author's collection.

Examples of Great Western passes for free travel. Unlike most Canadian roads, the Great Western was very conservative in issuing passes, due in part to the control of the British board of directors, since such passes were rare in the U.K.

Early in the railway's existence semi-annual meetings took place in Canada with a Canadian board of directors, which sent a report to the shareholder meeting in London, U.K. However, the English shareholders were really the financial backbone of the company (owning 92 percent of shares) and finally became so restive about what they considered to be the extravagant spending of the Canadian executive that they decided to take back more control into their own hands. From early in 1857 the Canadian board was gradually superseded by the English board and responsible, practical men in Canada were left to manage day-to-day operations.

By the end of 1856 locomotive and rolling stock numbers had increased to eight-six and 1,786 units, respectively. At this time, the company began planning and construction of a car works in Hamilton in which the company would build its own freight and passenger cars. There was also interest in the Detroit and Milwaukee Railway and the Great Western loaned £150,000 ($731,000 U.S.) to this line to assist in its completion across the lower peninsula of Michigan (Detroit to Grand Haven on Lake Michigan; see chapters 3 and 5).

In 1858 the company erected grain elevators in Hamilton and Sarnia, as well as a viaduct at St. Catharines and a steam hammer at the Hamilton Car Works. The Hamilton grain elevator was supported by forty-foot pilings underneath the stone foundation. It was one hundred feet tall with a capacity of 125,000 bushels. Water depth at the wharf was fourteen feet. A siding entered the building, which had three elevator machines. Three cars could be unloaded at the same time. Ships could be loaded directly from the elevator at dockside.

The first Toronto Union Station was erected in 1858 by the Grand Trunk, fifty feet west of Bay Street along Front Street. A small frame building, it housed two waiting rooms, a lunch room, a barber shop, a ticket office, a baggage room, and a telegraph office. The Great Western and Northern railways joined the Grand Trunk in joint use of this station on June 21, 1858.

Disaster struck again when the Chatham depot burned down on the night of Monday, November 15, 1858.

January 18, 1859, marked the opening of the Komoka-Sarnia line. A special excursion train left Sarnia at 0730 hours on a miserable cold and rainy day carrying about 250 passengers. It arrived in the "Forest City" (London) at 1130 hours. During the festivities in London, Great Western directors left in an official train travelling from London to Sarnia. Departing at 1400 hours and arriving in Sarnia at 1700 hours, Sarnia Mayor Henry Glass and a number of town councillors welcomed the directors at McAvoy's Hotel. Customary speeches and toasts followed. The depot was located at the foot of Cromwell Street. The Grand Trunk reached Sarnia in 1859 and erected an opulent depot. Traffic between the two depots mandated an easy means of transportation for customers and their baggage. Omnibuses fulfilled the need initially but, by 1875, a horse-powered street railway (Sarnia Street Railway Company) began operations between the depots. Its two cars were named *Sarnia* and *Huron.*

At the time of construction of the Great Western, a large wooden trestle had been erected over Twelve Mile Creek north of St. Catharines. Together with its approach tracks, it resembled a large letter S in the middle of a very straight line of track. In March 1859 this obstacle was removed by the erection of a new tubular bridge of riveted wrought iron at a new crossing a little downstream from the old trestlework. This resulted in a straightening of the east-west line. Heavy masonry abutments supported the cast-iron tubular beams at a span of about 184 feet. Trains passed over the bridge starting on March 18, 1859.

Library and Archives Canada, C-053563.

Photograph of the London Great Western station, date unknown.

Residents of Windsor were aroused from their slumber during the early morning hours on April 25, 1859, by the shrill whistles of a fire alarm. An inferno was raging in the repair shop and other buildings of the Great Western along the shore of the Detroit River. Firemen from Detroit came to the aid of their sister city using the ferry steamer *Windsor*. The fire quickly consumed the repair shop, which was located about a quarter mile east of the depot, including its valuable supply of tools and machinery and four locomotives: #72 *Medea* (2-2-2), #73 *Medusa* (2-2-2), #79 *Erebus* (0-6-0), and an unidentified locomotive built by Norris. The blacksmith shop and a

Southwestern Ontario Digital Archive, University of Windsor.

View of Windsor Great Western yard in the 1870s, facing west. Note dual-gauge track. On the left is Sandwich Street (Riverside Drive today) and the tallest building (top left) is the old city hall between Windsor Avenue and McDougall Street.

Windsor Community Museum.

View of Windsor Great Western yard, facing east. Various sheds (likely freight) and numerous examples of rolling stock can be seen. The many sheds were probably necessitated by the need to break bulk with the change in gauge at this terminal, until the third rail was installed so that standard gauge railcars could be interchanged. Note the two early cabooses near the centre of the image.

five-hundred-foot-long woodpile were soon consumed as well. Firemen were able to contain the blaze, protecting the roundhouse farther to the east. The cause of the fire was unknown, although some believed that it was the result of arson.

The year 1859 was a gloomy one for all railways, as the depression continued and a rate war was initiated by American railroads. Table 2-3 illustrates a summary of the Great Western public timetable of 1859, including the main line and three branches (Guelph, Sarnia, and Toronto). In 1860 large payments were still being made as a consequence of the Desjardins Canal and Flamborough accidents (see chapter 6). No dividend was paid. Table 2-4 provides a summary of Great Western operations and financial data for 1860. The average annual dividend paid to shareholders during the previous seven years had been 4.75 percent. In spite of this, the affairs of the company were not satisfactory to a large proportion of the shareholders and a committee of investigation was appointed. Further gloom was caused by the fact that passenger travel was severely depressed and that the cost of re-rolling damaged iron rails to allow them to be reused was very expensive (£6 per ton in Canada versus £3 per ton in England). The railway would react to these latter findings, although its response would be delayed until 1864.

The year 1860 saw a "bountiful harvest" and continued development of the first Canadian Oil Patch, discovered in 1858 in the area between the main line and the Sarnia branch around Petrolia. Conveyance of petroleum products in tank cars would become quite important to the company. Actually, a group led by John Henry Fairbank commissioned the building of the Petrolia–Wyoming

Burton Collection, Detroit Public Library.

Great Western Detroit ticket office in 1859, located at the corner of Third and Woodbridge.

Glenbow Museum.

Great Western Petrolia depot sometime between 1875 and 1898.

spur line, which was taken over by the Great Western at a cost of approximately £10,000 ($48,700). Mr. Fairbank also donated the land upon which the Petrolia station was erected. This line was fully open for business in November 1867. London business interests apparently influenced the Great Western to charge more to ship refined oil than crude oil, thus encouraging shipment of crude oil to east London refineries at the expense of Petrolia refineries. Traffic receipts for the first six months were almost £9,000 ($44,000 U.S.) and for the first four years were nearly £30,000 ($146,000). Complaints about unfair freight rates continued until 1877 when the Canada Southern built a spur line into Petrolia, thus ending the Great Western monopoly. Mr. Fairbank was instrumental in this latter action as well.

March 22, 1860, witnessed the opening of the new Desjardins Canal Swing Bridge. It had been tested the day before with the two heaviest locomotives on the roster: *Titan* (#75) and *Pollux* (#78) (total of one hundred tons).

Mr. Charles J. Brydges, managing director, resigned his position owing to his appointment as manager of the Grand Trunk Railway. (Obviously non-compete clauses were not used in managerial employment contracts in the mid-nineteenth century!) Mr. Thomas Swinyard of the London and North Western Railway of England was appointed general manager of the company on September 2, 1861.

Numbers of Great Western Railway personnel in 1860 included:

Head office = 38
Telegraphers = 43

Station agents = 90
Switchmen = 70
Others at stations = 218
Mechanics/others in shops = 602
On permanent way and works = 740
Enginemen = 51
Firemen = 51
Brakemen and baggagemen = 113
Conductors = 33
Total = 2,049

By 1860, the railway was finally beginning to emerge from the doldrums of the 1857 panic.

The departure of C.J. Brydges from the Great Western signalled the beginning of a general restructuring of railway personnel. The office of traffic superintendent was abolished. There was a very large turnover in personnel at all levels. As the editor of the *Essex Record* newspaper would note, on January 8, 1875, the directors had initiated an extensive movement to "sweep away the chaff." In addition, the "doubling-up" process initiated by Brydges was expanded by Swinyard, the new general manager. Most employees could expect sizeable increases in workload, since the positions of many employees who had been terminated would not be refilled. For example, a Mr. Levissey, a track inspector based in Windsor, had nearly the entire adjacent section of line added to his responsibilities. Due to the great length of line for which he was then responsible, he was forced to move to Chatham.

A bridge inventory effective January 11, 1861, read as follows:

- Wood (186 bridges): trestles (223 spans, 5,218 feet in length), pile (36 spans, 439 feet in length), bent & beam (359 spans, 9,213 feet in length), and arch & truss (61 spans, 6,014 feet in length)
- Iron (1 bridge): tube (1 span, 180 feet in length) and brick or stone arch (2 spans, 184 feet in length)
- Swing (wood or iron, 2 bridges): 2 spans, 232 feet in length
- Total bridging: 189 bridges, 684 spans, 21,480 feet in length

(Data compiled from the Report of Samuel Keefer, Inspector of Railways, for the years 1859 and 1860 to the Board of Railway Commissioners of Canada. Reproduced in *Railway & Locomotive Historical Society Bulletin*, No. 51, 1941.)

This inventory illustrates the ingredients for future financial woes, revealing a preponderance of wooden

Ian Cameron Collection, Elgin County Archives.

Great Western wood-steel trestle bridge, St. Thomas, 1872. Staged photograph, looking northeast, of the newly completed bridge, with a construction train and gandy dancers on top.

bridges that would soon have to be rebuilt due to the short lifespan of timber structures erected in the era before wood preservatives such as creosote. From a single firm (Phoenixville Bridge Works, Phoenixville, Pennsylvania), the Great Western would purchase 14,385 lineal feet (2.72 miles) of wrought-iron bridgework!

Toward the end of 1861, traffic again declined precipitously, this time due to the American Civil War. No dividend was paid in 1861. The chief engineer was still complaining bitterly about the quality of the iron rails. It was decided to erect a rail re-rolling mill in Hamilton to "rehabilitate" old rails more economically.

By 1862 traffic north-south via the Mississippi River had practically stopped. Canadian and "east-west" American roads now came into the welcome position of taking over this business. The very serious and ongoing loss of £7,000 ($34,000) by the Great Western alone during the first half of the year due to the depreciated value of the American dollar (below 30 cents to the Canadian dollar) led to a proposal. In it, the Grand Trunk, Great Western, and Buffalo and Lake Huron railways would combine to obtain prepayment of freight from Canada to the U.S. A bill to permit this arrangement was submitted to the Legislature of the Province of Canada but was rejected. Toward the end of 1862 Richard Eaton, locomotive superintendent, resigned and Samuel Sharp, car superintendent, replaced him. Although it was impossible at this time to raise freight rates, the recent large increase in traffic was gratifying.

On the afternoon of February 17, 1862, the Hamilton grain elevator, containing 30,000 bushels of grain, burned to the ground in a spectacular blaze. It was rebuilt on the same site and completed in the same year.

In 1863 the Grand Trunk terminated the agreement with the Great Western with regard to competition, much to the regret of the latter. New iron and stone bridges were erected over the Thames River at Woodstock, Ingersoll, and London, replacing wooden ones.

During 1864 the president of the company, Thomas Dakin, and director, Thomas Faulconer, visited Canada, inspecting the entire railway and its connecting lines (Michigan Central, New York Central, and Detroit and Milwaukee). It was made abundantly clear to them that, unless some drastic changes were made in the facilitation of transfer of passengers and freight between the Great Western and its U.S. affiliates, the Great Western was going to lose most of its valuable American business.

The principal cause of this trouble was the break in gauge between the broad-gauge Great Western and the standard-gauge American roads. This had become such a cause of delay, damage to goods, and inconvenience, generally, that the American roads concerned were offering to help finance the laying of a third rail on the Great Western to accommodate the interchange of American standard-gauge cars. The chief engineer of the Great Western estimated that this would cost $700,000.

The iron rail re-rolling mill established in the area of the Great Western Hamilton shops opened in 1864. The complex's footprint measured one hundred seventy feet by one hundred feet. The height to the roof was thirty-two feet at the side walls and the roof was supported by seven trusses. The main building was one hundred feet by one hundred feet with one-hundred-foot by thirty-two-foot lean-tos at both ends. The cupola was one hundred feet by twenty-two feet with six-foot-high side walls. Erected using 153,063 board-feet of pine and 5,477 board-feet of oak, the structure cost approximately $90,000. Goldie and McCulloch of Galt were responsible for supplying the machinery and boilers while John Gartshore of Dundas supplied castings. G.L. Reid, Great Western engineer, planned the building and supervised its construction.

On September 13, 1864, the steamer *Ottawa* arrived with the steam hammer. Built by Morrison and Co., its cylinder measurements were thirty-six inches (diameter) by sixty inches (stroke) and the main bracket base weighed nine tons. The side frames and bedplate weighed ten tons. The piston and piston rod were made in one solid forging, the rod being fourteen inches in diameter, seventeen feet long, and the forging weighed five tons. Its anvil was cast in two pieces by Dundas Foundry and had been delivered previously to the mill. The mill's annual capacity was 7,000 tons (seventy miles of track). At peak capacity, it employed 108 workers. It was operated under contract by Ward, Clement, and Potter of Detroit and Chicago. With the advent of steel rails in 1869, it became obvious that an iron rail re-rolling mill would not be needed much longer. In fact, the mill was closed for Great Western use on March 8, 1872. Mothballed for seven years, the railway leased the mill to the Ontario Rolling Mill Company in 1879 for custom steel rolling. This company eventually became a division of the Steel Company of Canada (STELCO) in 1909 and the former Great Western mill was enlarged and modernized. For many years it was in use as the Ontario Works of STELCO rolling, among other items, tie plates.

In a now familiar tune, the chief engineer complained about the much poorer quality of the fished rails in 1864 compared with those purchased only five to ten years previously. The iron rails being laid in the early to middle 1860s lasted but a few years. These rails were so poor in quality that freight trains of twenty to twenty-four cars running at thirty miles per hour were too much for them.

In 1864 the U.S. government instituted a passport system that, to a great extent, curtailed through-passenger traffic between eastern and western U.S. states. Fortunately, it was discontinued on March 8, 1865.

In 1865 the city of Toronto granted the Great Western the right to run a line along the Esplanade fronting Lake Ontario to a new terminal station to be built at the foot of Yonge Street. This station, which opened on March 5, 1866, was a great improvement on the previous shared station, which was out of the way and inconvenient. In addition, the provincial government and railway had

Canada Science and Technology Museum.

Great Western's impressive downtown Toronto station at the corner of Yonge and Esplanade Streets, built in 1866.

Archives of Ontario.

View of the Great Western Railway station in downtown Toronto at Yonge and Front Streets in 1867. An unidentified Great Western locomotive (likely a 4-4-0) followed by a probable baggage or baggage-mail-express car are also visible.

Toronto Reference Library.

View of the Great Western freight house at Toronto in 1873.

finally agreed on terms for a mail contract that would pay the railway $124 per mile per year, from September 1, 1865, for a term of four years.

In 1866 a dividend of 5 percent was paid to shareholders due to better economic conditions, but the company was still experiencing serious losses upon conversion of American to Canadian funds. Also at this time, new rails began arriving from England for use in laying the third rail planned months earlier.

On Saturday, March 3, 1866, the Great Western finally opened its own Toronto depot at the base of Yonge Street on reclaimed land. The extension to Yonge Street served two purposes. First, it gave the Great Western independent access to a number of wharves previously inaccessible.

Second, the railway secured accommodation in a depot entirely its own. The depot was supported by fifteen-foot-long timber pilings driven to bedrock. The base was built on large tiles due to its nature as reclaimed land. The depot had a large footprint of 150 by 211 feet. On the north side was the passenger station, including waiting rooms, a telegraph office, and refreshment areas. The south side was restricted to the freight offices. Between the passenger and freight operations was an enclosed trainshed that protected persons and materiel from the elements. This central portion was sixty-four feet wide with the side walls and top of the arch being thirty-four and fifty-four feet tall, respectively. The passenger platform was thirty-five feet by 195 feet. The depot was constructed using wood and was painted a neutral stone colour.

The opening of the Toronto depot was marked by excursion train service from the new depot to the Toronto Board of Trade thence to Niagara Falls. The train comprised five new elliptical-roofed passenger cars followed by the official (business) car at the rear. It was pulled by 4-4-0 #8 (*Dakin*). Departing at 0900 hours, it stopped at Hamilton to pick up Hamilton Board of Trade and Great Western officials. It then proceeded to Erie Junction, where the train used the Erie and Ontario line to stop in front of the Clifton House in Niagara Falls. After roaming about the falls area, including travelling over the ice bridge to the U.S. side, guests returned to the Clifton House for a banquet replete with speeches and toasts. Departing at 1800 hours, the train carrying tired but happy guests arrived at the Toronto depot at 2200 hours.

Niagara Falls (Ontario) Public Library.

A view down the platform of the original Clifton (Niagara Falls, Ontario) Great Western passenger station. The passenger deck (platform) was erected in 1855, followed by the station in 1863. In spring 1879 a fire razed the entire structure. A replacement station was opened on the site before New Year's Day 1880. All stations were located at the foot of Bridge Street, site of the current VIA station as well.

December 18, 1866, witnessed the advent of signal systems on the Great Western at the junction going into the major junction at the Toronto depot. The new signal tower used interlocking rods, which controlled all switches and signals.

January 9, 1867, saw the celebration of the opening of the Blue Line in Hamilton. Finally, the Great Western had been able to participate in a co-operative freight-hauling arrangement with U.S. railroads (for further details, see chapter 4). This celebration was attended by a large contingent of U.S. financiers and railroad owners/presidents who arrived in luxurious Michigan Central sleeping cars. Boarding in Chicago, they proceeded east to Hamilton and then to Rochester, New York. Passenger cars from Chicago arrived about 1500 hours, with Thomas Swinyard, general manager of the Great Western, meeting attendees at the Hamilton depot.

Third rail laying between the Suspension Bridge and Windsor was completed and opened for traffic on January 1, 1867, at a cost of £145,817 ($710,000). The Petrolia branch, extending five and a half miles from Wyoming to Petrolia, was opened for business in November 1867. McDonald and Brown of Hamilton had been the contractors on this tiny branch line.

The years 1867 and 1868 were difficult ones for the Great Western. The harvest was much smaller than expected and the continued rate-cutting war of the American roads reduced income substantially. A terribly hard winter resulted in numerous total interruptions of traffic due to snow storms and floods, culminating on March 12, 1868, with the Thames River overflowing its banks near Prairie Siding and destroying a four-foot-high railway embankment for half a mile. A dividend of only 2 percent was paid.

The opening of the U.S. transcontinental railway in 1869 was greeted with enthusiasm by Great Western officials, who felt that this road would bring considerable additional traffic that was formerly conveyed across the Isthmus of Panama or by ship around Cape Horn. The chief engineer strongly advocated adoption of new steel rails produced by the Bessemer process as they would be one-half the cost of English iron rails and would last at least five times longer. This year also saw a wage increase of ten to twenty cents daily for track (maintenance of way) men, in order to stem the wholesale emigration of men to the western U.S. where railway men were in real demand and commanded top wages. This modest wage hike raised track expenses by £2,504 ($12,200) annually.

In 1870 the Great Western, Detroit and Milwaukee, and Michigan Central signed a traffic agreement with respect to the splitting of profits of through traffic. The two-year agreement was based on the profits of each road compared with the other two roads over the preceding two years. Profits were to be split as follows: Great Western, 48.5 percent; Michigan Central, 44.5 percent; and Detroit and Milwaukee, 7 percent. The Detroit and Milwaukee received a much smaller proportion since through traffic was so infrequent on its line (most of its remuneration was generated by local traffic).

The year 1870 saw the initial replacement of iron rails with 1,100 tons of steel rails. No dividend was paid again, due to the great expense of mixing and working on two gauges at once as well as higher operating expenses. This year saw the "final act" played out in the fiasco of the provincial gauge. An amended act in 1870 repealed the act of 1851 requiring the use of the broad provincial gauge and authority was given to alter the gauge to standard (Dominion of Canada Statutes, 33 Victoria, chapter 50, 1870). As a result, preparations were immediately begun to take up the outside (broad gauge) rail from Windsor to Komoka (just outside London) and to sell the worn-out iron rails. The proceeds of this sale were then applied to the purchase of sixteen standard-gauge locomotives from the U.S. In addition, construction began on five standard-gauge locomotives in the company's locomotive works in Hamilton. The plan was then to take up the remainder of the outside rail on the main line and branches as broad-gauge locomotives were liquidated (converted to standard

Ian Cameron Collection, Elgin County Archives.

Great Western station, St. Thomas, circa 1890s. View of the north side, looking southeast. The station was located opposite the north end of Station Street. The photographer was likely located on top of a rail car.

gauge, sold, or scrapped; see chapter 4). Around this time, planning was begun for the construction of the Wellington, Grey and Bruce (see chapter 3) and Canada Air Line (aka Glencoe loop line) branches.

The charter of the Glencoe loop line required it to pass "through" St. Thomas and Cayuga and "at or near" Simcoe. This obviously limited the routing of the line. However, the line was practically straight throughout, being only four miles longer than a so-called "air line" (as the crow flies) over the entire 146 miles between Glencoe and the International Bridge at Buffalo. Gradients of this line were far less (238 feet in 96 miles or 0.05 percent) than those of the main lines of the Grand Trunk (967 feet in 38 miles or 0.48 percent) or the Great Western (762 feet in 44 miles or 0.33 percent). There were actually only five grades on the entire line:

- East of St. Thomas station, rose over 1,760 yards by one foot in 150 feet or 0.67 percent (rose toward the east)
- Approximately one mile west of Tillsonburg station, rose over 1,500 yards by one foot in 150 feet (0.67 percent) and over 900 yards by one foot in 188 feet (0.53 percent) (rose toward the west)
- East of Fredericksburg (Delhi) station, rose over 1,666 yards by one foot in 151.5 feet (0.66 percent) (rose toward the east)
- East of Simcoe station, rose over 2,000 yards by one foot in 154 feet (0.65 percent) (rose toward the east)
- West of Cayuga station, rose over 4,167 yards by one foot in 157.5 feet (0.63 percent) (rose toward the west)

The aggregate gradient was only 6.4 miles long and no helper services were needed along the entire loop line.

The company's rolling mill at this time was active night and day. A number of machines had been added, including a train of puddle rolls and a rotary squeezer for shingling the puddle balls; hot shears for cutting the puddle bars; a stationary engine of forty horsepower with two boilers; and an extension of the building to enclose the new machinery. The completion of these improvements had been one of the conditions of the contract entered into with Ward, Clement, and Potter in the previous March. The contract was for two years and specified re-rolling of all old iron rails with a very superior quality American iron at the rail heads at a cost of $27 (£5,11 shillings) per ton. It was also planned to replace iron rails with steel rails on the main line at a rate of five hundred tons per month.

By December 1870 alterations had been made to the Toronto depot, including an addition to the southeast corner of the Yonge Street building and one office being moved westward.

A dividend of 6 percent was declared for the final six months of 1870. By January 1, 1871, 111 miles of main line had been re-laid with steel rails or the best of the iron rails. Traffic had increased that winter with a reduction in accidents due to deficient rails. By this time, the following sections had been converted over completely to standard gauge:

- Windsor to Komoka (99.75 miles)
- Hamilton to Suspension Bridge (43.25 miles)
- Hamilton to Toronto (37.75 miles)

Revision of the gauge of the Sarnia, Petrolia, and Guelph branches (total of eighty-three and a quarter miles) would be the next track project. This would allow the car shops to convert all rolling stock over to standard gauge. At that time, the Wellington, Grey, and Bruce branch under construction (fifty and three quarter miles) was broad-gauged. The triple-railed section from Komoka to Hamilton (eighty-six and a half miles) would remain so in order to allow usage of the remaining broad-gauge locomotives until their standard-gauge replacements arrived on site. In a phenomenal feat of organization, revision of the gauge of the Hamilton-to-Toronto branch had interrupted traffic for only eight hours.

On January 21, 1871, a branch line was opened from Suspension Bridge to the city of Buffalo built by the Erie Railroad, producing a second eastbound connection in addition to the long-standing one with the New York Central. January 1871 witnessed the sod-turning ceremony initiating construction of the eight-mile-long Brantford branch. This branch left the Great Western main line at Harrisburg and ran south to Brantford on the Grand River. In the 1850s the city had backed the Buffalo, Brantford, and Goderich Railway (BB&G) over the Great Western. As a result, travellers had to journey west to Paris in order to board a Great Western passenger train to Toronto. The BB&G (later known as the Buffalo and Lake Huron) came under the influence of the Grand Trunk in 1864. Freight then had to travel west to Stratford before going east to Toronto. This short branch would eliminate these problems. See chapter 3 for further details regarding this branch.

A dividend for the first six months of 1871 of 5.5 percent annually was declared. A total of £5,895 ($28,710) was paid for repairs and victim compensation for the Nith River bridge accident on the night of June 5, 1871 (see chapter 6).

Some of the broad-gauge rolling stock that was not convertible to standard gauge was still in fair working condition and too good to scrap. It was decided that the triple-railed section between Komoka and Hamilton would remain in place for the present. Another factor supporting this decision was the inadequate number of standard-gauge locomotives to pull standard-gauge trains. Broad-gauge locomotives could be used with standard-gauge trains in this section of the railway.

A 6-percent dividend was declared for the last six months of 1871. Great satisfaction continued to be expressed regarding the performance of the steel rails, and steel replaced iron as quickly as the iron rails wore out. Steel rails allowed the passage of heavier locomotives, cars, and trains, with diminished wear and tear on the latter.

By January 31, 1872, the entire rolling stock of the company had been converted over to standard gauge. Arrangements were underway to purchase the Erie and Niagara Railway (31.25 miles), a line worked by the Great Western since the fall of 1866 (see chapter 3). At the October 16, 1872, shareholder meeting, a 6.5 percent dividend was declared for the previous six months.

Unfortunately, the proposed purchase of the Erie and Niagara fell through when no agreement could be reached. In place of this, the Great Western approached the Welland Railway and requested running rights over the approximately fifteen miles of line joining the eastern end of the Glencoe loop line with the main line at St. Catharines (see chapter 3).

In July 1872 it was reported that the Great Western would be moving its car shops to London, as part of the deal to lease the London and Port Stanley Railway. Over the next two years, despite the large number of cars that were needed due to gauge conversion, plans to enlarge the Hamilton car shops, even temporarily, were never acted upon. The car shops were easier to move than the locomotive shops for two major reasons. First, the tools, jigs, patterns, etc., were much larger for locomotive construction/maintenance than for car construction/maintenance. Second, the car shops were housed in inexpensive frame buildings as compared with the massive stone buildings housing the locomotive shops.

A dividend of 6 percent was declared for the last six months of 1872. Traffic had increased to such an extent during this period that consideration was being given to double-tracking the main line from Windsor to its junction with the loop line at Glencoe (eighty miles) and creating more and larger sidings.

The Wellington, Grey, and Bruce was completed and opened for business on November 29, 1872, from Guelph to Southampton on Lake Huron (102.25 miles). The Great Western worked this line from its opening. The same arrangement was pursued for the South Bruce division of the line from Palmerston to Kincardine (sixty-seven miles), which was expected to be completed and opened in the fall of 1873. A new line, the London, Huron and Bruce Railway, was under construction from near London to Wingham, a station on the Wellington, Grey, and Bruce (seventy miles) (see chapter 3 regarding all of these affiliated roads). On the Welland Railway, laying of a third rail to create a standard-gauge line was completed on the section between the Great Western main and loop lines.

In late 1872 rumours began circulating regarding the integrity of the Suspension Bridge built twenty years previously. Passenger traffic was interrupted until the rumour could be refuted or corroborated. The Great Western undertook a critical investigation of the bridge to reassure the public of its safety. Competent, independent engineers were chosen to carry this out. Inspection of the caps on the towers revealed no untoward findings. The cable anchorages were thoroughly inspected and, in fact, twelve feet of the masonry over one of these anchorages was removed, which was below the point where the wires were attached to anchor chains. This portion of the cable had been embedded in water lime cement. The exposed wires were "as bright and perfect as the day that they were installed." These findings were widely disseminated and served to reassure an anxious public. Passenger traffic over the bridge recommenced immediately.

The Detroit Tunnel project was abandoned toward the end of 1872, owing to tremendous water and sand leakage at several points. The tunnel had progressed 1,200 feet from the Detroit side and 350 feet from the Windsor side when the project was stopped. A rail tunnel below the Detroit River would not be successfully pursued until the Michigan Central Railroad opened its tunnel in 1910.

A 4.5 percent dividend was announced for the first six months of 1873. The year 1873 was marked by two important events. First, the outer line of rail for the broad gauge between Komoka and Hamilton was gradually taken up when the use of broad-gauge locomotives ceased, the last rail being removed at the end of June. Second, the rapid replacement of iron rails with steel ones meant that by June 30 only thirty miles of main line still had iron rails, and by the end of 1873 the entire main line had been laid with steel rails. In addition, the Hamilton-to-Toronto branch was converted to all steel rails by the end of 1873.

It was unfortunate for the Great Western that its gauge conversion took some seven years to accomplish when other railways of comparable length managed to complete theirs in much shorter periods of time. The third-rail method was the only course available to the company as it was completely unprepared with standard-gauge locomotives and rolling stock when the quick decision to change the gauge was made in 1866. It was fortunate that broad-gauge locomotives could easily haul American standard-gauge cars. An expensive, gut-wrenching experience had been precipitated by a colossal government blunder!

The wooden bridge at Oakville, approximately 575 feet long and sixty feet high, caught on fire and burned in its entirety on May 29, 1873. As a result, the Great Western Hamilton-to-Toronto branch was severed and somehow service had to be maintained while the bridge was rebuilt. Stairways were built up and down the embankments with adjoining chutes to handle baggage transfer. Omnibuses were provided for first-class passengers. Freight was sent from Hamilton to Toronto via steamships. It took approximately one month to build the replacement bridge.

On May 27, 1873, a government inspector went over the Glencoe loop line as far as it had been completed (Welland Junction, 128 miles) and was pleased with what he saw. An attempt was made to use it under unballasted conditions but that was soon given up. Why the company would even attempt this after the experience of 1853–54 is beyond comprehension. The full value of the line could not be realized until the Buffalo International Bridge was opened and a direct connection was made with the Suspension Bridge. In order to permit "immediate" use of the loop line for through-freight service via the Suspension Bridge and at the same time utilize that bridge for interchange traffic with the New York Central and Erie Railroads, a short branch, nine miles in length, was built. It ran from the main-line terminus at Suspension Bridge to the town of Allanburg on the Welland Railway. By this branch a through connection was formed from the loop line to the Suspension Bridge, making the distance to Detroit as short as that from the International Bridge in Buffalo and five miles shorter than the previous main-line route between those points. This branch benefitted the company greatly by facilitating through traffic along a line of much easier gradients than the main line east of London and the avoidance of tolls levied at the International Bridge at Buffalo. However, it was still recognized that the latter bridge was important for local and stockcar (cattle) traffic. Construction of the Allanburg branch was commenced on August 19 and the branch was opened to traffic on November 3, 1873.

The last section of the loop line from Welland Junction to the International Bridge at Buffalo was opened to traffic on December 15, 1873.

Old iron rails taken up on the main line were used, where possible, on branch lines and sidings. In 1873, 15.25 miles of new sidings were built, seven miles of which were at the Windsor and Suspension Bridge terminals.

During the winter of 1873–74, the easy gradients of the loop line enabled the company to run trains of twenty-seven loaded cars from Windsor to the Suspension Bridge via the Allanburg branch with only one locomotive. The previous "record" for the main line was twenty-four cars with the assistance of a helper locomotive at some locations. This additional three cars per train translated into a saving of 152 trains, or nearly two trains per day, during the period of observation.

An agreement was concluded with the London city council regarding the London and Port Stanley Railway on March 24, 1874, allowing the Great Western to lease the twenty-seven-mile north-south road for twenty-one years. Immediately upon taking possession of the property on September 1, 1874, the conversion to standard gauge was begun, a task completed by October (see chapter 3).

By mid-1874 the infrastructure of the railway had matured as evidenced by the following:

- Rail joints: along the main line, were strong fish plates, well-bolted and secured by lock washers and supported by a wrought-iron chair under each end. Along branches/sidings, were the same except for the absence of chairs.
- Ties: along main line, were white oak, eight inches wide by six inches thick by eight feet long, two feet centre-on-centre (no longer two and a half feet centre-to-centre). Along branch lines/sidings, were the same except could use additional species of wood.
- Bridges: all principal ones had been rebuilt in recent years, many in iron and stone. Only a small number (mainly west of Chatham) required heavy repairs or renewal in the near future (all were low structures).
  - Toronto branch: with few exceptions were masonry piers/abutments
  - Galt and Guelph branch: half had been renewed, including all principal ones but one
  - Sarnia branch: majority needed rebuilding but some had already been done and it was planned to do the rest before safety issues arose
  - London and Port Stanley: all were in excellent condition (iron and masonry)
  - New double-tracking; loop line; Brantford branch; Wellington, Grey, and Bruce (over half were new) — basically new stock

Trouble had been brewing for some time among some of the shareholders, regarding the condition and management of the company. As a result, a committee was appointed to examine the affairs of the company (called the Committee of Investigation). Also, the attitude of the Grand Trunk toward the Great Western was not at all friendly and was getting worse. By 1874 wood was becoming a problematic fuel due to its poorer quality, greater scarcity, and higher price. The chief engineer submitted a report to the directors and shareholders on the mileage of the Great Western's affiliated roads as of March 6, 1874 (Table 2-5).

A special general meeting of the shareholders was held in London, U.K., on August 26, 1874. Extreme dissatisfaction was expressed by some of the shareholders regarding company affairs. The Committee of Investigation recommended, among other measures, a complete turnover of the board of directors. After a heated debate at a meeting on September 9, a vote was taken and practically an entirely new board of directors was appointed. The shareholders immediately voted to increase the salaries of the new directors before seeing what improvements, if any, they could make, a deal that rankled the old board members.

The new board of directors, as recommended by the Committee of Investigation and a committee of shareholders, included:

- The Right Honourable Hugh Childers, MP, as president;
- Lieutenant-Colonel Grey as vice-president;
- T. Barkworth;
- Seymour Clarke;
- James Bald;
- L.W. McClure;
- John Stitt; and
- The Honourable W. McMaster (only Canadian) (three vacancies were left unfilled)

Table 2-6 illustrates the capital expenditures of the Great Western over the preceding five years (1870–74), which had been a factor in the British shareholder revolt, appointment of the Committee of Investigation and its subsequent adverse report, and mass resignation of the entire board of directors under Thomas Dakin.

The new president replacing Dakin, who had been president for the previous twelve years, was the Right Honourable Hugh C.E. Childers, MP (Member of British Parliament). He promised to visit Canada very soon. No dividends were paid for the first six months of 1874.

On October 1, 1874, there was a fire in the Clifton-Niagara Falls car shop that destroyed the 360-foot-long structure. Great Western baggage and passenger cars (one of each) and an Erie Railroad sleeping car were also consumed in the fire. Things were not going well due to a new financial panic in the U.S. A provisional agreement with the Canada Southern, by which it would gain access to the Suspension Bridge, was hammered out by the board. Double-tracking the main line had begun, with the Glencoe-to-Chatham and Windsor-to-Belle River segments (total fifty-one miles) being completed by early 1875. These were the first sections of double track in Canada.

President Childers travelled to Canada in the summer of 1875. He found relations with the Grand Trunk to be unsatisfactory, although they had recently improved a bit. Traffic had fallen off in the wake of the panic, though the effects were still acutely present. It is significant that three major managers of the railway resigned early in 1875: General Manager Price, Chief Engineer John Kennedy, and Locomotive Superintendent W.A. Robinson. No explanation is available for the resignations and no regrets were mentioned in the minutes of subsequent company meetings.

In May 1875 the Great Western Railway had requested relief from its property tax burden in Windsor at the Court of Revision (of Tax Assessment). This was flatly refused, considering that the real market value of the company's property of nearly one mile of waterfront was certainly around $700,000, far above the assessed value of $160,000.

By mid-1875, all main line, loop line, and branch mileage were laid with steel rails (513.75 miles). Sidings were of a total length of 178.33 miles. Average speeds of passenger and freight trains were twenty-six and thirteen miles per hour, respectively. By October 1875 F. Broughton had been appointed general manager and operating expenses (wages) and staff members had been cut back substantially. With the railway's extensive experience using steel rails, steel rail lifespan was estimated as being sixteen years, certainly an advance upon the one to three years seen with iron rails. Their cost had fallen to a very reasonable £3 ($14.60) per ton.

During 1875 President Childers spoke of the desirability of setting aside monies each year for rail renewal (£45,000 or $219,000) and bridge renewal (£15,000 or $73,000). At Hamilton, a brick passenger station three hundred fifty by forty feet was completed, as were additional tracks at the London car shops. A half-mile branch was opened at Southampton from the station to a new pier built by the Dominion government. The Kincardine branch was the victim of monstrous snowfalls that could not be overcome by the most powerful snow ploughs and a large workforce. It remained closed from the beginning of February until about the third week of March, while the line between Guelph and Southampton could be kept open only for light passenger traffic.

August 1875 saw the Great Western in the midst of an embarrassing controversy regarding passenger tickets. The controversy surrounded the question of the length of time that a ticket remained "good." The usual legal decision up to that time was that a ticket remained "good" until it was used, even if an expiration date existed on the ticket and that date had passed. The Great Western's policy was to refuse to accept a ticket after its expiration date had passed. Sheriff McEwen of Windsor personally objected to this company policy, and when he had a ticket refused by the company for this reason he entered into a legal action against it. There is no record regarding the outcome of this action.

Starting in 1875 a potentially explosive situation had developed wherein the Great Western was accused of obstructing navigation on navigable rivers in Essex and Kent counties. At the November 1875 Essex County council meeting, Mr. Chartrand gave notice that he would be introducing a resolution authorizing the county clerk to contact the Great Western Railway regarding its bridges built over Belle River and Ruscom River. The next day the resolution was introduced that railway bridges over navigable rivers are obstructions to navigation and violate the Railway Act. He had no problem with railways bridging waterways, but leaving only two or three feet of clearance made navigation impossible, seriously impacting the lumber/wood industries. The resolution was seconded and carried. It was also mentioned that the Baptiste Creek bridge, being constructed at that time, would block up the creek entirely.

At the June 1876 meeting, the county clerk read a letter from the county council's solicitor (lawyer) concerning the Great Western bridges over navigable waterways in Essex County. This letter was accompanied by extensive correspondence between the Grand Trunk and Kent County council where a similar situation existed. Councillor Trembly expressed hope that Essex County council would join with their Kent colleagues in resisting the encroachment of the railways on the rights of citizens negatively impacted by the bridges. The next day John

Langford, warden of Essex County, addressed the county council on the obstruction to navigation by the new Great Western bridge across Baptiste Creek. He explained the character of the obstruction, those who were impacted by it, and what Kent County had done to induce the railway company to modify bridges in its district in such a way as to allow small vessels to pass beneath. County council was left with a decision of whether or not to take legal action against the railway in order to compel it to remove the obstructions.

Table 2-7 illustrates a summary of the passenger timetable for 1875 for the Great Western and its affiliated lines, including the Sarnia; Toronto; Petrolia; Wellington, Grey, and Bruce (including south extension); Glencoe loop line, Welland; Brantford; London and Port Stanley; and Detroit and Milwaukee branches.

December 15, 1875, witnessed the completion of a new Great Western depot in Hamilton. It was a massive structure, thirty-six feet wide by three hundred fifty feet long, with the one-hundred-foot centre portion being two storeys high. The entire structure was built of red pressed Aldershot brick, with an ornamental roof of blue, red, and green slate shingles.

In 1870 work had commenced on the third Welland Canal, sponsored by the Dominion government under the auspices of the Department of Public Works. Railway-canal intersections had been the source of a number of railway mishaps over the years, with Desjardins Canal and Beloeil being the most tragic. To avoid this, the Great Western planned to dig a stone-lined tunnel only ten feet below the bottom of the canal. Commencing construction in 1875, the tunnel was completed in just one year. It was six hundred and sixty-five feet long and lined with limestone blocks shipped to the Queenston dock. It ran under locks 18 and 19.

The tunnel allowed only a single track. The line left the original alignment at Merritton, just east of the Welland Railway junction, and swung south in a downward arc, entering the tunnel. It emerged to climb up to the north and a connection with the original alignment near St. Davids. This single line became a traffic bottleneck and the tunnel was closed to traffic in 1915.

The London, Huron, and Bruce Railway was partially opened to traffic over sixty-nine miles of line in January 1876. Total cost was expected to be £170,000 ($828,000). In 1876 the conversion from pounds-shillings-pence to dollars-cents began in earnest in company financial documents.

The year 1876 saw a return to the rate wars of old between competing roads, leading to heavy losses in working the affiliated lines. Relations with the Grand Trunk continued to be unsatisfactory. Management of the Grand Trunk would not agree to any arrangement of fixed tariff rates and insisted on a pooling of traffic, which was not acceptable to the Great Western. Finally an accommodation was arrived at between the two lines, but it could not be depended upon until the disastrous rate war between the Grand Trunk and certain American lines came to an end. It should be noted that the Great Western directors were willing to pool traffic with the Grand Trunk, which was actually competitive. However, the Grand Trunk wanted, in the interests of some large Grand Trunk shareholders, to force the Great Western to accept a pooling of traffic over the entirety of the compact and reasonably prosperous Great Western and the entirety of the Grand Trunk, much of which it may be doubted had ever paid for itself. Of course, the Great Western could not agree to this. At this time, a few shareholders proposed to amalgamate the two companies, but this attempt was not successful.

An American railway trade journal in 1876 did not mince words about the precarious position of the Great Western:

> Its revenue is insufficient to pay the interest on its mortgage debt by over £100,000 a year. It has the Canada Southern on its south, controlled by Vanderbilt. It has an internal cancer of its own in the form of the loop line, and it has the Buffalo and Lake Huron section of the Grand Trunk running side by side, while the Grand Trunk proper has the shortest line to the seaboard, viz, from Chicago to Montreal. The Great Western of Canada has felt some of the plagues of Egypt, not the least of which are a president and general manager [and a board of directors] who know nothing of American railway administration.

The Toronto *Globe* newspaper contracted with the Great Western in August 1876 to operate a special early morning train from Toronto to London via Hamilton for the exclusive delivery of the newspaper. The *Globe* set the rules, prohibiting passenger and mail traffic between Toronto and Hamilton and specifying the departure time from Toronto (0500 hours) and arrival time at London (1000 hours). The "*Globe* train" was the best-known of all of the Great Western "flyers." Occasionally, passengers would be carried west of Hamilton. The "*Globe* train" always had a clear track!

Starting in 1876 and continuing into 1877, the Great Western began filling in the mouth of the Desjardins Canal with earth. There was great difficulty in finding a solid bottom (similar to the case near Copetown in 1853). When an attempt was made to build a bridge on wooden piles, it gained the nickname "bottomless pit," for it was found that as fast as piles were driven down during the day, they would disappear during the night in the quicksand on the canal bottom. As a consequence, the old canal was filled in and a new one was cut through Burlington Heights to the west.

On the Toronto branch at the outlet of the Desjardins Canal into Hamilton Bay, the Great Western still had a wood trestle built in 1855. This had not been planned to be a permanent structure and the railway was determined to fill in the old canal and dispense with the bridge, thus securing a permanent line. Immense quantities of material were thrown into the gulch. By the end of summer 1877 the embankment had risen two-thirds of the height from the water to the rails (about eighty feet). The huge amount of fill caused some curvature in the trestle, which worsened as the fill amount increased over time.

On Wednesday September 19, 1877, while a large number of men and teams were at work under the trestle, there was a large subsidence of the fill which extended from the centre of the trestle for several hundred feet to the western edge near Hamilton. In only one hour, the embankment subsided twenty-two feet. A large mound was raised several feet from the bed of the adjacent marsh on the side of the embankment next to the bay. The trestle was left twisted, with a large bow into the bay. At one point the trestle sank two feet. Work began immediately on filling and repairing the wooden structure so as to allow trains to creep across the bridge.

On Saturday December 22, 1877, shortly after 2200 hours, the watchman at the trestle over the old canal discovered that another earth slide had occurred. The previous slide in September had occurred on the Hamilton side. This slide had occurred at the eastern (Toronto) end. Great Western personnel were immediately summoned. The amount of damage was impossible to ascertain in the dark of night. It was decided to not let the night train pass. Omnibuses were dispatched from Hamilton to transport passengers in the early morning. Although examination the next day revealed that a large slide had occurred, the actual damage was modest. Slowly, a heavy freight train with twenty full cars and two locomotives passed safely over the remaining wood trestle. Some 6,000 to 7,000 yards had given way, but since nearly 200,000 tons of clay and gravel had been deposited the actual proportion lost was quite small. It appeared that finally the fill had reached the bottom of the old canal/swamp and the embankment had become more stable.

The cut between the west main line at the west junction (Hamilton West Junction) and the Toronto line at Junction Cut (later known as Bayview Junction) was completed. Completion of the remainder of the work took about three weeks.

The winter of 1876–77 was extremely severe and, for weeks, the interchange of traffic with railroads in New York State was significantly compromised and even stopped on some days. As many as three thousand cars were, at one time, detained between Detroit and Suspension Bridge, resulting in a loss to the company of £28,000 ($136,000). The company continued to suffer as a result of the Grand Trunk versus American railroads rate war. The Brantford, Norfolk and Port Burwell Railway was acquired for £12,000 ($58,400), forming another connection between the main line and air line divisions (see chapter 3).

The Great Western in 1877 proposed to lease the Detroit and Milwaukee Railway and issue first mortgage bonds in the amount of $2 million and second mortgage bonds in the amount of $3 million, all guaranteed by the Great Western. In return, it would take up the entire indebtedness of the line. The proposition was laid before the English Detroit and Milwaukee shareholders who were "disposed to accept it." The English Detroit and Milwaukee and Great Western bondholders owned a controlling interest and, acting together, would undoubtedly win.

John S. Newberry, on behalf of Detroit capitalists, offered to buy the Detroit and Milwaukee for $4.5 million ($500,000 in cash, $4 million as 5 percent bonds). In this case, the railway would end up with "home management." The whole matter was referred to a committee of Henry N. Walker, S.T. Douglass, H.B. Ledyard, Captain F. Davy, E.W. Meddaugh, and F. Martin. The bondholders met on September 28 and assigned yet another committee to review all offers (Douglass, Taylor, Ledyard). Finally, the committees and shareholders voted in favour of the Great Western offer late in the year.

In early June 1877 trains on the Sarnia and London and Port Stanley branches were very delayed by caterpillars on the rails, since when they were crushed, locomotive traction was substantially reduced. Crews began on August 10 to convert the old wooden trestle bridge on the Toronto branch across the old outlet of the Desjardins Canal into an embankment. It was hoped that the project would be completed before winter. Ballasting of the London, Huron, and Bruce line was proceeding very slowly due to a lack of labourers. A small fireproof building, thirty feet by twenty feet in size, was erected near the general offices in Hamilton for the storage of old books and other company records.

On October 1, 1877, the Michigan Central withdrew from all passenger agencies in eastern seaboard cities that were being operated in conjunction with the Great Western. The Great Western continued these agencies on its own. The Michigan Central continued its western agencies. Up to this time, the Michigan Central and Great Western contributions to joint agencies had been 55 and 45 percent, respectively.

In October 1877 the situation continued poorly for the company. Traffic was still poor and rates were low. The agreement with the Grand Trunk was presented to the shareholders. The mileage report noted a total of 866.22 miles of line, the Great Western proper having 590.07 miles and the four affiliated lines (Wellington, Grey, and Bruce; Galt and Guelph; London and Port Stanley; and London, Huron, and Bruce) having 276.15 miles. The embankment at the Desjardins Canal was not completed until January 15, 1878, using material obtained from the excavation for a quarter-mile loop line joining the Hamilton-to-Toronto division with the main line. A new wooden passenger depot, forty-seven feet by twenty feet in size, was erected at Welland Junction.

In 1878 the embankment of the Great Western at Jarvis was raised in order to allow an underpass for the Hamilton and North Western Railway. The Hamilton and North Western and Great Western Railways contributed $2,000 and £920 ($4,500), respectively, to pay for this improvement. The Detroit and Milwaukee defaulted on its interest payment and was placed in receivership. An agreement was reached between the Great Western and bondholders of the Detroit and Milwaukee, allowing it to be reorganized under the new title of the Detroit, Grand Haven, and Milwaukee Railway. From this time forward, the railway would be run as part of the Great Western system rather than as a semi-autonomous organization dealing at arm's length with the parent company. Traffic arrangements with the Canada Southern, also recently reorganized, were completed on August 1, 1878.

On April 27, 1878, the new permanent drawbridge (as required by the Dominion government) over the newly enlarged Welland Canal on the loop line was ready for traffic, a mere six days before the canal would be opened for the navigation season. The draw girders of this bridge were those formerly used in the infamous 1858 Desjardins Canal bridge (the latter having been converted from a drawbridge to an embankment). New stations had also been completed at Nixon and East London. The double-track iron superstructure built across the Desjardins Canal and the double-tracking of the Hamilton-to-Toronto branch were opened for traffic on October 12, 1878. These did away with the need for day and night telegraphers and switchmen at the old junction, prevented delays, and removed all risk of collision. The quarter-mile loop line at Burlington Heights was opened on September 16, 1878, connecting the main line to the Hamilton-to-Toronto branch. Trains could now run between Toronto and stations west of Hamilton without having to enter Hamilton yard, saving three miles on their journeys. Also in 1878 the Brantford, Norfolk and Port Burwell branch was substantially improved, new sidings being installed and the line being extended to the Glencoe loop line (extension was opened on December 19, 1878).

July 1878 was a time of tension between the Credit Valley Railway and the Great Western in the environs of Woodstock. The Credit Valley had built west from Toronto to the north of the Great Western main line but, as it proceeded toward St. Thomas, a crossing of the two lines was planned one mile west of Woodstock. The Great Western objected to this plan since the crossing would be located on a rising grade on the Great Western, making it difficult for Great Western trains to proceed after having come to a complete stop at the crossing. The Great Western wished it to be relocated. However, the Credit Valley was seeking its bonuses/subsidies for completing construction and would brook no delay. On Saturday July 20, 1878, the Credit Valley attempted to lay track over the Great Western main line. Expecting this move, the engineer of Great Western freight train #36 was told to "hold the fort" and wait for reinforcements. Shortly afterward, a special train arrived with Mr. Domville (mechanical superintendent), Mr. McGuiness (roadmaster), and a number of men. The Great Western put locomotives from passing freight trains on the crossing to prevent use by the Credit Valley. Although a fight would eventually develop, the Great Western prevailed until the matter could be settled in Chancellery Court.

In November 1878 the Maidstone (Essex County) town clerk was instructed by county council to notify the Great Western that it must remove certain obstructions at the Great Western bridge over "Brown's Creek," and also that a culvert just west of the bridge needed to be repaired.

The year 1879 was to be a significant year in the history of the Great Western. The first serious discussion of amalgamation with the Grand Trunk would occur during this year. In May the annual shareholder meetings of both railways occurred simultaneously. Sir Henry Tyler of the Grand Trunk supported amalgamation while the Honourable Mr. Childers did not. Mr. Abbott (London, U.K.), on behalf of the Grand Trunk shareholders, put together a proposal for amalgamation of the two roads. The proposal included a proposition to place the two lines under one authority, in the form of a joint committee formed out of the two boards of directors. The proportions of revenue division would be settled by arbitration.

The Great Western board meeting in Manchester, U.K., on July 25 featured a large attendance and unanimous passage of a resolution in favour of amalgamation. A committee was appointed to safeguard the shareholders' interests and to urge the board of directors to approve amalgamation.

The Great Western board agreed to refer conditions of amalgamation with the Grand Trunk to arbitration. Five chairmen of important railways were nominated as arbitrators. It should be noted that fusion of the capital of both companies was not being entertained.

The Honourable Mr. Childers had had enough by this time and resigned from the presidency. The Great Western published its answer to the proposition of Sir Henry Tyler to fuse the receipts of both roads. The Great Western preferred a division of traffic at competitive points only, rather than a plan for a joint purse arrangement. In response, the Grand Trunk stated that if the Great Western board adhered to this decision, the Grand Trunk board would appeal to the shareholders of both companies to whom they could guarantee up to £200,000 ($975,000) as an immediate advantage of fusion. The Grand Trunk also offered to seek the formal sanction of the Canadian government for a joint purse arrangement "so as to guarantee the Great Western company against the risk of capricious withdrawal." The Grand Trunk was even prepared to place the two roads under one management based in Canada.

Tyler responded that the Great Western had only two courses: continue the disastrous policy adopted over so many years, or join the Grand Trunk, which was then acquiring an independent position in Chicago and elsewhere.

Lieutenant-Colonel Grey, on behalf of the Great Western board, welcomed a detailed fusion proposal, which would be carefully considered by the board and then submitted to a special meeting of the shareholders.

The Great Western board released a special report on the proposal to fuse with the Grand Trunk, which was to be given to shareholders at a special meeting on October 2, 1879. This report stated that the Great Western had always demonstrated a peaceful response to Grand Trunk aggression. The inability of the Great Western to pay dividends had been due to the Grand Trunk's persistent competition. The board insisted on the division of all competitive traffic and maintained that Tyler's amalgamation proposals were illegal, since no such arrangement would be binding without the approval of the Canadian government. The Great Western would enter into any arrangement that would put an end to competition, but not on the terms proposed by the Grand Trunk.

The Great Western stockholders meeting adopted a resolution approving the board of directors' policy on the question of fusion of net receipts with the Grand Trunk. Two members of the board of directors (Lieutenant-Colonel Grey and James Bald) left for the U.S. on October 4 to confer with W.H. Vanderbilt of the New York Central and other railway authorities. It was rumoured that the reason for the October trip was to take measures to protect the company from Grand Trunk attacks.

On April 2 a fire started in the early morning hours in the Great Western Clifton (Niagara Falls) depot. Starting in one of the wings, the fire soon overtaxed the local and Great Western fire brigades and razed the entire building. However, the heroic efforts of the firemen did save many buildings fronting on Bridge Street. On January 10, 1880, a new, large depot opened on the same site. Built of brick and stone in a semi-Gothic style, it was three hundred feet in length, comprising a central two-storey portion sixty feet in length and two single-storey wings, each being one hundred twenty feet in length. The building was thirty-five feet wide. Waiting rooms and the ticket office were located in the centre block. The east wing had a large dining room, lunch counter, wine room, and U.S. Customs office. The west wing had a telegraph battery room, agent's office, baggage room, and Canadian Customs office.

In the summer of 1879 the Great Western was considering entering into a traffic arrangement with the Rome, Watertown, and Ogdensburg Railroad (RWO).

An eye-popping advertisement for the Great Western and Michigan Central Railways' "Only Route Via Niagara Falls and Suspension Bridge." The bottom of the poster reads: "For Detroit, Chicago, San Francisco, and all points west, take the Great Western and Michigan Central R Line. Palace, sleeping and drawing room cars between New York, Boston, and Chicago without change."

Niagara Falls, Ontario Public Library collection.

This line stretched from the Suspension Bridge, along the southern shore of Lake Ontario, almost to Montreal. A connection with the New York, Ontario, and Western would open up the way to New York City. The two roads were examining the potential for a shared bridge at Lewiston, New York, on the lower Niagara River. Alas, it was not meant to be. The Vanderbilts would swallow up the RWO.

The town of Chatham and the Great Western Railway, the latter being represented by General Manager Broughton, celebrated the opening of the new Chatham depot on Friday September 27, 1879.

A very influential committee of shareholders of the Great Western was formed in December 1879 to arrange, with the Great Western board, a plan to end the unsatisfactory relations with the Grand Trunk. In 1880 the Great Western appealed its Windsor property tax assessment to the Court of Revision, saying that it was $32,000 too high. The appeal was rejected.

There had been fear for some time that Cornelius Vanderbilt, obtaining control of the Michigan Central, would cut off the Great Western from through-freight business between the west and east. In July 1878 his son W.H. Vanderbilt (representing the Canada Southern) and F. Broughton (representing the Great Western) and T. Scott as arbitrator came to an agreement on the division of Michigan Central business to the two roads. Broughton claimed that the Great Western was carrying 75 percent of the east-west business between Buffalo Suspension Bridge and Detroit, with the Canada Southern carrying only 25 percent. While not claiming that the same proportions should still apply, he felt that the Great Western was entitled to the largest share. Vanderbilt claimed that the relationship had changed, since the Michigan Central formerly had discriminated against the Canada Southern while they were now natural allies (both being under the control of the Vanderbilts). Mr. Scott announced the decision as follows: for through passenger traffic the Great Western/Canada Southern proportions would be 60/40 percent, and for through-freight traffic they would be 55/45 percent. The agreement was to last for six months and at the end either party could withdraw by giving three months' notice (for practical purposes, it was a nine-month agreement).

On June 3, 1880, the Wabash, St. Louis and Pacific Railroad and the Great Western signed a twenty-one-year traffic agreement with the following terms:

- The Wabash would pay a $20,000 annual fee plus $5/ loaded twelve-ton car or $1.80/empty car for ferrying across the Detroit River from Detroit, transit across southern Ontario and transit across the International Bridge at Buffalo.
- Gross receipts of the traffic would be collected by the Great Western and, after expenses were deducted, the profits would be split 50/50 between the two railways.
- If the Great Western wished the Wabash to ship its through cars to/from Ashburn (south Chicago), it would have to pay a $10,000 annual fee plus $2.50/ loaded twelve-ton car or $0.90/empty car. In this case, the Wabash would collect the gross receipts to be followed by the same division of the profits after the deduction of expenses.
- If the Great Western wished the Wabash to ship cars between Detroit and Toledo, Ohio, it would have to pay only the usual pro rata mileage divisions of rates and fares and no annual fee.

There is no mention in the document of binding the Wabash to send all through traffic via the Great Western. In fact, as it turned out, Wabash through traffic was almost equally split between the Great Western, Canada Southern, and Lake Shore and Michigan Southern. In addition, how could the Great Western make such a favourable (to the Wabash) arrangement and not expect that the same would have to be granted to its old ally, the Michigan Central, especially with the huge through traffic forwarded by the latter over the Great Western? By making this agreement with the Wabash, would the Great Western reduce its profits on all through traffic by 50 percent? In any case, this is how the relationship would stand, at least until the 1882 Grand Trunk takeover.

A dividend of 1.5 percent for the half year was declared at the April 22, 1880, shareholder meeting. Traffic had increased by 28 percent and rates had improved. Despite this, the leased lines were still being worked at a loss although the Detroit, Grand Haven, and Milwaukee line was working satisfactorily. Mr. Brackstone Baker, secretary of the company for twenty-six years, retired on January 1, 1880. In appreciation of his services, an annuity of £650 ($3,166) per year (50 percent of his annual salary) was voted for him. Mr. Walter Lindley became the new secretary.

Table 2-8 illustrates company financials for several years prior to amalgamation. The October 30, 1880, shareholder meeting was somewhat more cheerful. A surplus of £34,847 ($169,700) was shown and a dividend of 1 percent was declared. Earnings of the main line and branches showed an increase of £71,662 ($349,000) (19.5 percent) over the same period one year previously, while leased lines showed a deficit of £15,201 ($74,029). The Detroit, Grand Haven, and Milwaukee had better results and a 3 percent dividend was declared.

During 1880 the replacement of old wooden bridges by stone and/or iron structures was accelerated throughout the system. Wire fencing was also introduced on an experimental basis on a six-mile stretch and proved quite satisfactory. The Tillsonburg and Delhi viaducts were rebuilt with more permanent materials. The Tillsonburg viaduct was 1,287 feet long and 112 feet high, while corresponding figures for the Delhi viaduct were 1,087 feet and ninety feet. These were the two largest structures on the Great Western system.

In 1881 the Great Western appealed against the Court of Revision finding in terms of property tax levied for its Windsor properties. The mayor of Windsor voiced his doubts that railway personnel had honestly reported the extent of the railway's property holdings. The mayor felt that this needed to be investigated before the trial began. Augustin McDonell was selected to conduct the survey of Great Western property.

By 1882 the juggernaut of the pro-amalgamation forces could not be stopped. In the final tally, the votes for amalgamation were a landslide, with 1,072 shareholders controlling 83,409 votes supporting amalgamation and eight shareholders controlling only 1,100 votes not supporting amalgamation. Amalgamation occurred at 2300 hours on August 11, 1882.

The first board of directors of the amalgamated company, split as one-third Great Western-affiliated and two-thirds Grand Trunk-affiliated, included:

Sir Henry W. Tyler, MP
Sir Charles L. Young
Baronet Lord Cland J. Hamilton, MP
Robert Young
Robert Gillespie
William U. Heygate
James Charles
Right Honourable David R. Plunket, MP
Honourable James Ferrier
Viscount Bury
Henry D. Browne
Colonel E. Chaplin
John Marnham and
Major Alexander G. Dickson, MP

Just two weeks after the August 12, 1882, amalgamation, the last ticket was sold at the Great Western Railway Toronto depot on Saturday night, August 26.

Posted on the door was a single note reading "Go to Union Station." The dining room was locked and the staff had departed. The freight house would continue to be used. It would become a bonded freight warehouse for the Grand Trunk.

The loss of the Great Western as an independent line was bemoaned by the editor of the *Acton Free Press* in its editorial pages on August 17, 1882. Within this editorial the author warned that the Grand Trunk would become a virtual monopoly in the province of Ontario, since it would be years until the Canadian Pacific Railway would play any significant role in rail transportation in southern Ontario. The loss of the Great Western would be especially injurious to the large tract of counties that had formerly enjoyed the advantage and competition of two railway companies. The public could now expect higher freight and passenger rates, fewer trains, and less accommodation for local traffic. The Grand Trunk would only have its own interests to keep in mind in the future: "One can now only hope against hope that greater consideration will be given by the Grand Trunk than has heretofore been seen with other monopolies."

* * *

The Appendix provides details of the ten extant Great Western stations in Ontario. These were built between 1855 and 1890. Half were of brick and half were of frame construction. Seven of ten are in either good (1) or excellent (6) condition, with the remainder in unknown (1), fair (1), or poor (1) condition at present. Details of two extant Detroit and Milwaukee/Detroit, Grand Haven, and Milwaukee stations in Michigan are also provided (1 each being in excellent and poor condition at present). The presence of these stations is a tribute to local citizens who organized and overcame sentiments to demolish these historic structures and then arranged for their restoration and subsequent use.

TABLE 2-1. COMPARATIVE TRAFFIC GROWTH OVER THE FIRST TWO YEARS AFTER OPENING OF THE GREAT WESTERN RAILWAY

Values (£) of Half-Year Ending	Local Passenger Traffic	Foreign Passenger Traffic	Local Freight	Foreign Freight	Local Livestock	Foreign Livestock
7/31/54	59,962	58,724	18,966	11,227	777	449
1/31/55	66,928	76,458	36,349	12,401	1,332	1,250
7/31/55	66,832	104,068	40,969	29,844	1,017	6,462
1/31/56	93,128	109,221	61,372	34,666	3,040	18,438
7/31/56	100,018	110,112	65,707	54,081	4,016	20,541

In addition, average weekly traffic receipts rose from £5,773 in 1854 to £13,633 in 1856. To convert £ to U.S. $, multiply by 4.87.

TABLE 2-2. ELEVATION PROFILES OF THE GREAT WESTERN RAILWAY AND ITS AFFILIATED LINES

Distance (miles) from	Localities	Elevation Above Lake Ontario (feet)
Niagara Falls	Great Western Main line	
	Niagara River (east canyon side)	300
	Niagara River (west canyon side)	308
0.00	Niagara Falls, ON	326
2.84	Track	362
2.84	Summit (sand and gravel)	386
	St. Davids valley, track over	292
9.19	Meritton	143
9.39	Welland Canal crossing	142
10.61		120
10.70	Bed of creek	20
11.10	St. Catharines	110
14.26	Bed of Fifteen-Mile Creek	00
15.34	Sixteen-Mile Creek	-4
15.45		65
16.95	Jordan Station	64
17.23	Twenty-Mile Creek, bed	-8
22.69	Beamsville station	47
26.80	Grimsby station	40
31.72	Winona station	38
37.22	Stoney Creek station	28
43.33	Hamilton station	8
45.02	Toronto Branch junction	58
49.00	Mile post	234
49.41	Summit of gravel ridge (original surface)	308
	Spencer's Creek:	
49.53	Bed	160
49.53	Track	260
49.73	Dundas station	270
51.70	Flamboro station (old)	368
53.75	Summit of drift hills	520
54.73	Copetown station	502
54.92	Bed of Elliot's Pond	475
59.09	Lynden station	504
61.84	Bed of valley	415
	Harrisburg station:	
62.25	Track	487
62.25	Original ground	504
64.01	Fairchild's Creek, bridge	480
64.01	Fairchild's Creek, bed	420
67.23		595
	Grand River:	
69.50	East side	577
69.92	Bed	495
72.06	West side	577
74.90	Paris station	595
75.19		610

75.23	Bed of valley of Nith's Creek	550
		620
78.98	Princeton station	685
79.92	Horner's Creek, bed	635
84.00	Governor's Road, siding	720
86.27	Eastwood station	726
87.69	Summit	775
90.72	Woodstock station	710
95.55	Beechville station	660
100.00	Ingersoll station	632
109.66	Dorchester station	605
119.28	London, Richmond Street	559
	Thames River:	
119.50	East Side	553
	Bed	507
119.73	West side	560
	Cove of Thames:	
120.17	East side	550
120.64	Bottom	505
122.82	West Side	680
129.17	Komoka station	564
139.96	Longwood station	505
142.50	Canada Southern Railway crossing	
144.89	Oppin station	496
149.62	Glencoe station	453
155.87	Newburg station	455
160.70	Bothwell station	444
169.51	Thamesville bridge	376
169.51	Bed of river	340
174.34	Lewisville station	368
183.33	Chatham station	351
198.11	Baptiste Creek station	348
202.84	Stoney Point station	340
211.66	Belle River, bed	320
220.81	Tecumseh station	343
228.82	Windsor station	335

Hamilton Station	Great Western –Toronto Branch	
0.00	Hamilton station	8
1.62	Toronto junction	58
2.15	Track over old outlet of Dundas marsh	82
2.15	Piles driven in marsh to below Lake Ontario	-40
4.08	Waterdown station, ground	98
4.57	Lake Terrace (Ballast Hill)	118
7.02	Burlington station	93
	Twelve-Mile Creek:	
12.94	Track	98
12.94	Bed of creek	29
13.50	Bronte station	99
17.07	Bed of creek	6
17.51	Oakville station	93
20.62		104
	Credit Valley:	
24.46	South side	36
	Piles driven to	-20
25.88	North side	34

29.30	Track	55
29.30	Bed of valley	10
32.19	Mimico station	60
32.69	Mimico River, bed	-2
39.00	Toronto station	8

Harrisburg Jct	Great Western –Brantford and Tillsonburg Line	
0.00	Harrisburg junction	487
0.75	Fairchild's Creek, bed	412
7.31	Grand Trunk Railway crossing	439
	Brantford:	
8.14	Bridge over Grand River	412
8.14	Bed of Grand River	398
12.60	Mount Pleasant station	563
15.57	Mount Vernon station	592
17.30	Burford station	597
21.00	Harley station	590
28.05	Norwich station	597
	Tillsonburg:	
39.12	Canada Southern Railway crossing	550
40.25	Station	538
42.75	Junction	

London	Great Western–Sarnia Branch	
0.00	London station	559
4.22	Hyde Park station	639
10.00	Komoka junction	575
20.23	Strathroy station	500
	Sydenham River bed	475
33.38	Watford station	540
41.81	Wanstead station	455
45.38	Wyoming station	465
51.10	Mandamin station	400
60.89	Sarnia (near Lake Huron)	342

Port Stanley	Great Western –London and Port Stanley Branch	
0.00	Port Stanley, level of Lake Erie	327
3.70		443
4.55	Kettle Creek bridge	488
7.87	St. Thomas station	511
16.18	Summit of track	673
23.58	London	567

London	Great Western –London, Huron, and Bruce Branch	
0.00	London (Richmond Street)	559
4.22	Hyde Park junction	639
11.22	Ilderton station	690
15.58	Brecon station	653
19.22	AuSable River, track	624
	Bed	598
20.69	Clandeboye station	641
26.50	Centralia station	620

31.11	Exeter station	628
37.17	Hensall station	652
43.23	Brucefield station	643
50.06	Clinton station	672
56.20	Maitland River, bed	695
56.86	Londesborough station	727
60.80	Blyth station	834
62.55	Summit	877
67.23	Belgrave station	815
72.06	Bed of valley	765
74.00	Wingham station	834

Glencoe Jct.	Great Western –Air Line	
0.00	Glencoe junction	48
	Thames River:	
11.70	Track	453
11.70	Bed	383
15.20	Lawrence (near)	495
	Kettle Creek:	
26.75	Bridge	500
	Bed of	420
28.00	St. Thomas (near)	520
37.75	Aylmer (near)	514
46.20	Corinth station	520
52.00	Otter Creek, bed	404
53.25	Tillsonburg (near)	538
56.50	Courtland (near)	529
	Big Creek:	
63.00	Track	515
63.00	Bed	424
64.25	Delhi (near)	548

73.00	Simcoe station	472
83.50	Jarvis station	454
92.00		468
96.60	Grand River bridge, near Cayuga station	368
96.60	Bed	324
103.20	Grand Trunk Railway crossing	369
123.00	Frank's Creek	328
125.75	Welland Canal feeder	339
128.50	Welland Railway crossing	330
138.00	Stevensville station	345
142.75	Erie and Niagara Railway crossing	348
145.40	Niagara River	325

Harrisburg Jct.	Wellington, Grey and Bruce Railway	
0.00	Harrisburg junction, with main line of GWR	487
2.40	Fairchild's Creek (Dumfriesbranch), track	513
6.13	Branchton station	650
11.82	Galt station	641
16.00	Preston station	680
17.22	Ballast hill	718
19.07	Speed River, track	686
19.38	Hespeler station	695
27.33	Guelph station	832

Guelph		
0.00	Guelph station	832
8.70	Hurst's Creek, bed	902
	Swan Creek:	
11.02	Track	970
11.02	Bed	911
13.31	Elora station	1050
	Grand River:	
14.75	East side	1080
14.75	Bed	992
16.00	Fergus station	1111
	Irwine River:	
19.00	East side	1135
19.00	Bed	1074
24.60	Summit	1235
27.30	Goldstone station	1214
31.10	Drayton station	1147
35.00	Moorefield station	1104
42.10	Palmerston station	1067
47.80	Harriston station	1017
54.23	Clifford station	987
63.23	Mildmay station	783
69.01	Walkerton station	686
77.80	Pinkerton station	614
84.29	Paisley station	529
	Teeswater River:	
84.61	Bed	462
84.61	Track over	525
97.00	Port Elgin station	428
101.14	Southampton station	369
101.30	Lake Huron, August 1872	335

Palmerston	Wellington, Grey and Bruce Railway –South Extension	
0.00	Palmerston station	1067
5.62	Gowanstown station	1038
8.71	Listowel station	1016
14.68	Newry station	957
18.81	Henfryn station	919
21.78	Ethel station	927
27.35	Brussels station	875
30.00	Gravel bed	848
34.15	Bluevale station	832
35.00	Maitland River, bed	797
37.22	Wingham station	835
38.54	Maitland River, bed	757
43.64	Kinloss (Whitechurch) station	799
50.00	Lucknow station	663
57.00	Pine River, bed	536
58.18	Ripley siding	560
66.38	Kincardine station	343
66.41	Kincardine, Lake Huron	335

TABLE 2-3. SUMMARY OF THE 1859 GREAT WESTERN RAILWAY PUBLIC TIMETABLE

A. Main Line	
Eastbound	
Accommodation (London to Suspension Bridge)	0600–1145 hrs.
Morning Express (Windsor to Suspension Bridge)	0815–1655 hrs.
Mixed (Thamesville to London)	1110–1450 hrs.
Day Express (Windsor to Suspension Bridge)	1255–2200 hrs.
Night Express (Windsor to Suspension Bridge)	1930–0400 hrs.

Westbound	
Accommodation (Suspension Bridge to London)	1615–2155 hrs.
Morning Express (Suspension Bridge to Windsor)	0420–1250 hrs.
Mixed (Hamilton to London)	0930–1710 hrs.
Mixed (London to Thamesville)	0630–1000 hrs.
Day Express (Suspension Bridge to Windsor)	1020–1920 hrs.
Night Express (Suspension Bridge to Windsor)	2120–0545 hrs.

B. Guelph Branch	
Harrisburg to Guelph	1140–1320 hrs.
	1930–2055 hrs.
Guelph to Harrisburg	0645–0815 hrs.
	1700–1835 hrs.

C. Sarnia Branch	
Sarnia to Komoka	0825–1120 hrs.
Komoka to Sarnia	1610–1905 hrs.

D. Toronto Branch	
Hamilton to Toronto	
Accommodation	0910–1045 hrs.
Accommodation	1220–1405 hrs.
Express	1500–1635 hrs.
Accommodation	1930–2140 hrs.

Toronto to Hamilton	
Accommodation	0710–0855 hrs.
Accommodation	1645–1835 hrs.
Express	1030–1215 hrs.
Accommodation	2050–2250 hrs.

TABLE 2-4. SUMMARY OF GREAT WESTERN RAILWAY OPERATIONS AND FINANCIALS FOR 1860

Earnings	
Passengers	$1,021,701
Freight	$1,090,978
Mail/Express	$73,330
Other	$11,934
Total	$2,197,943
Earnings/mile/week	$122.51
Expenses	
Total	$1,993,806
Expenses/mile/week	$111.13
Net Income	$204,043
Percent of expenses to earnings	91
Operations	
Number of Miles	
Passenger trains	54,782
Freight trains	67,885
Other	36,937
Number of Passengers Carried	525,632
Number of Tons of Freight Carried	311,443

TABLE 2-5. SUMMARY OF THE GREAT WESTERN-AFFILIATED RAILWAY MILEAGE, EFFECTIVE MARCH 6, 1874

Description	Main Line Miles	Siding Miles	Mileage of Standing Room for Cars on Sidings	
Main line,				
Single-track				
Air line,				Glencoe to Fort Erie
Single-track loop line	145.50	28.67	21.31	
Welland Railway	14.50	1.29	1.04	Welland Jct. to Merriton
Allanburg branch	8.25	1.41	1.25	Allanburg Jct. to Clifton
Toronto branch	39.50	5.25	3.73	Hamilton to Toronto
WG&B	111.00	NA	NA	Harrisburg to Southampton
G&G	15.50	11.08	7.66	
Galt branch	2.50			
Brantford branch	8.00	0.64	0.42	Harrisburg to Brantford
Sarnia branch	51.00	6.12	4.88	Komoka to Sarnia
Petrolia branch	4.75	3.25	2.58	Petrolia Jct. to Petrolia
L&PS	25.00	2.39	1.95	London to Port Stanley
Totals	425.50	60.1	44.82	

Abbreviations: WG&B = Wellington, Grey, and Bruce; G&G = Galt and Guelph; L&PS = London and Port Stanley; NA = not available (under construction); Jct. = Junction

Note that this summary from the chief engineer does not include Suspension Bridge to Windsor main line or siding mileage.

TABLE 2-6. CAPITAL EXPENDITURES OF THE GREAT WESTERN RAILWAY (1870-74, INCLUSIVE)

	£	$
Glencoe "loop-line"[a]	966,687	4,707,766
General improvements on main line[b]	577,054	2,810,253
New locomotives[c], cars[d], ferry steamers[e]	770,107	3,750,421
Brantford branch	25,659	124,959
Allanburg branch[f]	37,759	183,886
Detroit River bridge survey	924	4,500
Commissions, exchanges, discounts, etc., on stocks and bonds	238,114	1,159,615
Total	£2,616,304	$12,741,400

Also done in these years: 20,020 tons of iron rails re-rolled, 22,916 tons of steel rails purchased, 707,225 ties purchased.

[a] Includes £113,513 ($552,808) for interest during construction and discounts.

[b] Included "doubling-up" of main line from London to Glencoe (79.25 miles); installation of sidings at virtually every station; improvements in roadbed; new station works/yards at Clifton, London, and Windsor; new car shops at London; new wharf at Sarnia; new warehouse at Detroit.

[c] N=113

[d] Passenger/baggage (N=74), Freight (N=2,119), Platform (Flat) (N=524)

[e] *Michigan* and *Saginaw*

[f] Saved £50,000 ($243,500) annually in bridge tolls

TABLE 2-7. SUMMARY OF THE 1875 GREAT WESTERN RAILWAY PLUS AFFILIATES' PUBLIC TIMETABLES

A. Main Line	
Eastbound	
Accommodation (London to Niagara Falls)	0600–1055 hrs.
Atlantic Express* (Windsor to Niagara Falls)	0440–1315 hrs.
Mixed (Windsor to London)	0835–1715 hrs.
Accommodation (Harrisburg to Hamilton)	1040–1140 hrs.
London Express (London to Niagara Falls)	1745–2300 hrs.
Day Express* (Windsor to Niagara Falls)	0900–1920 hrs.
New York Express* (Windsor to Niagara Falls)	1935–0400 hrs.
Buffalo Express (Windsor to Niagara Falls)	0030–1125 hrs.

Westbound	
Mixed (London to Windsor)	0645–1655 hrs.
Morning Express* (Niagara Falls to Windsor)	0615–1725 hrs.
Pacific Express* (Niagara Falls to Windsor)	1235–2120 hrs.
Accommodation (Hamilton to Harrisburg)	1615–1715 hrs.
Accommodation (London to Windsor)	1830–0920 hrs.
Accommodation (Niagara Falls to London)	1525–2045 hrs.
Steamboat Express* (Niagara Falls to Windsor)	2105–0645 hrs.
Chicago Express* (Niagara Falls to Windsor)	0110–0930 hrs.

B. Sarnia Branch	
Eastbound (Sarnia to London)	
Accommodation	0700–1000 hrs.
Accommodation	1020–1305 hrs.
Accommodation	2000–2300 hrs.

Westbound (London to Sarnia)	
Accommodation	0645–0945 hrs.
Mixed	0745–1145 hrs. (ends at Wyoming)
Accommodation	1325–1615 hrs.
Accommodation	1815–2110 hrs.

C. Toronto Branch	
Hamilton to Toronto	
Mixed	0315–0615 hrs.
Accommodation	0915–1100 hrs.
Steamboat Express	1145–1330 hrs.
Mail	1455–1640 hrs.
Express	1725–1905 hrs.
Accommodation	2135–2330 hrs.

Toronto to Hamilton	
Express	0700–0845 hrs.
Express	0935–1125 hrs.
Accommodation	1240–1425 hrs.
Accommodation	1515–1705 hrs.
Express	1945–2130 hrs.
Mixed	2300–0150 hrs.

D. Petrolia Branch	
Petrolia Jct. to Wyoming	
Passenger	0700–0730 hrs.
Passenger	1020–1055 hrs.
Passenger	1310–1340 hrs.
Passenger	1950–2020 hrs.

Wyoming to Petrolia Jct.	
Passenger	0905–0935 hrs.
Passenger	1110–1145 hrs.
Passenger	1540–1610 hrs.
Passenger	2040–2110 hrs.

E. Wellington, Grey, and Bruce, South Extension	
Palmerston to Kincardine	
Accommodation	1405–1645 hrs.
Accommodation	2035–2315 hrs.
Kincardine to Palmerston	
Accommodation	0500–0740 hrs.
Accommodation	1400–1650 hrs.

F. Wellington, Grey, and Bruce, Main Line	
Harrisburg to Southampton	
Accommodation	1040–1630 hrs.
Accommodation	1715–2300 hrs.
Southampton to Harrisburg	
Accommodation	0515–1225 hrs.
Accommodation	1430–2020 hrs.

G. Air Line Division	
Welland Jct. to St. Thomas	
Mixed	0800–1645 hrs.
Express	0840–1112 hrs.
Accommodation	1721–2150 hrs.

St. Thomas to Welland Jct.	
Express	1520–1947 hrs. (originates at Glencoe)
Accommodation	0730–1142 hrs.
Mixed	1015–2020 hrs.

H. Welland Railway	
Welland Jct. to Meritton Jct.	0830–0950 hrs.
Merritton Jct. to Welland Jct.	1040–1250 hrs.

I. London and Port Stanley Railway	
Northbound	
Accommodation	0700–0830 hrs.
Mail	1135–1250 hrs.
Accommodation	1620–1755 hrs.

Southbound	
Accommodation	0900–1035 hrs.
Mail	1430–1535 hrs.
Accommodation	1835–1955 hrs.

J. Brantford Branch	
Harrisburg to Brantford	
Passenger	0835–0905 hrs.
Passenger	1040–1110 hrs.
Passenger	1615–1645 hrs.
Passenger	1840–1910 hrs.

Brantford to Harrisburg	
Passenger	0730–0800 hrs.
Passenger	0945–1015 hrs.
Passenger	1500–1530 hrs.
Passenger	1745–1815 hrs.

K. Detroit and Milwaukee Railway	
Westbound	
B City Express (Detroit to Bay City)	0830–1320 hrs.
Mixed (Owosso to Grand Rapids)	0730–1530 hrs.
Mail (Detroit to Grand Haven)	1000–1915 hrs.
Express (Detroit to Grand Rapids)	1740–0000 hrs.
Night Express (Detroit to Grand Haven)	2315–0840 hrs.
Mixed (Detroit to Pontiac)	0600–0730 hrs.

Eastbound	
Express (Grand Rapids to Detroit)	0600–1230 hrs.
Mail (Grand Haven to Detroit)	0820–1820 hrs.
Express (Grand Rapids to Owosso)	1215–2015 hrs.
Express (Holly to Detroit)	1320–1530 hrs.
Night Express (Grand Haven to Detroit)	2025–0820 hrs.

*Connections made with trains to/from Chicago via Detroit.

Railway connections:
Suspension Bridge — with New York Central and Erie RRs
St. Catharines — with Welland Railway
Toronto — with Grand Trunk Railway
Paris — with Grand Trunk Railway
London — with L&PS branch
Detroit — with Michigan Central, Detroit and Milwaukee, and Michigan Southern lines

TABLE 2-8. SUMMARY OF GREAT WESTERN RAILWAY OPERATIONS AND FINANCIALS FROM 1872 THROUGH 1881[a]

	1872	1873	1874	1875	1876	1877	1878	1879	1880	1881
Passengers carried	930,678	1,031,491	1,095,239	1,103,122	1,110,184	1,196,150	1,206,332	1,227,825	1,314,872	1,380,749
Freight moved (tons)	1,263,179	1,492,208	1,582,275	1,408,175	1,572,538	1,622,342	1,854,663	1,789,214	2,011,930	2,302,571
Earnings										
Passenger	362,914 (1,767,391)	393,627 (1,916,963)	377,092 (1,836,438)	334,097 (1,627,052)	309,083 (1,505,234)	298,962 (1,455,945)	276,693 (1,347,495)	264,736 (1,289,264)	292,784 (1,425,858)	319,880 (1,557,816)
Freight	687,777 (3,349,474)	792,554 (3,859,738)	769,894 (3,749,384)	530,875 (2,585,361)	462,485 (2,252,302)	416,799 (2,029,811)	510,207 (2,484,708)	434,173 (2,114,423)	540,874 (2,634,056)	631,955 (3,077,621)
Other	27,395 (133,414)	29,498 (143,655)	32,188 (156,756)	28,367 (138,147)	59,289 (288,737)	56,382 (274,580)	74,035 (360,550)	54,157 (263,745)	64,915 (316,136)	31,933 (155,514)
Total	1,078,086 (5,250,279)	1,215,679 (5,920,357)	1,179,174 (5,742,577)	893,339 (4,350,561)	830,857 (4,046,274)	772,143 (3,760,336)	860,935 (4,192,753)	753,066 (3,667,431)	898,573 (4,376,051)	983,768 (4,790,950)
Expenses/taxes	662,928 (3,228,459)	807,480 (3,932,428)	872,228 (4,247,750)	758,725 (3,694,991)	653,332 (3,181,727)	558,302 (2,718,931)	583,856 (2,843,379)	509,855 (2,482,994)	560,379 (2,729,046)	619,069 (3,014,866)
Net earnings	415,158 (2,021,819)	406,199 (1,978,189)	306,946 (1,494,827)	134,614 (655,570)	177,525 (864,547)	183,841 (895,306)	277,079 (1,349,375)	243,211 (1,184,438)	338,194 (1,647,005)	364,699 (1,776,084)
Loss on leased lines	---	---	---	30,006 (146,129)	18,385 (89,535)	27,231 (132,615)	18,915 (92,116)	28,661 (139,579)	27,033 (131,651)	29,825 (145,248)
Bond and debenture stock interest	77,914 (379,441)	72,226 (351,741)	198,586 (967,114)	197,725 (962,921)	197,420 (961,435)	191,571 (932,931)	188,867 (919,782)	193,749 (943,558)	196,442 (956,673)	195,197 (950,609)
Balance		-7,666 (-37,333)	+9,051 (+44,078)	-24,209 (-117,898)	-124,894 (-608,234)	-82,060 (-399,632)	-81,292 (-395,892)	+4,344 (+21,155)	-25,604 (-124,691)	

[a] Financial data are expressed as pounds Sterling (U.S. dollars).

CHAPTER THREE

AFFILIATED RAILWAYS

Several railways were affiliated with the Great Western Railway. The characteristics of these affiliations were quite varied. In some cases, the railway promoters and the Great Western worked together from before the incorporation; in others the Great Western entered the "partnership" later, principally as a rescuer of a failing road. In one case, the only affiliation involved the granting of running rights. Sometimes time-limited leases were used, other leases were in perpetuity, and some railways were purchased outright. Summaries of the histories of the affiliated lines up to the time of amalgamation with the Grand Trunk follow in alphabetical order. Unfortunately for the Great Western, these lines were financial liabilities, as attested to in Table 3-1. The positive result for the Detroit, Grand Haven, and Milwaukee was an unusual event.

BRANTFORD, NORFOLK, AND PORT BURWELL RAILWAY

The Norfolk Railway Company was incorporated under provincial statutes on January 23, 1869, to build from Simcoe, Port Dover, or Port Ryerse to Caledonia, Brantford, or Paris. Provisional directors were Daniel Mathews, Thomas W. Walsh, William M. Wilson, Isaac Austin, Thomas W. Clark, and H.J. Sutton. Capital of the company was set at $200,000. Construction of the railway had to commence within two years and be completed within five years of the assent date (Provincial Statutes of Ontario, 32 Victoria, chapter 58, assent date January 23, 1869)

With no progress being made on the railway, an extension in deadlines was requested and approved on

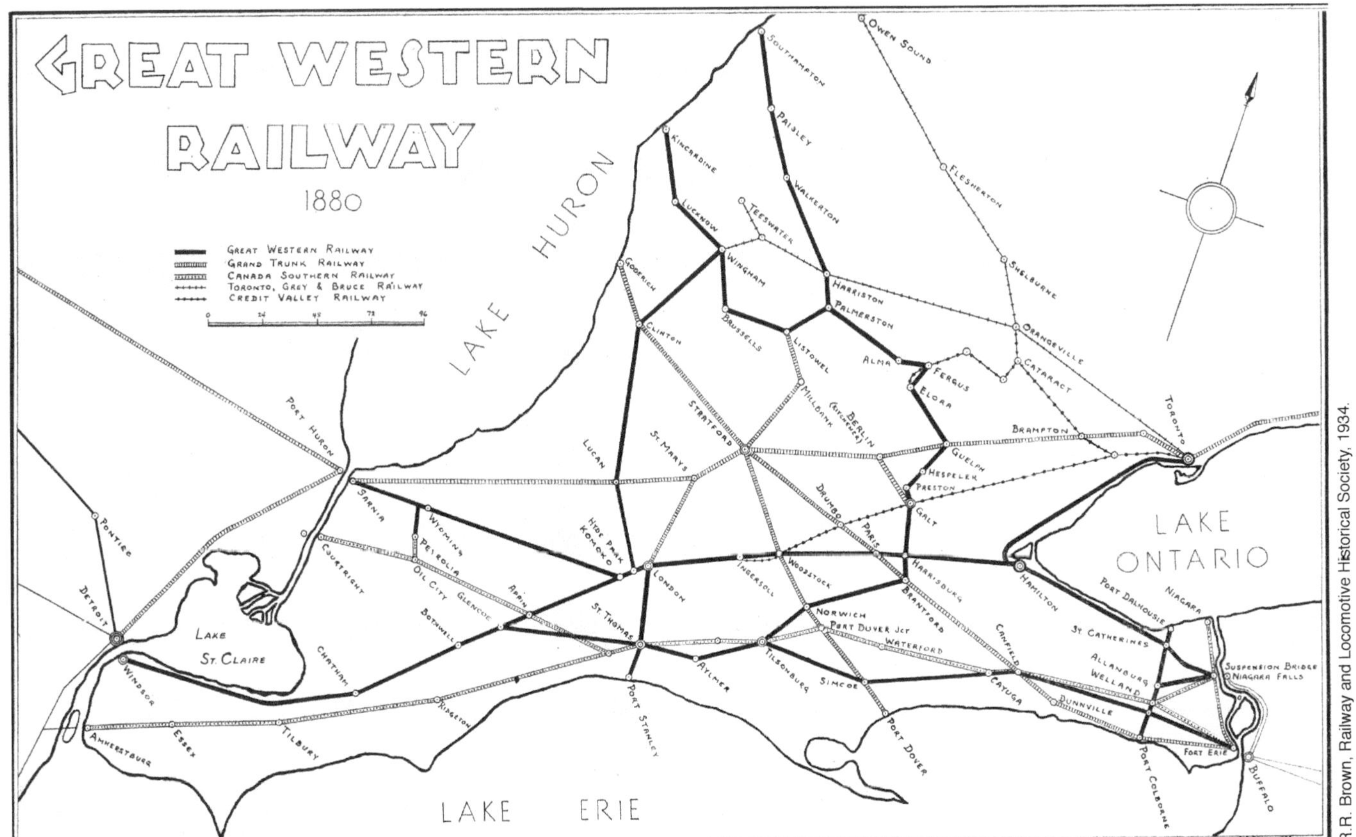

R.R. Brown, Railway and Locomotive Historical Society, 1934.

Map of the Entire Great Western System, 1880.

February 15, 1871. From that date, the deadlines to initiate and complete construction were one and three years, respectively (Provincial Statutes of Ontario, 34 Victoria, chapter 52).

In 1872 the charter of the railway was amended to allow the construction of a branch line to Port Rowan. In addition, the railway would be able to enter into leasing arrangements with other railways. As expected, another request was made for deadline extensions, these extensions to initiate and complete construction being two and five years, respectively, from the assent date (Provincial Statutes of Ontario, 35 Victoria, chapter 52, assent date March 2, 1872).

In a letter dated February 8, 1872, President Mathews made a formal request to the province for a grant of $2,000 per mile of the planned forty-mile line. The other sources of capital for the project were detailed, including a rather dismal $10,000 in private stock paid up, $160,000 in municipal bonuses, and $400,000 from the Great Western. In addition, it was mentioned that the Great Western would complete and run the railway after being paid a bonus of $6,000 per mile. In fact, the municipal bonuses totalled more than $160,000 (Town of Brantford, $70,000; Township of Burford, $30,000; Township of North Norwich, $30,000; Town of Tillsonburg, $8,000; Township of Houghton, $10,000; Township of Bayham, $30,000; and Village of Vienna, $4,000 [total=$182,000]).

An application for amendment of the charter was made in 1873 to allow the line to be routed through to a different port on Lake Erie (Port Burwell instead of Port Ryerse) and to extend north from Brantford to the line of the Credit Valley Railway or any other railway northeast of Brantford. This amendment, assent date on March 28, 1873, also extended the time for the initiation of the railway by one year from the assent date (Province of Ontario Statutes, 36 Victoria, chapter 92).

The year 1874 saw the name of the railway changed to the Brantford, Norfolk, and Port Burwell Railway. The legislation also allowed the issue of bonds, not to exceed $12,000 per mile of line, and allowed the railway to enter into leasing arrangements with other railways. As usual, it extended the initiation and completion dates of the railway to two and five years, respectively, from the assent date (Provincial Statutes of Ontario, 37 Victoria, chapter 53, assent date March 24, 1874). On March 16 the railway secured a provincial grant of $2,000 per mile of completed line. In 1876 the portion of the line from Brantford to Tillsonburg at a junction with the Great Western Air Line extension was finally open to traffic. The remainder of the road was never built. As provided for, the Great Western Railway began operations over the forty-seven-and-a-quarter-mile line. In 1878 the Great Western leased the line in perpetuity.

The Brantford, Norfolk, and Port Burwell was put into "first-class shape" by the Great Western in 1880, with new iron bridges being installed between Brantford and Harrisburg. The line had also been entirely equipped with steel rails by this time.

DETROIT AND MILWAUKEE RAILWAY

The Detroit and Milwaukee Railway Company was composed of two predecessor lines, the Oakland and Ottawa Rail Road Company (incorporated in Michigan on April 3, 1838) and the Detroit and Pontiac Rail Road Company (incorporated in Michigan on March 7, 1834). These two lines were consolidated on April 21, 1855. The first through train (Grand Haven to Detroit) ran on September 1, 1858, while the first Grand Rapids to Detroit through train ran July 12, 1858. The Detroit and Milwaukee Railway Company, in turn, was sold at foreclosure on October 4, 1860, and acquired by the Detroit and Milwaukee Railroad Company on October 22, 1860. This latter line, in turn, went into receivership on April 15, 1875 (C.C. Trowbridge, receiver), and was sold at foreclosure on September 4, 1878. It subsequently was reorganized on November 9, 1878, as the Detroit, Grand Haven, and Milwaukee Railway Company.

The main line of the railway stretched from Detroit to Grand Haven, Michigan, on the eastern shore of Lake Michigan. Construction can be summarized as follows:

- Constructed by Detroit and Pontiac: Detroit to Royal Oak (1838), Royal Oak to Birmingham (1841), and Birmingham to Pontiac (1844).
- Constructed partly by the Oakland and Ottawa and completed by the Detroit and Milwaukee Railway: Pontiac to Fentonville (1855).

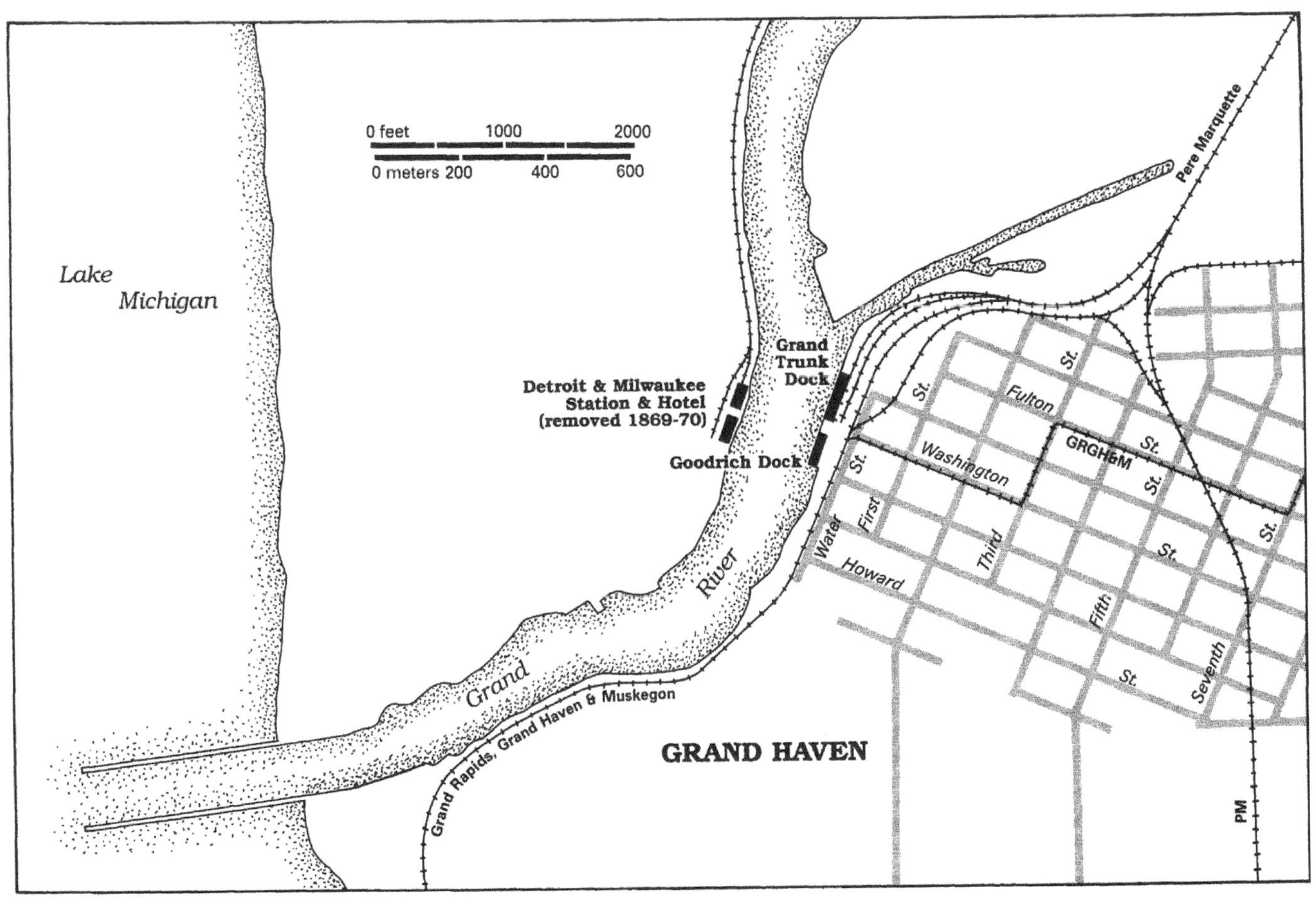

Schematic of the city of Grand Haven, illustrating the locations of the Detroit and Milwaukee, Grand Trunk, and Goodrich Transportation facilities on the Grand River. The Grand Rapids, Grand Haven, and Muskegon Railway was an electric interurban line that operated from 1902 until 1928. G.W. Hilton, *Lake Michigan Passenger Steamers*, Redwood, CA: Stanford University Press, 2002.

Burton Collection, Detroit Public Library.

Detroit and Milwaukee Detroit freight yard, circa 1857.

Burton Collection, Detroit Public Library.

View from above of the Detroit and Milwaukee Detroit passenger depot on Atwater Street, circa 1860. A broad-gauge locomotive is proceeding toward the covered train shed.

- Constructed by the Detroit and Milwaukee Railway: Pontiac to Fentonville (1855), Fentonville to Grand Haven (west side of river) (1856–58), and Ferrysburg to Grand Haven (east side of river) (1870).

Total mileage of the line was 189.73 miles.

The preceding, rather dry, listing of facts hides a lineage of corruption and collusion in the financing and construction of this line, in which the Great Western was to play a pivotal role.

From November 1852 to June 1855 the Canadian government made loans totalling £770,000 ($3.75 million U.S.) to the Great Western. During these years the Great Western was represented by Sir Allan MacNab, who was also the leader of the government for many years. In 1852 he moved a resolution in the Railway Committee, as set forth by the company, which aimed to give the Great Western a monopoly in the Ontario peninsula. However, the bill failed to pass; the obvious reason being the increasingly dominant

Burton Collection, Detroit Public Library.

Detroit and Milwaukee/Great Western Detroit freight depot in 1860.

Loutit District Museum, Grand Haven, Michigan.

An overview of 1869 Grand Haven taken from Dewey Hill. The Detroit and Milwaukee passenger depot is in the foreground, on the channel between the Grand River and Lake Michigan.

position of influence of the Grand Trunk Railway at all levels of government.

In 1863 Finance Minister John Rose accused the Great Western of misappropriating a total of approximately $1.225 million dollars and doing what it was never chartered to do and what it had no legal right doing — constructing a railway in the United States known as the Detroit and Milwaukee. Rose also asserted that $4 million of Great Western capital was thusly used, as well as used in building other lines and investing in steamships on Lake Michigan.

The Commercial Bank of Canada had also advanced the Detroit and Milwaukee a loan of £250,000 ($1.22 million U.S.), its value being substantially greater than this by 1863 with accumulated interest being unpaid. The bank, however, had no recourse since the Great Western had foreclosed two mortgages in 1860 against the railway. A lawsuit also failed. Charles John Brydges, a former Great Western managing director, was one of

Grand Rapids (Michigan) Public Library.

An 1875 view of the first union station in Grand Rapids located at the corner of Island (now Western) Street and South Ionia Avenue. It was built in 1870 and served two major roads, the Detroit and Milwaukee and the Grand Rapids and Indiana. A locomotive of the latter road and an unidentified passenger coach are also pictured.

Author's collection.

Detroit, Grand Haven, and Milwaukee Railway depot in Gaines, Michigan. Built in 1884, it has been lovingly restored and is currently a branch library. Note the extensive use of three-dimensional brick trim around the windows, doors, and eaves. This building "yearned to be a big stone building but lacked the budget."

Author's collection.

Detroit and Milwaukee/Flint and Pere Marquette joint depot at Holly, Michigan. Built in 1886, it is in poor condition, awaiting restoration. Like the depot in Gaines, this depot is a very functional brick cottage style which, in Europe, is called a "railroad style" or "Italian villa."

the Canadian directors of the Detroit and Milwaukee line with the other two being politicians (James Ferrer and William Molson). Brydges was appointed receiver and soon the Great Western bought the line for a nominal $1 million. Down went the Commercial Bank of Canada in ruin, one of Canada's largest banks, with shockwaves reverberating across a Canadian economy already depressed by the American Civil War. The Great Western, in the meantime, was "laughing all the way to the bank."

In the late 1860s the railway began to plan a relocation of the Grand Haven depot from the north side (Dewey Hill) to the south side of the Grand River at Harbour and Washington Streets. To lay track on the south side of the river, train equipment was ferried across, track was laid to the shoreline, and sand was brought into the city to make a solid bed in marshy areas. New docks were built near the depot to maintain connections with steamships plying Lake Michigan. The new depot opened January 1, 1870. Freight trains did not take advantage of the new trackage until six months later.

In the year ending December 31, 1871, the Detroit and Milwaukee had thirty-four locomotives (fourteen passenger, sixteen freight, and four switchers), fifty-seven passenger cars (thirty first-class coaches, twenty baggage-mail cars, and seven emigrant or second-class coaches), 518 freight cars (330 box or stock [cattle] cars and 188 flatcars), and one auxiliary car.

In the year ending December 31, 1879, the locomotive and car inventories for the Detroit, Grand Haven, and Milwaukee (successor to the Detroit and Milwaukee Railway) were as follows:

Clinton Northern Railway, St. Johns, Michigan.

A view of the 1869 Detroit and Milwaukee St. Johns depot after the great tornado of 1920. A new station replaced this one and is still standing, fully restored.

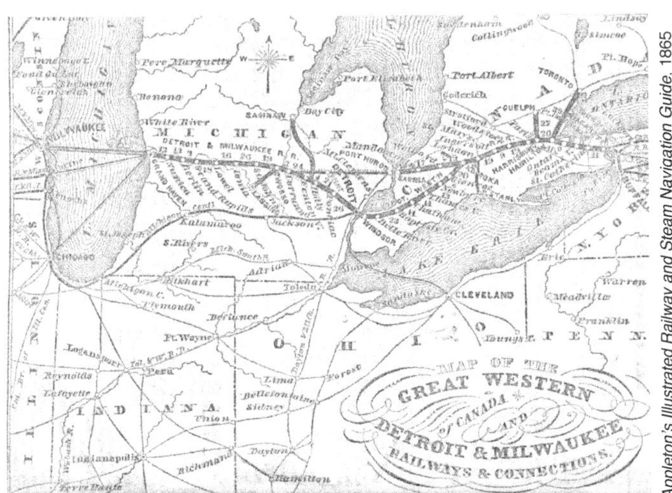

Appleton's *Illustrated Railway and Steam Navigation Guide*, 1865 edition.

Map of Detroit and Milwaukee/Detroit, Grand Haven, and Milwaukee Railways in 1865.

Grand Rapids (Michigan) Public Library.

Grand Haven Detroit and Milwaukee depot post 1869, with nearby stock pen, water tank, three-stall enginehouse, and three major hotels: the Baldwin to the far left, the Parnell to the right of the Baldwin, and the Sherman near the centre of the photograph.

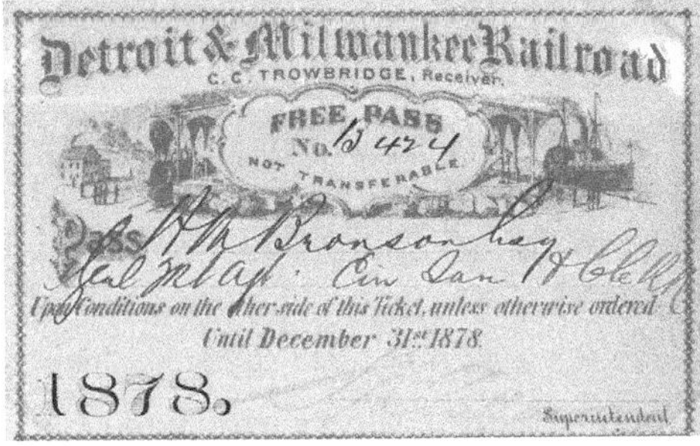

Detroit & Milwaukee Railroad
C. C. TROWBRIDGE, Receiver.
FREE PASS
No. 13424
NOT TRANSFERABLE
Pass H. H. Bronson, Esq.
Genl. Mgr. Cin San. H. Clk.
Upon Conditions on the other side of this Ticket, unless otherwise ordered.
Until December 31st 1878.
1878.
Superintendent

1889.
DETROIT, GRAND HAVEN & MILWAUKEE
RAILWAY.
Pass Mr. J. D. Hawks
Chief Engineer M. C. Rd.
UNTIL DECEMBER 31ST 1889, UNLESS OTHERWISE ORDERED AND SUBJECT TO CONDITIONS ON BACK.
No. 29/238
GENERAL MANAGER.

Author's collection.

Examples of Detroit and Milwaukee and Detroit, Grand Haven and Milwaukee passes for free travel.

Locomotives — 36
Passenger coaches — 28
Baggage/mail/express cars — 16
Boxcars — 324
Stock (cattle) cars — 26
Flatcars — 124
Freight Total — 474
Service cars — 4

Further details regarding the locomotive and passenger car rosters of the Detroit and Milwaukee/Detroit, Grand Haven and Milwaukee are available in chapter 4.

ERIE AND ONTARIO RAILROAD ERIE AND NIAGARA RAILWAY

In light of the revenue lost to the "new" Welland canal starting in 1829, several businessmen from communities along the Niagara River sought a charter to build a railway to bypass Niagara Falls. They were led by John and Alexander Hamilton, sons of the Honourable Robert Hamilton, the builder of the original Niagara Portage Road.

Due, at least in part, to the bitter fight waged by William Merritt and others of the Welland Canal Company, charter legislation failed in the Legislature of Upper Canada in 1831 and 1832. However, the Hamiltons and their colleagues were not to be denied, and assent to the charter of the Erie and Ontario Railroad occurred on April 16, 1835. Of interest, this legislation was delayed by the need to obtain the assent of the Board of Ordnance, which was responsible for military fortifications. Assent was given, provided the railway did not "intrude" within one thousand yards of military fortifications. It appears that the War of 1812 had not been forgotten. Capital stock for the railway was fixed at £75,000 ($365,250 U.S.) and it was to be completed by April 16, 1840 (Acts of the Legislature of Upper Canada, 6 William IV, chapter 19).

Construction began in 1835 but proceeded slowly. By 1837 the line was far from complete and money was running short. A provincial loan of £5,000 ($24,350 U.S.) was arranged. The line has been variously described as beginning operation in 1838 or 1839. Likely both answers are correct in that sections were probably opened as they were completed. The railway was "fully completed" by 1841. However, this may not be entirely correct since there is good evidence that the wharf at Queenston was not completed until 1846!

The railway was an animal tramway in the beginning. Railcars (coaches or freight wagons) were drawn by horses (two to four per car, draught horses for freight wagons and trotting horses for passenger coaches). Coaches/wagons rode upon wooden rails topped with iron strapping. Coaches had the appearance of Stockton and Darlington Railway coaches of 1840s England. Each held twenty to twenty-four people with baggage being carried on the roof. As one might imagine, on both economic and pragmatic bases, the railway closed for the winter, operating only in the high tourist season of summer. The line followed a path nearly parallel with Stanley Street in present-day Niagara Falls.

In 1852 the charter was revised to allow the line to be rebuilt and equipped with steam locomotives as motive power (Provincial Statutes of Canada, 15 Victoria, chapter 50, assent date November 10, 1852). In addition, the line was extended to Niagara-on-the-Lake, this section being opened on July 3, 1854.

The Erie and Ontario only owned one locomotive, *Niagara*, an inside-connected 4-4-0 with sixteen-by-twenty-inch cylinders and sixty-inch-diameter driving wheels. It was built in 1854 by Amoskeag Manufacturing Company of Manchester, New Hampshire. In all likelihood, this locomotive was the *Clifton* (Amoskeag construction number 169), built for Zimmerman and Balch, contractors. It was disposed of early in 1860 and replaced by the leased locomotive to be next described. *Niagara* (2nd) was an outside-connected 4-4-0 with eighteen-by-twenty-inch cylinders and sixty-six-inch-diameter driving wheels (Amoskeag 1854, construction number unknown). The identity of the locomotive's owner is unknown.

In addition, the rolling stock of the road as of December 31, 1860, was as follows:

- four first-class passenger coaches (six-wheeled trucks)
- one baggage car (four-wheeled trucks)
- one boxcar (four-wheeled trucks)
- eight flatcars (four-wheeled trucks)
- ten gravel cars (four-wheeled)
- two handcars

The ever-present Samuel Zimmerman was involved in the rebuilding process of the railway, as well as in the ordering of the only locomotive on the railway's roster (see above). Zimmerman took over the railway in 1854, but his ownership was cut short by his death at the Desjardins Canal disaster on the Great Western Railway on March 12, 1857 (see chapter 6). During the rebuilding process, the line was relocated closer to the villages of Clifton and Elgin and bypassed Queenston and its heavy grades.

In 1857 the Fort Erie Railway Company was formed to construct a line from Fort Erie to Chippewa (completed in 1860) (Provincial Statutes of Canada, 20 Victoria, chapter 151, assent date June 10, 1857). In 1862 the town of Niagara, which had previously acquired all of the assets of the Erie and Ontario Railroad, sold them to William A. Thomson of Fort Erie.

Legislation introduced in 1863 was to change the Erie and Ontario forever. This act empowered the Fort Erie Railway Company to build a line from "some point at or above the wharf of Samuel Cowtherd" (Fort Erie) to Chippewa and acquire the line of the Erie and Ontario Railroad, ending at Niagara-on-the-Lake. In addition, the name of the resulting railway was to be changed to the Erie and Niagara Railway Company. This railway was now capitalized at $2 million and could amalgamate with or engage in leasing arrangements with any other railway. The Erie and Niagara could likewise buy the Erie and Ontario from William Thomson. Branch lines were permitted to the Buffalo (New York) Railway Depot and to Port Robinson on the Welland Canal (as well as a junction with the Welland Railway). An optimistic completion date of October 15, 1865, was set. Lastly, provision was made for incorporating very broad-gauge track (six feet) with the normal Erie and Niagara broad gauge of five feet six inches, such that the Erie and Atlantic and Great Western Railways would be able to run trains over the Erie and Niagara (Provincial Statutes of Canada, 26 Victoria, chapter 59, assent date October 15, 1863).

At the London (U.K.) Great Western Railway shareholders meeting in April 1865, President Thomas Dakin announced that a twenty-one-year-long agreement had been concluded with the Erie and Niagara even before its thirty-one-mile line had been completed. The road would be operated by the Great Western. The advantage of this agreement for the Great Western lay in its provision of a direct line into Buffalo, and direct connections with the Erie and Atlantic and Great Western lines. This line would shorten the Buffalo-to-Detroit distance by twelve miles.

In the fall of 1867 the Great Western closed down the Erie and Niagara, bringing about legal action to reopen the line. The judge ruled in favour of the Erie and Niagara in 1868, forcing the Great Western to reopen the line, allow connections with other railways in the spirit of the agreement, run the line continuously, and give W.A. Thomson of Queenston his proper place as joint comptroller of the Erie and Niagara. If the Great Western failed to perform any of these required actions, the contract would be rescinded. Damages were also awarded to the railway for past Great Western misdeeds.

In 1872 the Great Western board of directors suggested that the Erie and Niagara be purchased, hopefully for a price of £75,000 ($365,250). The board wanted to join the eastern end of the main line to the Glencoe Loop Line using the Erie and Niagara. However, negotiations were to bog down due to the multiple "owners" of the Erie and Niagara. Finally, the Great Western achieved its aims by another means; that is, by negotiating an agreement with the Welland Railway instead (see Welland Railway monograph in this chapter). It was not long before the Canada Southern Railway would approach the Erie and Niagara to complete the "Great Southern Route." The incident that concludes this section illustrates just how low railway companies would stoop to outcompete each other.

In April 1872, along the line of the Erie and Niagara Railway, it appeared as though the Great Western and Canada Southern Railways were at war. Early in the morning of April 22 William A. Thomson and N. Kingsmill, with an accompanying gang of men, took possession of all stations from Fort Erie downstream, locking the drawbridge at Chippewa open to prevent Great Western trains from passing. Arriving at Niagara at 0500 hours, they ran a Great Western freight car off the rails and took possession of the station. The scheduled train from Fort Erie arrived at 1030 hours, Great Western officials having broken the locks on the drawbridge at Chippewa and having repatriated the stations at Fort Erie and Chippewa along the way. The train brought a gang of Great Western employees who attempted to regain possession of the station. However, Thomson's gang prevented this from happening and the Great Western men returned to the Suspension Bridge. Thomson's gang now began to lift rails in several places to prevent passage of Great Western trains. Fortunately, it appears that cooler heads prevailed and that there was no escalation in tensions or violent confrontations. The Canada Southern would win the Erie and Niagara in the end, amalgamation occurring in 1875.

In an ironic twist, the last Great Western cars to undergo gauge conversion (broad to standard) were the nineteen reserved in 1871 for use on the Erie and Niagara.

GALT AND GUELPH RAILWAY

The act incorporating the Galt and Guelph Railway gained assent on November 10, 1852 (Provincial Statutes of Canada, 15 Victoria, chapter 42). Its promoters included some of the wealthiest men in the area, including Absalom Shade, Andrew Elliott, William Dickson Jr., and Jacob Hespeler. It provided for the construction of a railway from the terminus of the Great Western Harrisburg-Galt branch line to Guelph. Capital stock would be a maximum of £140,000 ($681,800 U.S.) and the maximum borrowing capacity was £50,000 ($243,500 U.S.). Promoters planned to lease it to the Great Western once completed.

Investors were initially reluctant to participate based, in part, on the results seen in other railway promotions in the area. Several public meetings were held to bolster support and encourage investment in the line.

Soon a dispute broke out between the Galt and Preston factions regarding the best route for the line. This, of course, was based upon the self-interest of the combatants. The Galt faction wished the line to proceed through Hespeler to Guelph, while the Preston faction wanted the line to proceed through Preston then Hespeler to Guelph. Eventually, the Preston faction won out because it seated more individuals on the board of directors by less than transparent and ethical means.

A contract was signed in January 1854 to build the line, with the official sod turning being done by President Grange (who was also the sheriff) on May 12, 1854. From the start, financial woes plagued the project. Finally, in spring 1855, the Great Western stepped in and agreed to complete the line.

However, the Act of Incorporation of the Galt and Guelph Railway would have to be amended. The final amendment bill passed was nothing like the grandiose bill submitted. However, it did contain the minimum required elements. It allowed each municipality investing at least £5,000 ($24,350 U.S.) in company stock to gain a seat on the board of directors. It allowed extensions to be built from Guelph to Sydenham and Preston to Berlin (now Kitchener). It also allowed an extension to be built to Owen Sound and/or a suitable port on the eastern shore of Lake Huron. Capital stock was increased from £140,000 to £550,000 ($2.68 million U.S.). The Berlin line could not be started until £50,000 ($243,500 U.S.) in stock had been sold, with a 10 percent deposit being paid thereon. The Owen Sound and Sydenham line could not be started until £350,000 ($1.7 million U.S.) in stock had been sold, with a 10 percent deposit being paid thereon. Sections 5 and 6 dealt with the working relationship between the Galt and Guelph and the Great Western. The Great Western was allowed to supply materials and/or labour to build the line, and to take out a mortgage on their value. Finally, the extensions to Owen Sound and Berlin had to be started within three years and finished within seven years of the assent date (Provincial Statutes of Canada, 18 Victoria, chapter 70, assent date April 3, 1855).

The city of Guelph was heavily involved financially with the railway. Not only had the city subscribed to £10,000 ($48,700 U.S.) worth of stock, but in October 1855, when the line was out of money, the city provided a £20,000 ($97,400 U.S.) loan from the municipal fund (endorsed at a public meeting on October 4) to keep it afloat. The line was opened to Preston in December 1856 and finally to Guelph in September 1857.

The Galt and Guelph Railway, only fifteen miles long and being now open, linked the two arch-rivals of the Great Western and the Grand Trunk. More important, for the Great Western, the way was open, through the amended act of 1855, to expand both east and west of Guelph.

Unfortunately, the line never earned or paid any interest upon the amount spent by the Great Western. In light of this, the mortgage taken out for the advance by the Great Western was foreclosed in 1860, effectively making the Great Western Railway the owner of the Galt and Guelph. Amalgamation could not be effected until some legal formalities were completed. For the sum of $12,000, the board of directors of the Galt and Guelph would cease all further disputes with the Great Western and allow the railway to be fully incorporated into the Great Western. The five individuals sharing the $12,000 surrendered by the Great Western were Alexander McDonnell ($1,333.33), Rose Anderson ($2,666.67), and Isaac Buchanan, Charles Davidson, and Donald Guthrie (split $8,000) (Provincial Statutes of Ontario, 41Victoria, chapter 46, assent date March 7, 1878).

HARRISBURG AND BRANTFORD RAILWAY

The Great Western Railway began planning the Harrisburg and Brantford branch in 1870. A provincial act sanctioned the construction of the branch line through the Town of Brantford via Water Street. It also legalized the bylaw providing a $75,000 bonus from the town, a significant

Paris Museum and Historical Society, Paris, Ontario.

Joint Great Western (GTR)/Buffalo and Lake Huron (GTR) station in Paris in 1885.

factor in the line's creation. Lastly, it set out the route of the line, payment schedule for the bonus, and scheduling of the construction. In regard to the latter, one year would be allowed to complete the section between Harrisburg and the line's crossing of the Buffalo and Lake Huron (B&LH) (Grand Trunk subsidiary) and an additional year to complete the section between the B&LH crossing and Water Street (Provincial Statutes of Ontario, 34 Victoria, chapter 55, assent date February 15, 1871). Construction was commenced and completed in 1871.

LAKE HURON AND BRUCE RAILWAY

The Lake Huron and Bruce Railway was incorporated in 1871, with the proposed line originating in London, proceeding to some point in the township of Stanley or Tuckersmith (or both), with power to extend to Goderich or Kincardine (or both). The Honourable

John Carling (of Carling Brewing Company fame) was one of the provisional directors. Capital was established at $400,000. Bond issues were limited to $400,000, or the sum of paid-up share capital plus paid-up bonus installments, whichever was lower. Deadlines for initiating and completing construction of the line were set at one and five years, respectively, after the assent date (Provincial Statutes of Ontario, 34 Victoria, chapter 42, assent date February 15, 1871).

As reported to the London (U.K.) board of directors of the Great Western in January 1873, the London, Huron, and Bruce wished the Great Western to work the line, when completed, for 70 percent of gross earnings and to apply a sum equivalent to 20 percent of the traffic interchanged between the two companies toward the purchase of London, Huron, and Bruce bonds at par. Bonds were limited by charter to $12,000 per mile of line. This was approved, in principle, by the London board. As it happened, the president of the Great Western, Thomas Dakin, was in Canada around this time and chaired a Canadian board meeting on September 5, where the draft agreement was submitted and approved. Arrangements were made to transfer the majority of London, Huron, and Bruce stocks to the Great Western. The two companies signed and sealed the agreement on September 10, 1873, pending ratification by shareholders. To say that the London stockholders were angry at the lack of prior consultation by the board was putting it mildly. The seals were hurriedly torn off the signed documents, rendering them useless (*London* [Ontario] *Daily Advertiser*, July 4, 1874).

In spring 1875 the railway secured a provincial government grant of $2,000 per mile of line (approximately $138,000). By December 6, 1875, the railway had secured $272,500 in municipal support (Townships of Goderich, $15,000; Hay, $15,000; Hullet, $25,000; London, $15,000; Stephen, $17,500; Tuckersmith, $10,000; Turnberry, $5,000; Usborne, $25,000; and Wawanosh East, $25,000; Town of Clinton, $20,000; and the City of London, $100,000).

Construction did not begin until 1875. Contracts were bid out early in the year and the successful bidders of five sections of the line were notified in June. Robert Steele contracted to build sections 1 (14.57 miles) and 2 (15.38 miles) while C.C. Smith would build sections 3 (15.44 miles) and 4 (10.36 miles). Lastly Angus D. MacDonald would build section 5 (approximately 11 miles). At this time, Charles John Brydges and George Masson were president and chief engineer, respectively, of the London, Huron, and Bruce.

The Act of Incorporation of the road was amended in 1876. The time to completion of the line was extended to December 31, 1878. The Great Western was allowed to merge with and own the stock of the London, Huron, and Bruce (Provincial Statutes of Ontario, 39 Victoria, chapter 77, assent date February 10, 1876). The road, as built from London to Wingham, was deemed completed, effective December 31, 1875.

The sixty-nine-mile line had the following route: it began with a junction with the Great Western in London; crossed the Grand Trunk main and branch lines at Lucan and Clinton, respectively; and ended at a junction with the Wellington, Grey, and Bruce at Wingham.

LONDON AND PORT STANLEY RAILWAY

The London and Port Stanley had many problems to contend with, the biggest being the lack of any profit. Very seldom did the railway operate in the black. Up until electrification during the First World War, things got so bad that the line was leased to other railways in the hope that they could make it turn a profit. The Great Western Railway was to be the first of these railways.

Effective March 24, 1874, the Great Western began a twenty-year lease of the London and Port Stanley Railway. All of the physical plant was to be repaired and updated within one year and kept in the same condition throughout the lease. The annual rent was fixed at $20,000 and taxes were the responsibility of the Great Western Railway. Freight rates and passenger fares were fixed at the lowest of the "usual and customary fares into London" charged by the Great Western, Grand Trunk, and Canada Southern lines. Passenger trains were to run a minimum of twice daily each way (except Sundays). If requested, the Great Western was to lay a third rail to accommodate the London, Huron, and Bruce Railway from London to Port Stanley, and allow it reasonable running rights. Car and other workshops were to be maintained in London to work on the locomotives and rolling stock assigned to the leased line. The Great Western even agreed to employ two hundred more workmen than already employed in the present shop. A broad-to-standard gauge conversion of the leased road was to be performed at the expense of the Great Western Railway within one year. Running of weekly excursion trains was to continue without change, as were the rates to be charged to passengers. There were even limits to the rate that could be charged should the Great Western develop the harbour facilities of Port Stanley. Finally, the Great Western was to absorb the obsolete broad-gauge rolling stock of the leased line at a mutually agreed-upon price (through arbitration, if necessary).

It is difficult to think of the benefits that would accrue to the Great Western Railway by leasing a chronically nonpaying short-line railway under seemingly excessive terms. In fact, this was the viewpoint of the London (U.K.) board of directors, who viewed this lease as poorly reasoned and precipitate. The line was in a wholly unsatisfying condition when taken over and needed £12,473 ($60,744) in immediate aid just to get the trains running. Mr. Reid, the Great Western engineer, reported that the line was in unsatisfactory condition in every way and, even with emergency cash infusion was still in a deficient state.

The Great Western made some immediate changes at Port Stanley. The London and Port Stanley rails were extended south of Bridge Street. By 1877 there were three separate lines running along the west side of Kettle Creek harbour. Under the direction, and at the expense, of the Great Western, the piers on both sides of Port Stanley harbour were improved in 1874 and the harbour was dredged in the following two years. It appeared that the Great Western was attempting to make Port Stanley a commercial shipping hub in order to improve the "bottom line."

The Great Western lease of the London and Port Stanley Railway was destined to continue until its amalgamation with the Grand Trunk in 1882, and the latter was to continue the lease for some time after that.

WELLINGTON, GREY, AND BRUCE RAILWAY

The Wellington, Grey, and Bruce Railway was incorporated in 1864, at the request of a large contingent of promoters headed by the Honourable John McMurrich and Francis Shanley, the famous railway contractor. The route of the proposed road started at Guelph, proceeded to or near the town of Fergus, crossing the Grand River midway between Fergus and Elora, and terminated at Southampton. A branch line to Owen Sound was also planned. Capital was set at $1.5 million. Time limits called for construction to begin within three years and to be completed within seven years of the assent date. A clause was present allowing the road to seek arrangements (merger, lease, etc.) with other railways (Provincial Statutes of Canada, 27 Victoria, chapter 93, assent date June 30, 1864).

Even though Guelph was one of the road's two termini, its citizens failed to support it. It was felt that should the line be built, farmers and businessmen from the north would no longer have to come to Guelph to sell produce/products and/or pick up supplies. In fact, the subsequent trade loss was enormous, just as had been feared.

Although a local flurry was created by the incorporation, the lack of initial investment cooled subsequent investor interest. In 1866 there arose two new "threats" to the Wellington, Grey, and Bruce. One was a proposed extension of the Northern Railway to Owen Sound with a branch line (the Grey and Simcoe) to run from Angus to Durham. The second was a proposed railway from Weston or Brampton to Arthur or Mount Forest and on to Owen Sound (the principal promoter being J. Fowler). These threats, in the interests of the two Toronto-based schemes, stimulated Hamiltonians to support the Wellington, Grey, and Bruce. Even the Guelph business community began to support the Wellington, Grey, and Bruce, sensing that Guelph being a terminus would at least get business during construction of the line, as well as the transfer trade. It was also felt that too vigorous opposition may lead to trade being driven elsewhere in retaliation.

On June 15, 1869, the Wellington, Grey, and Bruce entered into a lease in perpetuity with the Great Western such that the latter would supply all motive power and rolling stock and repair/maintain the line. The Great Western would also pay 30 percent of gross traffic receipts as a rental fee. It would also set aside 20 percent of gross receipts from new interchange traffic and buy, at par, Wellington, Grey, and Bruce bonds (initially issued at $10,000 per mile, later increased to $12,000 per mile).

The railway enjoyed tremendous support from the municipalities through which it would pass. From the townships alone, it gained $680,000 in bonuses! The following illustrates the level of support:

- Bruce County: $250,000
- City of Hamilton: $100,000
- Municipality of Fergus: $10,000
- Village of Elora: $10,000
- Town of Kincardine: $8,000
- Town of Durham: $20,000
- Village/Town of Listowel: $15,000
- Townships of Howick ($20,000), Minto ($65,000), Maryborough ($40,000), Normanby ($50,000), Nichol ($10,000), Peel ($40,000), Wallace ($10,000),

Elma ($30,000), Grey ($35,000), Turnberry ($28,000), Wawanosh West ($18,000), Glenelg ($5,000), Bentinck ($25,000), Kinlass, Huron, Kincardine ($51,000).

Construction proceeded slowly but surely. The Guelph to Elora section opened in 1870 while the line from Guelph to Southampton (102 miles) opened in 1872. In 1873, construction began on the circuitous branch from Palmerston to Listowel to Kincardine (sixty-six miles), being completed in 1876.

Unfortunately for the Great Western, the Wellington, Grey, and Bruce turned out to be a poor investment due to its poor construction. The line consumed 81 percent of its gross revenue in maintenance and construction costs. In addition, the Great Western would assume all costs for the conversion of iron to steel rails on the Wellington, Grey, and Bruce.

THE WELLAND RAILWAY

The Welland Railway initially emerged as the Port Dalhousie and Thorold Railway, incorporated in 1853. Its projected route was from Merriton (the station for Thorold on the Great Western) to Port Dalhousie on Lake Ontario. The railway was strongly supported by William Merritt, creator of the Welland Canal, since he felt the railway and canal would be complementary. The canal would be best suited to hauling bulky, heavy, long-distance goods, while the railway would be best for the lighter, more valuable cargoes and could operate in the winter time when the canal was closed. In fact, William Merritt was one of the directors of the Port Dalhousie and Thorold Railway. The railway was capitalized at £75,000 ($365,250 U.S.) and was authorized to own and operate steamships to/from Port Dalhousie. No deadlines were provided for the initiation and completion of construction (Provincial Statutes of Canada, 16 Victoria, chapter 136, assent date May 23, 1853).

In 1856 legislation was introduced to allow the line to be extended to Port Colborne. Capitalization was increased to £100,000 ($487,000 U.S.). The town council of the Town of St. Catharines could now purchase stock in the road. Deadlines for the initiation and completion of the line were two and five years after the assent date, respectively (Provincial Statutes of Canada, 19 Victoria, chapter 23, assent date May 16, 1856).

In 1857 the name of the railway was changed to the Welland Railway, and the railway could own up to twenty-five acres of property at the two port termini (Provincial Statutes of Canada, 20 Victoria, chapter 141, assent date May 27, 1857). Grain elevators were built at both termini.

The line was reasonably rapidly built, opening for service on April 5, 1859, with the first through trains. The route ran from Port Dalhousie, southeast through St. Catharines and Merritton to Thorold, then due south through Welland to Port Colborne.

Legislation in 1864 provided for the sale of £50,000 ($243,500) worth of preference bonds, paying a maximum rate of return of 8 percent. Share capital was increased to $1 million, with an additional $1 million allowable for double-tracking of the line or enhancing port facilities, vessels, and/or rolling stock (Provincial Statutes of Canada, 27 Victoria, chapter 89, assent date June 30, 1864).

The Welland Railway proved its value as a troop transporter during the Fenian Raids in 1866. Using the Welland Railway, troops could be delivered to meet the Fenian invaders wherever they crossed the Niagara frontier since the railway traversed the Niagara peninsula from north (Port Dalhousie) to south (Port Colborne). General Napier's troops were transported to Port Dalhousie by ship and then via the Welland Railway to Port Colborne where they rapidly met the Fenians who had crossed at Fort Erie.

In 1873 the Great Western obtained running rights over a portion of the Welland Railway (from Welland Junction as far north as Allanburg). This was to force gauge conversion (broad-to-standard) onto the Welland Railway. The Welland Railway was to receive $9,000 annually for the twenty-one-year term of the lease agreement. The Welland Railway became a part of the Grand Trunk Railway in 1884.

TABLE 3-1. SINGLE-YEAR SUMMARY OF FINANCIALS OF AFFILIATED RAILWAYS (1880-81)[a]

	BN&PB	LH&B	L&PS	WG&B	DGH&M (12/31/79)
Earnings					
Passenger	3196/0/9	12791/19/6	8549/6/10	33063/18/11	406,761
Freight	7217/3/9	16745/6/3	5183/1/4	38678/8/3	663,629
Other				4435/6/5	42,073
Total	10413/4/6	29537/5/9	13732/8/2	76177/13/7	1,112,463
Expenses/Taxes	10068/13/4	21798/6/3	13074/2/9	71799/6/3	744,384
Net Earnings	N/A	7738/19/6	658/5/5	4378/7/4	368,079
Interest	4231/15/3	11210/14/4	N/A	N/A	280,000
Surplus/loss for GWR	-4427/4/1	-3471/14/10	-3451/6/5	-18474/18/9	+51,873

[a] Financial data are expressed in pounds/shillings/pence except DGH&M ($).

Abbreviations: BN&PB = Brantford, Norfolk and Port Burwell Railway; LH&B = London, Huron and Bruce Railway; L&PS = London and Port Stanley Railway; WG&B = Wellington, Grey and Bruce Railway; DGH&M = Detroit, Grand Haven and Milwaukee Railway; GWR = Great Western Railway, N/A= not available

CHAPTER 4

LOCOMOTIVES AND ROLLING STOCK

LOCOMOTIVES

In keeping with the traditions of other pioneer railways in Canada and the U.S., early Great Western locomotives were personalized. It was considered to be a great honour to have one's name emblazoned upon the sides of a locomotive cab or running board. Perusing the leftmost column of table 4-1, the wide variety of types of names can be appreciated. These included the names of mythological persons, deities, and animals; geographic and political names; animal names; and names of officers of the railway. Geopolitical names included the names of local lakes, rivers, counties, cities, and towns. Examples of officers' names included Adam Brown (leading Hamilton businessman and president, Wellington, Grey and Bruce), Thomas Dakin

Canadian National Photo Archives.

Great Western #8 (*Dakin*) was built as *Woodstock*, a very early broad-gauge Schenectady inside-connected product with fifteen-by-twenty-two-inch cylinders and sixty-six-inch-diameter drivers. Personnel posing on the locomotive are as follows, left to right: Robinson, Forsyth, McMillan, Sharp, Robertson, Hall. On step: Payne, unidentified conductor, and Penny. On ground, left to right: Reid, Wallace, G.H. Howard, Faulconer, Dakin, J. Howard, Swinyard, Baker, unidentified man, Weatherston, Ward, Neilson, and Wilson.

Canadian National Photo Archives.

Great Western #41 *(Spitfire)* was one of six locomotives built by Fairbairn in 1855 as 2-4-0s and rebuilt into 4-4-0s about 1860. Note the classy covered turntable pit!

Canadian National Photo Archives.

Great Western #55 (named *Adam Brown* in 1870) was delivered in November 1855 as *Minos*, a Canada Works (Birkenhead) 2-4-0 which was rebuilt into a 4-4-0 about 1860. About 1873 it was sold to the Wellington, Grey, and Bruce Railway. Thus, this photograph dates from 1870–73.

(president, Great Western), Brackstone Baker (secretary, Great Western), and John Fildes, Gilson Homan, George Smith, and W. Weir (directors, Great Western).

Table 4-1 illustrates the broad-gauge (five-foot six-inch gauge) locomotives first utilized by the Great Western

Canadian National Photo Archives.

Great Western #52 (*Prospero*), built in 1856 by Stephenson, still looked very un-(North)American despite alterations in the cab, pilot beam, stack, and headlamp. The "NG" (for "narrow-gauge") sign on the pilot beam warned switchtenders that there were standard-gauge (four-foot eight-and-a-half-inch-gauge) cars in tow. From the "NG" sign and the dual rails in the picture, it is possible to date the photograph to 1867–70. In 1873 the locomotive was sold to the Midland Railway of Canada.

Canadian National Photo Archives.

Great Western 2nd #14 (*Brackstone Baker*) and 2nd #47 (*Stag*), although built only one year apart in the company's Hamilton shops (1867 and 1868, respectively), varied considerably in dimensions and details. The former was sold in 1871 to the Grand Trunk, while the latter was sold in 1872 to the Northern Railway of Canada.

Railway, some dating back to 1852. The numbers noted under the first column (under "Original Name/#") may not have actually appeared on the locomotives. They may have only been used for record-keeping purposes, and some sources list entirely different numbers that conflict with these. The second set of numbers (under "GWR 1862 renumbering") lists still other numbers that were definitely in use after 1862.

North American builders were predominantly used by the Great Western Railway although five British firms produced forty-four broad-gauge locomotives for the railway: three from Peto, Brassey, Betts, and Jackson, Canada Works, Birkenhead, England; twelve from W. Fairbairn and Son, Canal St. Works, Ancoats, Manchester, England; twenty from Stothert, Slaughter and Company (until 1855) and Slaughter, Gruning and Company (1856 onwards), Bristol, England; six from Robert Stephenson and Company, Darlington, England; and three from John Jones and Son, Liverpool, England.

The original fourteen (#s 1–14) were light locomotives, principally used in construction of the railway, which proved too light for a working railway. The *Elk* (#28/45) was the first locomotive to cross the Niagara Falls Suspension Bridge. The *Oxford* was wrecked as a result of the terrible Desjardins Canal Bridge accident on May 12, 1857 (see chapter 6).

Richard Eaton, the first locomotive superintendent of the Great Western Railway, reported in 1858 that, during the conversion of the Fairbairn and Stephenson 2-4-0s to 4-4-0s, he had planned some novel uses for the two-wheeled lead trucks. He was going to use these now "spare" items to convert the four-wheeled tenders of the

Canadian National Photo Archives.

Great Western #27 (*Niagara*), a 4-4-0 built by Lowell in 1851 and delivered in May 1853. Originally #4, it was both renumbered (to #27) and scrapped in 1862. Note in the foreground the dual-gauge trackage characteristic of the Great Western between 1867 and 1873. Note also the "NG" sign on the pilot beam, signalling the presence of narrow-gauge (i.e., standard-gauge, or four-foot eight-and-a-half-inch-gauge) cars in the consist, and the two accessory head or signal lamps on the pilot beam.

Canada Science and Technology Museum.

Oberon (#51), an inside-connected Great Western 2-4-0 with a British-style six-wheeled tender and the seemingly ubiquitous "NG" sign and dual lamps on the pilot beam. Originally #83, it was renumbered in 1862. Its subsequent disposition is unknown, although two of its stablemates were sold to the Midland Railway of Canada in 1873, while the remaining two were scrapped during the same year.

Canadian National Photo Archives.

Great Western #15 (*Essex*), an inside-connected 4-4-0 built by Lowell in 1853. Cylinders were fourteen inches by twenty-two inches and drivers were sixty-six inches in diameter. Note the single dome atop the boiler and the absent bell. Inside-connected locomotives were less likely to be converted over to standard gauge than those that were outside-connected because the cost of doing so was about four-fold greater (about $2,400 versus $600, respectively).

Canada Science and Technology Museum.

Great Western #3 (*Canada*), a very early 4-4-0 built by Lowell (1851), had sixteen-by-twenty-two-inch cylinders and seventy-two-inch-diameter drivers. Although having a freight consist in tow, those seventy-two-inch drivers made the locomotive more suitable as a passenger locomotive. Rebuilt in June 1861, the locomotive was scrapped by 1873.

Birkenhead and Stephenson locomotives to six-wheeled tenders, due to their excessive weight. He was also going to use them to replace the tender wheels on the Amoskeag tenders, which were nearly worn out.

Obviously wood was chosen early on in middle and eastern North America as the fuel for steam locomotives as it was cheap, plentiful, and readily available near trackside. However, by the 1850s this was no longer the case. In addition, during the winter when there was little or no snow and sleighing was impossible, or during the spring thaw when the roads were dreadful, cordwood for fuel could be difficult to obtain and transport to rail lines. In terms of alternatives, the Great Western Railway of Canada was among the leaders in developing peat as a locomotive fuel. From 1859 onward the Great Western experimented with its use, on and off, until coal became a practical fuel. At the time, peat was much less costly than wood. In an experiment comparing wood, coal, and peat as fuel sources in the same locomotive over 171 miles, 2.95 tons, 4.41 cords, and 3.5 tons of coal, wood, and peat, respectively, were used. At costs of $10/ton, $7/cord, and $5/ton for coal, wood, and peat, respectively, the corresponding fuel costs were $29.50, $30.87, and $17.50. Even with the cost of condensing the raw (surface) peat at $2.50 per ton, substantial savings would accrue with the use of peat. A one acre peat bog produced about one thousand tons of condensed peat. In the end, the relatively limited availability of peat compared with coal led to the use of coal as the fuel-of-choice for steam locomotives.

Experimentation with other fuel sources did not end with peat. The Great Western, along with the Pittsburgh, Fort Wayne, and Chicago, claimed success

Canada Science and Technology Museum.

An engraving of 0-6-0 #67 (*Lioness*), a product of the British firm of Slaughter in December 1855. It was converted to standard gauge in 1873. Details of its further disposition are unknown. Although 0-6-0 locomotives were considered acceptable for road and switcher use in Great Britain, locomotives without pilot wheels were considered only yard switchers in North America, predominantly due to the rougher track, which demanded pilot wheels to prevent derailment at usual main-line speeds.

Library and Archives Canada, PA-138681.

Great Western Railway #42 (*Diadem*), a Fairbairn 2-4-0 rebuilt into a 4-4-0 in 1860, is shown exiting from the Suspension Bridge in 1864. This locomotive would be retired by 1873.

with coke as a fuel source. Coke, better known for its use in steel production, is a result of combustion leading to the extraction of gas from bituminous coal. One advantage of this fuel was its lack of smoke as a byproduct of combustion. This would be of obvious value in urban areas, especially in yard settings. However, unless precautions were taken, the firebox and flues were susceptible to clogging. Precautions involved the use of much larger than usual fireboxes and expensive retrofitting was necessary for existing locomotives. Coke was thus discarded as a locomotive fuel.

As discussed previously, oil was an important commodity on the Great Western Railway, leading to the purchase of a total of seventy-five, and later ninety-six, oil tank cars. Most oil was refined to produce kerosene for use in lighting fixtures and lanterns of the day. Canadian oil, being heavier, was more difficult to refine than oil from Pennsylvania. Supply of Canadian oil far exceeded the demand. In order to create more demand for Canadian oil, oil entrepreneur Charles Ribighini experimented with using crude oil to fuel steam engines. Oil was found to work with stationary steam engines. Would it work in steam locomotives?

The Great Western allowed Mr. Ribighini to experiment with the old broad-gauge locomotive #56 *St. Catharines*. A small oil tank was placed in the tender, from which a hose pipe ran to within about a foot of the stoking hole in the firebox. At this point, the pipe divided in the shape of a "T" into two half-inch pipes that, at a distance of two feet apart and a few inches above the platform of the cab, entered the boiler. At the entrance point, two holes, about 2.5 inches in diameter, were cut through the front of the firebox. These were larger than the diameter of the smaller oil-delivery pipe in order to allow a draught of cold air from the outside to reach the heat within, so as to keep the internal apparatus cool.

From the boiler, a pipe conducted steam to the locomotive cab where, branching into two smaller ones, hot vapours descended to the floor and into a short pipe that surrounded (with a space between) the smaller pipe through which the oil was projected into the firebox. Thus, the oil entered the firebox by the pressure or suction of the steam which was being directed through it in jets.

A fire was started in the firebox and kept going until steam was generated in the boiler. At this point, the oil flow was started and, the steam playing around and upon the flaming petroleum, the totality of heat was directed to the flues so that all of the heat was used. The trial using the *St. Catharines* appeared to be a success, but was not repeated. Oil would not become a commonly used locomotive fuel in Canada until the 1950s, after the development of the Alberta oil industry. Most oil-fired locomotives would exist in the Canadian West as a result. The *St. Catharines* was none the worse for wear for participating in the experiment, as it was to remain on the roster until the end of broad-gauge trackage (scrapped circa 1875).

The Great Western was also among the first to use steel, instead of iron, in locomotive boilers. Cammell & Company steel was used in the fireboxes of two Great Western heavy freight locomotives with "constant and satisfactory use for up to 15 months." In the largest locomotives, use of steel would save one to two tons in locomotive weight compared with iron.

A drawing and photograph of Great Western 0-6-0 *Scotia*, the first North American locomotive with a steel boiler. The drawing illustrates the pre-1862 locomotive (#90), since during 1862 its number was changed to 82.

Canada Science and Technology Museum.

In 1861 the *Scotia* became the first locomotive in Canada, if not North America, with a steel boiler. The *George Stephenson*, *Scotia*, *Erin*, *Sarnia*, and *Saxon* (#s 89–93/81–85) were the first locomotives built in the shops of the Great Western Railway in Hamilton (1860–62).

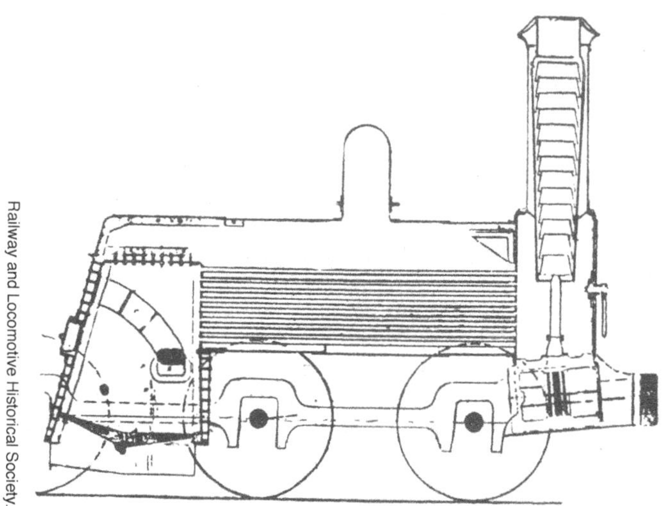

Railway and Locomotive Historical Society.

This is a schematic of Eaton's Smoke Consuming Boiler (Richard Eaton being the Locomotive Superintendent of the Great Western until late 1862). This boiler was designed to burn coal. The firebox had a water arch, projecting from near the top of the back sheet and extending downward below the lower row of flues. Mark's patent stack was fitted, containing a series of flounces intended to regulate the draft, with a lubricator supplying oil regularly to slide valves and cylinders. A tubular feedwater heater, comprising a tube passing through from the tender tank to the firebox, preheated the water, saving 15 percent on fuel. The total heating surface was 1,100 square feet, of which the feedwater heater provided one hundred square feet.

They also became the first coal-burners on the railway as an experiment of Mr. Eaton's. These locomotives had the following characteristics. The firebox had a water arch projecting from near the top of the back sheet and extending downward below the lower row of flues. Mark's patent stack was fitted with a lubricator to supply a regular supply of oil to slide valves and cylinders. A tubular feedwater heater, patented by Eaton, comprised a tube passing through from the tank to the firebox which heated the water, resulting in a cost savings of 15 percent on fuel. Unfortunately, the experiment was not successful and, by February 1863, Mr. S. Sharp (Eaton's successor) had had the five locomotives converted back to wood-burners. Despite this setback, it was abundantly clear that a conversion to coal-burning was absolutely necessary since the forests were rapidly disappearing. Eventually, all wood-burners were converted to coal-burners or were retired. Of interest, during rebuilding of some of the tank locomotives, a pair of trailing wheels had to be added due to the increased weight of coal, compared with wood, in the rear bunkers.

All locomotives of British origin had their copper fireboxes and tubes switched out to iron replacements during their first heavy servicing at the Hamilton shops.

In 1862 Mr. Sharp, mechanical superintendent of the Great Western, successfully used petroleum oil (kerosene) in locomotive marker lamps and headlights. The reward for this switch was much greater illumination at 20 percent of the cost of the former illuminating fluid, whale oil. This was among the first uses of kerosene on railways. In late 1872 the Great Western was the first line to use locomotive marker lamps integrated with locomotive number boards. In addition, these were the first lamps in which the indication colour could be readily changed (white to red and vice versa). Only two lines at this time provided train numbers in a readily-assessed form: the Great Western and Eastern (of Massachusetts). Train numbers were illuminated by placing dark numbers across the centre of locomotive headlamps. In 1880, John Hall of the Great Western invented a novel air brake, which was highly regarded by the editors of the periodical *Scientific American*.

Canadian National Photo Archive.

Great Western #103, delivered in August 1870, was among the first group of Rhode Island standard-gauge passenger motive power. This locomotive was one of the earliest in the group to be scrapped (June 1906).

Canadian National Photo Archives.

This one-hundred-series Great Western locomotive was typical of dozens of locomotives delivered from Rhode Island in the early 1870s. Note the distinctive touches: the warrior figure atop the headlamp and the bell atop the pilot beam.

Canadian National Photo Archive.

#126 was one of five freight locomotives built at the Company's Hamilton shops in 1870. Even numbers were assigned to all Great Western standard-gauge freight motive power.

Canadian National Photo Archives.

#92 (*Gilson Homan*), an 0-4-4 tank locomotive, was rebuilt in 1870 from a then-obsolete 1853 Globe (Souther) 4-4-0 called *Huron* (#24).

Beginning in 1870, the Great Western changed from broad gauge (five feet six inches) to standard gauge (four feet eight-and-a-half inches). Unlike the Grand Trunk Railway, the Great Western Railway converted relatively few locomotives over to standard gauge (only 19.1 percent or twenty-two of one hundred fifteen units), relying instead on placing huge orders for new road power. An unusual numbering scheme was adopted, assigning odd numbers starting at #101 to passenger units and even numbers starting at #102 to freight units. Switcher numbers started

Canadian National Photo Archives.

No records list Great Western 0-4-2T #208. Outshopped by Baldwin in 1872, the construction number is illegible.

Canadian National Photo Archives.

#102, a 4-4-0 from the Rhode Island Works in Providence, Rhode Island, illustrates the beautiful lines of later 4-4-0s with a minimum of extravagant ornamentation. The sixty-three-inch-diameter drivers favoured use as a freight locomotive (even numbers on the Great Western connoted freight power, while odd numbers connoted passenger power in the standard-gauge era). This locomotive would serve the Grand Trunk as #s 775 and 324, until it met the scrapper in April 1908.

Author's collection.

A large group of distinguished gentlemen, including members of the English board of directors of the Great Western, join the crew in front of the *William Weir* (#87), an 0-4-4 tank switcher rebuilt from #87 (*Erie*), a 4-4-0 from Globe (Souther) built in September 1853, rebuilt in 1871. This locomotive is outside the front entrance to the Great Western's Toronto waterfront depot.

Canada Science and Technology Museum.

John Fildes (#91), an 0-4-4 tank locomotive without a headlamp! This photo appears to have been taken shortly after its arrival from Baldwin Locomotive Works in Philadelphia (build date: September 1870). Note the ornate lettering and striping on a lowly switcher.

with #301 and were renumbered to #401 and up as the road engine fleet grew past three hundred units. Tables 4-2 and 4-3 illustrate the standard-gauge passenger and freight locomotives on the Great Western Railway, respectively.

The *Gilson Homan* (#92) was probably the first standard-gauge locomotive on the railway, while the *Lincoln* (#10/4) was likely the last broad-gauge locomotive. The last seven broad-gauge locomotives were *Middlesex* (#7/1), *Chatham* (#12/6), *Paris* (#13/7), *Woodstock* (*Dakin*) (#14/8), *Welland* (#55/9), *St. Catharines* (#56/10), and *Lincoln*. The *Gilson Homan* enjoyed a long life, largely, it is believed, because it ended up as a stationary steam engine powering the cliff railway at Port Stanley.

The construction of three 4-4-0s was commenced in the Great Western Hamilton shops before amalgamation with the Grand Trunk, with subsequent completion well after amalgamation had been completed. The locomotives *Empress*, *Princess*, and *Duchess* retained these names and became Grand Trunk Class H4 #s 728 to 730, respectively. Completion dates were October 1887, July 1888, and August 1888, respectively. Corresponding renumberings were to #s 581 to 583 (in 1898), #s 597 to 599 (in November 1899), and #s 455 to 457 (in 1904). Only the original #730 (*Duchess*) survived until the 1910 renumbering (to #2213). Respective scrapping dates were November 1906, September 1909, and May 1918.

Unfortunately the Great Western Railway did not place more orders with the nascent Canadian locomotive builders of the time, placing only the small order for two locomotives with Daniel C. Gunn and the orders placed for twenty-five locomotives with the Ontario Foundry/Canadian Engine and Machine Company/Canadian Locomotive and Engine Company. Additional orders, especially during the terrible depression of 1857, may have saved Gunn's firm and promoted a broader-based Canadian locomotive industry.

Gunn was a pioneer Canadian locomotive builder located in Hamilton, headquarters city of the Great Western. He had actually worked on behalf of or for the Great Western from 1850 to 1856. As a result of attending a meeting on April 22, 1850, Gunn was appointed to a committee of sixty Hamiltonians charged with selling stock in the Great Western. At the time of the 1851 Canada Census, Gunn listed his occupation as "agent for the Great Western Ry." For the next few years he worked for the railway in at least two capacities. First, he served as a land agent, acquiring real estate for right-of-way and buildings. Second, he "attended to the transportation and distribution" of rails, hardware, and other materials "to the various points where required for laying the superstructure of the Road" (his description of his duties). In the first Hamilton city directory (1853) his occupation was given as "R.R. land agent" and he was likewise described three years later as a "land-agent." By 1856 Gunn had severed his ties to the Great Western and headed into the foundry/machine shop business.

In 1857 Gunn delivered two 0-6-0 freight locomotives to the Great Western, named *Achilles* and *Bacchus*, respectively. These proved to be the only locomotives bought by the Great Western from Gunn as Gunn went bankrupt on March 7, 1859, as a consequence of the decline in orders due to the financial panic of 1857 and his overextended borrowing.

Canada Science and Technology Museum.

Great Western 4-4-0 #318 became Grand Trunk #74 in 1898 after having been renumbered to #865 in 1882. A Rhode Island product of September 1873, it was rebuilt in December 1885 and was sold in July 1902 to the Sun Portland Cement Company.

Library and Archives Canada, DAPDCAP 142112.

Great Western Rhode Island–built standard-gauge passenger 4-4-0 locomotive #107 at St. Thomas. Built in September 1870, it was scrapped in March 1915.

Ian Cameron Collection, Elgin County Archives.

Great Western locomotive #292. This 4-4-0 freight locomotive would subsequently become Grand Trunk #s 852, 26, 110, and 118, being sold in November 1905 to Quebec Railway, Light and Power, becoming its #1. Photograph was taken in St. Thomas in 1872.

Library and Archives Canada, DAPDCAP 141992.

Great Western 0-4-4 tank switcher #403 (*George Smith*), at St. Thomas in 1881, was the product of a 4-4-0 rebuilding project in 1870.

Certainly, had Gunn survived as a locomotive builder, he may well have garnered many more locomotive orders based on the favourable impression of *Achilles* and *Bacchus*. One and one-half years after their delivery, the Great Western locomotive superintendent was asked to comment on them for a prospective buyer of another Gunn locomotive. This Great Western official was Richard Eaton, the most brilliant locomotive engineer in Canada in the 1860s and 1870s. Since his endorsement was written well after Gunn's bankruptcy, one can be sure that he had no possible motive for flattery in writing concerning "the Two Engines made by D.C. Gunn for the above Company":

> I beg to state that with the exception of the Cylinders and Tyres being rather soft I consider the said Engines to be equal in every respect to any of our best English or American locomotives. They work very economically both on Fuel and repairs — and as to the latter shew a lower figure than the American and English Fre[igh]t engines.... In conclusion I wish to state emphatically that the *Bacchus* and *Achilles* made by Messr. Gunn & Co. are very good Engines and from what I have seen during the past 12 months, I have every reason to think that considerable improvements have been made upon those Engines which have been constructed by them since the *Bacchus* and *Achilles* were set to work.

This was high praise indeed, coming as it was from a premier locomotive expert. Gunn's locomotives had been ordered and delivered to the Great Western before Eaton took his job there. Thus, he had no motive to exaggerate or falsify his judgment in order to vindicate the decision to buy them.

Orders were also sent to three of the predecessor companies of the Canadian Locomotive Company in Kingston (The Ontario Foundry, 1854–64; Canadian Engine and Machine Company, 1865–78; and Canadian Locomotive and Engine Company, 1878–87). All orders involved 4-4-0 types. Definite build orders numbered eighteen units and definite rebuild orders numbered four units. Build orders for three units should be classified as possible-probable due to deficiencies in documentation.

In 1882 the Great Western Railway (and Welland Railway) contributed to the Grand Trunk Railway (GTR) 203 modern locomotives (in the 701–909 less 728–733 and 354, 356, 358, and 360 GTR number groups, respectively), of which 162 (79.8 percent) were Rhode Island 4-4-0s (acquired new for standard gauge) accompanied by other modern (or rebuilt) 4-4-0s and a respectable fleet of 0-4-0/0-4-2 tank switchers (tables 4-2 and 4-3). Of interest, of twenty-two broad-gauge Great Western Railway locomotives undergoing conversion to standard gauge, fifteen (68.2 percent) were turned over to the Grand Trunk Railway.

Unfortunately, no official record of the 1882 renumbering of Great Western locomotives into the Grand Trunk system has been found. The Rhode Island and Baldwin construction records show original road numbers only and the Grand Trunk records for #s 701-909 show dates built but no builder's construction numbers

Canadian National Photo Archives.

One of the two steam "dummies" (#s 1 and 2) delivered to the Great Western from Baldwin in 1878, with ten-by-twelve-inch cylinders and forty-two-inch drivers. These were specially ordered for the short (4.75-mile) Petrolia branch line to Canada's first "Oil Patch." Dummy #1 was wrecked in Toronto in 1882, while #2 was sold to J.B. Smith (contractor) in October 1892 (as ex-Grand Trunk #760).

Library and Archives Canada, DAPDCAP 142268.

Great Western steam dummy (# unknown) used for passenger service between Wyoming and Petrolia, alleged to have been purchased second-hand in the U.S., photographed in 1873. The car is characterized by extensive external gilding and the unexpected presence of a mural with an eagle and shield motif on the frontispiece of the car. One would usually associate the latter with U.S. equipment, not Canadian (British Empire) equipment. Perhaps this was a holdover from the prior owner that had not yet been removed.

or former road numbering. By matching these records, it has been possible to identify some renumbering, which must have taken place, apparently to keep similar power grouped together and keep the entire series uninterrupted.

The two steam dummies from Baldwin Locomotive Works were specifically designed for use on the five-and-a-half-mile Wyoming-Petrolia branch. They were characterized by an upright boiler and a direct connection between the boiler and the axles of the wheelset below. Since each dummy contained no seating for passengers, one or more coaches would have to be hauled behind these dummies. The decision to use these in lieu of traditional passenger trains was based on the much lower cost of the former versus the latter, while still maintaining a satisfactory speed. In addition to data supporting the purchase of the two steam dummies as new equipment from Baldwin Locomotive Works, Lepkey and West have advanced the following hypothesis for another dummy. According to these authors, the Great Western acquired a second-hand full-sized steam dummy (capacity of forty-five to fifty passengers) in February 1873, which subsequently burned on the Petrolia branch in August 1873. It was sold to the Grand Trunk, possibly rebuilt by the Portland Company, renumbered as GTR [*International Bridge*] #1, and placed in service on September 9, 1874. It had been built in 1871 or before, by Grice and Long of Trenton, New Jersey, and Philadelphia, Pennsylvania. The source(s) of these data were not provided.

Table 4-4 provides details of the fifteen Great Western locomotives that entered service with the Canadian National Railways (CNR) at the time of the absorption of

Canada Science and Technology Museum.

Grand Trunk 4-4-0 #2125 originated from Great Western #123, another Rhode Island product of December 1870. It had been rebuilt in November 1885 and would not be scrapped until after it had been accepted as Canadian National #248. One of the last Great Western locomotives in existence, scrapping occurred in September 1925.

Claude Stoner Collection, Bentley Historical Library, University of Michigan.

Detroit and Milwaukee #30 (*Detroit*) was a Baldwin product from February 1861. This 0-4-0 tank locomotive was no longer around at the time of the 1881 renumbering.

Author's collection.

Detroit and Milwaukee #19 (*Michigan*) was typical of numerous Hinkley locomotives purchased by the road. The design was suggestive of motive power built by other manufacturers many years later.

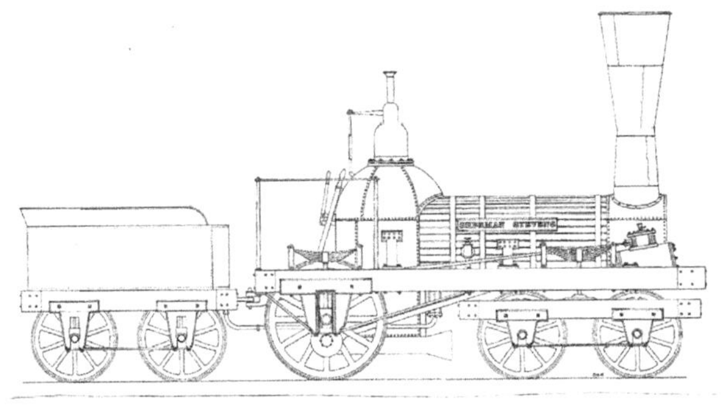

Denis Hoffman, Grand Haven, Michigan.

Wood-burning Detroit and Pontiac Railroad locomotive *Sherman Stevens*, built by Baldwin in 1838.

the Grand Trunk Railway (thirteen 4-4-0s and two 0-4-0Ts). The 4-4-0s were retired and scrapped reasonably early in the CNR era, all but one by September 1925. Similarly, the two tank switchers were sold early, in July 1923 and February 1925.

Table 4-5 illustrates the locomotive roster of the U.S. subsidiary of the Great Western, known initially as the Detroit and Milwaukee and later as the Detroit, Grand

Haven, and Milwaukee. Forty-one locomotives built for the D&M/DGH&M (in the 200–240 GTR number group) were absorbed by the Grand Trunk in 1882. As with the Great Western, the vast majority of absorbed locomotives were 4-4-0s but there were also four Dickson 2-6-0s (213–216) and two Baldwin 0-4-2Ts (217 and 218).

ROLLING STOCK

Initially, the Great Western Railway board of directors, which was largely composed of residents of the British Isles, favoured the use of traditional four- or six-wheeled British-style rolling stock. Specifications for use in bidding for contracts were developed for the following British-style passenger car types: second-class carriages (1850), six-wheeled third-class carriage (not dated), four-wheeled standard-gauge third-class carriage (four compartments, ten persons in each; not dated), six-wheeled first- and second-class composite carriage (1850), four-wheeled composite standard-gauge carriage (three compartments, six persons in each, 1856), six-wheeled second-class carriage (1850), and iron passengers' luggage brake van (1852). Specifications were also developed for the following British-style freight car types: standard-gauge hopper-bottomed coal wagon (1857), four-wheeled iron tilt wagon (with Brotherhood's patent tilt cover, 1852), covered goods wagon (1857), four-wheeled iron, coal, and c. truck (1852), four-wheeled iron box wagon (1852), and four-wheeled iron goods brake van fitted with two entire brakes (1852).

Great Western rolling stock as of December 31, 1859/1860, were as follows:

- 25/26 first-class passenger coaches (6-wheeled trucks, 35,000 lbs.)
- 58/57 first-class passenger coaches (4-wheeled trucks, 30,000 lbs.)
- 44/44 second-class passenger coaches/emigrant cars (4-wheeled, 20,000 lbs)*
- 10/7 baggage-mail-express cars (4-wheeled trucks, 20,000 lbs.)
- 10/13 baggage-mail-express cars (6-wheeled trucks, 30,000 lbs.)
- 860/860 box-freight/stock-cattle cars (4-wheeled, 18,500 lbs)*
- 100/100 box-freight/ stock-cattle cars (4-wheeled, 12,000 lbs)*
- 250/246 flatcars (4-wheeled trucks, 18,000 lbs.)
- 0/4 flatcars (6-wheeled trucks, 30,000 lbs.)
- 6/6 timber trucks (4-wheeled)
- 6/0 timber cars (16-wheeled)
- 120/409 gravel cars (4-wheeled, 10,000 lbs.)*
- 50/50 hand cars
- 33/33 conductor's cars (4-wheeled trucks)

(* = British-style cars)

At the end of 1859 rolling stock totalled 1,572 units (95.9 percent in good repair, 3.1 percent needed slight repairs, and 1 percent needed heavy repairs). Corresponding figures at the end of 1860 were 1,855 units, 87.8 percent, 7.4 percent, and 4.8 percent (data were compiled from the Report of Samuel Keefer, inspector of railways, for the years 1859 and 1860 to the Board of Railway Commissioners of Canada — reproduced in Bulletin No. 56 of the Railway & Locomotive Historical Society, 1941).

Windsor Community Museum, Windsor, Ontario.

View of Detroit from the Great Western terminal in Windsor, circa 1860. This watercolour, by an unknown artist, illustrates the terminal of the first railway to serve Windsor. It is also important because it is one of the few illustrations of the lettering schema for Great Western freight cars.

Toronto Public Library.

A variety of freight and passenger cars are evident in this photograph of the Toronto yards of the Grand Trunk near Front and John Streets. An important component of this photograph is the lower left corner, where a Great Western boxcar can be found. Few examples exist of the lettering schema of Great Western freight cars. It is unfortunate that the smaller lettering inside the six-pointed star and the diamond cannot be deciphered.

Table 4-6 illustrates the Great Western rolling stock rosters on eight separate occasions from 1871 through 1881.

Table 4-7 illustrates the Detroit and Milwaukee/ Detroit, Grand Haven, and Milwaukee rolling stock rosters on eight separate occasions from 1868 through 1882.

FREIGHT CARS

The 1859/1860 listing by Samuel Keefer confirmed that at least four British-style rolling stock types (second-class passenger coaches, box-freight/cattle cars of two capacities, and gravel cars) actually were built and used on the Great Western. However, these cars were not used for very long since four-wheeled cars were eminently unsuited to the rough roadbeds of this era in North America, leading to frequent derailments. The stability of eight-wheeled (in the form of a pair of four-wheeled trucks) freight cars was so superior to that of the four-wheeled cars that construction of the latter was soon terminated and their use was rapidly phased out.

PRIVATE FREIGHT-CAR BUILDING FIRMS USED BY THE GREAT WESTERN

During the existence of the Great Western as an independent line, there were fourteen small car-building firms in Canada that were open for business from one to eleven (average three) years. There are only four companies where reasonable evidence exists that they produced freight cars for the Great Western: Canada Car and Manufacturing Company, Ontario Car Company (T. Muir), William Hamilton and Sons (St. Lawrence Foundry and Machine Shop), and James Crossen (Crossen Car Manufacturing).

1. Canada Car and Manufacturing Company, Central Prison, Toronto

This company opened its prison shops on February 7, 1874, for the purpose of building railway cars using convict labour at Toronto's Central Prison. The prison was located on the west side of Strachan Avenue, near the Great Western tracks (present Canadian National Oakville subdivision). A mechanical engineer, Hugh Baines, was the managing director.

In the yard outside the cell blocks were a foundry, storage shop, erecting shop, coal house, paint shop, dry kiln, saw and stave mill, and various sheds. In addition, there was a turntable accessing various leads to the erecting and paint shops and storage areas.

Rail access direct to the prison workshops/grounds was provided by the Great Western. Apparently, Canada Car and Manufacturing spent all of 1874 filling orders from the Great Western, but no details are available, with two exceptions. In 1873 the firm won a contract to build one hundred platform (flat) cars at a price of $525 each. These were delivered by July 31, 1874. In addition, it was awarded a contract to build two hundred and twenty Erie & North Shore boxcars at $750 each. These were delivered between September 1, 1874, and January 31, 1875. The Erie and North Shore cars were intended for through services between Michigan and New York, resulting from a co-operative freight-sharing agreement between several railways (see later in this chapter for more details regarding such lines). In an unpublished manuscript by the late Andrew Merrilees (1963), it was stated that several orders for freight cars were placed with the firm, but no details were provided. If additional orders existed, all of them would have had to be concurrent with or have preceded the two orders just described since further orders for several years would be unlikely due to the 1873 panic. Over half of the approximate six-hundred-car output of the firm went to the Great Western and it is possible that this proportion may have even been higher. The firm closed its prison operation in February 1875, although it briefly reopened in August 1875 to complete an order for which a buyer had been found.

2. Ontario Car Company (T. Muir), London

Incorporated in 1872, the physical plant was located on the east side of Rectory Street, immediately south of the Grand Trunk Railway (present site of the CNR London car repair tracks). Its first president was James McMillan, who had previously been secretary of the Michigan Car Company of Detroit. This has led to speculation that Ontario Car Company was, perhaps, a Canadian subsidiary of Michigan Car Company, the latter being a firm that built many cars for the Great Western and Grand Trunk Railways at the time of gauge conversion in the 1860s and early 1870s. The manager of the business was Thomas Muir and, for some time, the business was operated under the moniker of "T. Muir and Son." It was also known as the London Car Works for a time. This firm was established in London two years before the Great Western moved its car repair shops from Hamilton to London in 1874.

Just what experience Muir had as a builder of railway cars is unknown, but it is certainly true that he had a loyal following among Canadian railways. It is thought that the firm produced only freight cars for the Great Western. Of course, the firm produced freight and passenger cars for other central and eastern Canadian railways as well as millwork materials from the millwork division for use in passenger cars. All that is known of its production for the Great Western Railway is that it produced a "large volume of freight cars of all types" with no details provided.

In close connection with this entity, a wheel foundry was established by William Gartshore (of the well-known Canadian railway supply family of that name) which operated until the gauge conversion era was over.

3. William Hamilton & Sons Ltd. (St. Lawrence Foundry and Machine Shop), Toronto

This establishment was a very active foundry, which flourished in Toronto throughout most of the latter half of the nineteenth century. Products included all types of mill machinery, cast-iron water pipe, hydraulic valves, railway car trucks, fences, grilles, cast-iron staircases, set and cap screws, and cold-pressed nuts. Also supplied were structural steel beams. The firm contracted for the fabrication and erection of bridges and other types of steel work. The firm was located on the north side of Front Street East (#206) between Berkeley and Parliament Streets and was managed by the William Hamiltons — Senior and Junior.

In the autumn of 1871 the St. Lawrence Foundry secured a large order from the Great Western Railway for fifty standard-gauge platform (flat) cars at $460 each and 150 standard-gauge Michigan Line boxcars at $595 each. The Michigan Line cars were intended for through service between Michigan and Ontario, resulting from a traffic-sharing agreement entered into in 1869 between the Great Western, Michigan Central, and Detroit and Milwaukee lines. See later in this chapter for more details regarding these co-operative freight lines. Car building in this firm only occurred from 1870 to 1874.

4. James Crossen (Crossen Car Manufacturing of Cobourg Limited), Cobourg

This prolific builder started in 1866 with the manufacture of freight and passenger railway cars. At that time, James Crossen was the owner of a small foundry in Cobourg known as the Ontario Foundry or Helm Foundry. This establishment produced castings for the metal parts of the cars and the balance of needed materials, lumber and timber, were readily available locally.

This was an ideal time to commence car building, since gauge conversion on lines such as the Great Western and Grand Trunk created a demand for large quantities of new rolling stock. Taking pride in his work and delivering quality product on time, Crossen Car Manufacturing quickly became the largest car factory in Canada.

Founder of this firm, James Crossen, was born at Comber, County Down, Ireland, on March 9, 1826. In 1842 his father emigrated to the U.S. with his wife and nine children, settling on a farm in western New York State, near Batavia. In 1843 James crossed Lake Ontario and started a foundry. His business in fitting out grist mills entailed much travel in the hinterland of Cobourg (also called the Newcastle District). Beginning in 1866 he commenced initially with simpler cars, such as flatcars or gondolas, before graduating eventually to the production of cars of all types, including sleeping cars. The firm is listed as having produced boxcars for the Great Western Railway, but details are not available.

Among U.S. car builders, only for the Michigan Car Company is there reasonable evidence that the Great Western Railway purchased freight cars. This company was founded in Detroit in 1863–64 by James McMillan and John S. Newberry, together with E.C. Dean and George Eaton, with capital of just $20,000. Their works were established in 1865. In 1873 the company built a large plant at Grand Trunk Junction (now West Detroit). At this time, John Newberry was president, Z.R. Brockway was vice president and general manager, James McMillan was treasurer and manager, Hugh McMillan was secretary, and James McGregor was superintendent. Offices were at #2 in the Moffat Block in Detroit. In 1890 the Grand Trunk Junction plant, together with the associated Detroit Car Wheel Company, occupied thirty acres.

Within ten years, Michigan Car had grown into one of the major U.S. freight car builders. In 1881 and 1882 the business brought in $6 million annually. By 1883 it had produced 48,731 cars. With one exception, the types of freight cars produced by the Michigan Car Company for the Great Western Railway are unknown. This one exception involved an 1867 contract with the Michigan Car Company for thirty Blue Line freight cars (Merrilees fonds, Library and Archives Canada). The Blue Line was yet another co-operative freight line formed by several railways.

GREAT WESTERN CAR SHOPS

Another source of freight cars for the Great Western was its own car shops in Hamilton (later, London). In April 1852 bids were solicited by the road for an outside contractor to rent the car shops for one year and produce 434 cars of various types and fifteen handcars. The contractor would be responsible for providing all machinery except the steam engine and main shafting (i.e., power source). The successful bidder was Brainard, Williams, Fisher and Company. Over the one year period, one hundred eight-wheeled flatcars, one hundred fifty eight-wheeled boxcars, one hundred four-wheeled gravel cars, twenty-five four-wheeled repair cars, and fifteen handcars were produced.

Only after the shops expansion in 1859 could railway staff build cars in volume. In the middle to late 1860s and early 1870s, much work was expended on the conversion of cars from broad to standard gauge. This was also a time of scrapping much of the old rolling stock.

Barely after the end of the frenetic activity of the shops during gauge conversion, it was announced that the car shops, but not locomotive shops, would be moved to London. Completely new car shops were subsequently opened in September 1874.

There are virtually no data available with respect to the numbers and types of freight cars built by the Great Western at its Hamilton and London car shops. In the January 3, 1880, issue of *Railway World*, it was revealed that the Great Western was currently building one hundred grain cars with a capacity of 500 bushels each.

CAR LEASING

There is also evidence that the Great Western and its U.S. affiliate leased freight cars. In mid-1882, on the day before amalgamation of the Grand Trunk and Great Western, the Erie and Chicago Car Company, a company that leased cars to railways, seized all of the property of the Great Western Railway in the U.S. Predominantly at Detroit, this included one ferry transit steamer, another vessel, plus much rolling stock. This, obviously, led to an embargo on Great Western rail traffic, but traffic exchange was later resumed with the one non-seized ferry transit steamer without further seizures. In 1870 the Erie and Chicago Car Company had entered into a contract with the Great Western and the Detroit and Milwaukee. When the Great Western subsequently took over the Detroit and Milwaukee line, it also assumed the accumulated indebtedness of the latter, which included $740,000 owed to the Erie and Chicago Car Company! This $800,000 debt led to the court-authorized seizure of Great Western assets in the U.S. Fortunately, the Grand Trunk manager Joseph Hickson came to the rescue.

IMPROVEMENT AND INNOVATION

In 1873 Joseph Taylor, assistant to the general superintendent in Hamilton, invented an "improved" boxcar. In contrast to the usual boxcars of the era, which had two doors opposite each other and centred on the sides and, occasionally, an end door for special types of freight, the "improved" car had two doors opposite each other but located next to the end of the car. In addition, there was no end door. This design improved the strength of the car (and, hence, its capacity) since the side bracing ran continuously with no break in the middle. The car was no longer subject to sagging in the middle or twisting/spreading of the roof leading to leaks, since all sections had the same degree of strength. This car was much easier to load with long items such as lumber or rails. In the usual thirty-two-foot-long boxcar without an end door, the longest item that could be loaded was sixteen feet in length. In the thirty-two-foot-long "improved" car, the longest item that could be loaded was thirty feet in length. The use of end doors in usual boxcars to load long

Glenbow Museum.

Barrel-filling house at the Imperial Oil Company refinery, Petrolia between 1875 and 1898. Note the rolling stock and motive power on the spur. From left to right are two oil-tank cars with horizontal tanks of metal construction, followed by a stock car (likely preferred for barrel transport due to its ventilation characteristics, which would reduce the risk of explosion and fire), a conductor's car (caboose) with a small rectangular window, side door, and a bay window on each side, and, finally, a locomotive of unknown wheel arrangement with a spark-arresting smokestack, a reasonable risk-reducing strategy in a high-risk environment.

items mandated the cutting of the train and provision of empty space next to the end door before loading could proceed. The "improved" car made end doors obsolete. The Great Western built a prototype "improved" car and sent it around the system as a trial. Apparently pleased with the feedback on the trial unit, seventy-five home-built boxcars were approved. Additional information on these boxcars is not available. Obviously this design did not become popular with other roads, probably because the advent of longer cars made of steel eliminated the negatives of short wooden cars.

Interestingly, the rail lines located in areas with climate extremes, such as Canada and New England, were not the originators of what has been variously called the cabin car, conductor's car (van), way car, or caboose. In a comprehensive survey of Canadian railways conducted by Samuel Keefer in 1858, not one caboose was recorded. In Keefer's report of 1859, the Great Western had taken mercy on its crews by providing thirty-three ten-ton, eight-wheeled conductor's cars. In 1860 Keefer found that the Northern Railway had put seven caboose cars into service. Big roads like the Grand Trunk held off until the early 1860s, when they began to convert boxcars into cabin cars. According to Omer Lavallee, caboose cars were not commonly used in Canada until the 1870s.

Great Western conductor's cars in 1872 were divided into two compartments. In the smaller one, there were accommodations for the conductor and crew, with a stove, comfortable seating, a writing desk, washstand, locker, and a brake wheel mounted like a ship's wheel. This was in addition to the usual platform-mounted brake wheel, so that in bad weather or an emergency brakes could be applied as quickly as possible. There were also projecting side windows (primitive bay windows) to allow for front and rear viewing. Viewing was augmented through use of a series of mirrors, allowing adequate viewing without the need to go outside. The lamps lighting this compartment were mounted in such a way that they also illuminated, through red glass lenses, the end of the car ("guard lights").

In the larger compartment, along one side there were seats for passengers while along the other side there were lockers for crewmen. The "lids" of these lockers served as beds. In addition, there were the usual stove, saloon, and washroom facilities. Underneath the car was a large compartment for storing ancillary materials.

The development of commercial oil wells in southwestern Ontario at Oil Springs, beginning in August 1858, was to provide a welcome, albeit temporary, boost in revenue for the Great Western, since its main line was only five miles from Oil Springs. As in Pennsylvania after the development of its first commercial oil well (Drake well near Titusville) in August 1859, crude oil was hauled to refineries in forty-two-gallon barrels in boxcars or on flatcars. Regardless of the type of car used, hauling bulk liquids in barrels was inefficient and, because of the labour needed for handling, filling, and emptying individual barrels, expensive. Barrels were expensive, seldom costing less than $3.00 each, and were prone to damage, loss, and theft. In addition, barrels tended to explode due to the gaseous nature of crude oil. There was no practical means of venting every barrel. These deficiencies brought about investigations into the use of tanks for the transportation of petroleum products.

Tank cars for the haulage of bulk liquids (especially petroleum products) initially comprised two vertically oriented wooden tanks mounted onto a standard wooden flatcar with the tanks centred over the trucks. Tanks were made of pine planks, which were glued and banded together and each tank had a capacity of approximately forty barrels (1,680 gallons) of oil. A major problem was the development of leaks with wooden tanks, made worse by the large number of joints between pine boards making up the individual tank. Generally, wooden tanks would lose 10 percent of their volume and, occasionally, up to 33 percent. Leaks occurred since crude oil contains insufficient water to cause the wooden staves to swell and seal the joints. The only known Canadian involved in the development of tank cars was an anonymous inventor who made a test run of an iron tank car over the Grand Trunk to Portland, Maine, in 1862. The oil was transshipped to the U.K. No description of the test vehicle is known to exist. However, based upon the 1862 date, it was likely based upon the Densmore vertically oriented "tub" design.

In an attempt to improve on the design, metal vertically oriented tanks were substituted for the wooden ones. Being top-heavy when full and with the contents sloshing about, especially when negotiating curves or undergoing sudden stops, tanks would occasionally tip over with nasty consequences! Due to space limitations on the flatcars of the era, the only way to increase capacity was to build taller tanks. Obviously, this would raise the centre of gravity, which would aggravate the tipping problem.

In 1868 the horizontally oriented boiler-type tank car was born. It had the desired low centre of gravity and also a dome to allow for the expansion of liquid content with increasing temperature without damage to the sealed horizontal container. This allowed the tank to be completely filled. At first, they were of wooden construction with the tank fixed to the flatcar through the use of saddles. However, these were quickly replaced by iron, and later, steel versions of larger capacities. In the 1870s tanks were approximately twenty-four and a half feet long by five and a half feet in diameter (capacity of one hundred barrels or 4,200 gallons), while in the 1890s the dimensions had increased to thirty-two feet long by six feet in diameter (capacity of 190 barrels or 7,980 gallons). In 1873 the Great Western bought seventy-five tank cars (source unknown), the first such freight car order in Canada. The railway would buy additional tank cars such that at the time of amalgamation with the Grand Trunk it would own ninety-six such cars.

PSEUDO-PRIVATE LINES

The Great Western participated in railway-controlled fast freight lines or what might be called pseudo-private car lines. These were outright railway-sponsored corporations, financed, set-up, and controlled by the railways themselves and yet presented to the public as independent operations. These "puppet organizations" were designed to solicit freight that might otherwise go elsewhere and they appeared to serve little more than marketing and traffic generation functions. They did help to facilitate interchange traffic and also acted as a transitory arrangement until better financing mechanisms became available through which individual rail lines could buy rolling stock (i.e., equipment trusts). Most of these lines worked on the co-operative plan whereby each railway contributed a fixed number of cars to the line as required for the anticipated traffic. The number of cars to be contributed was based on either the length of the road or the amount of revenue the road derived from through traffic. The cars were managed by the corporation, which also controlled mileage payments. Earnings were divided proportionally among the partners, those contributing the most cars receiving the largest payments. Cars of the co-operative lines could travel over lines other than those who were members of the co-operative. For example, in November 1872 there were only twenty lines participating in the Blue Line co-operative, but co-operative cars travelled over 124 different lines!

The New York Central found this scheme quite appealing and may even have been the first railway to organize this type of freight service in establishing the Red Line in 1866. The basic scheme was to offer through service between Boston, New York, and Chicago via Toledo, Cleveland, Buffalo, and Albany. It was the beginning of this service that led to the creation of the Master Car Builders Association, for it marked the true commencement of long-distance interchange service. The Red Line was a co-operative that included the New York Central and all of its associated lines to the north and west. Each railway was required to furnish three cars per mile of line. Cars were painted an English vermillion then coated with varnish, and sported broad-head wheels. In less than a year, the Central had set up a second line, the Central Transit Company or White Line. The Central supplied one hundred cars while affiliates supplied thirty or forty cars each, making up a total of 270 cars. The Great Western had not been able to participate in these lines, although it was perfectly poised to do so, being able to function as the intermediary between the Central at Niagara Falls and other affiliates at Detroit. The source of its difficulties was the broad gauge of its track. Until this could be overcome, either by installing a third rail to accommodate standard-gauge cars or converting over to standard gauge, it could not participate. As it turned out, the Great Western, for better or worse, delayed the inevitable (gauge conversion) and added a third rail to accommodate standard-gauge cars. It also began a car ferry service between Windsor and Detroit to facilitate through car service (see chapter 5).

When the Blue Line came into being on January 1, 1867, the Great Western and co-operative partners outside the usual family of affiliates (e.g., Burlington and Illinois Central) became members. In fact, twenty-seven roads were members. The basic scheme was to offer through services between Boston, New York, and Chicago, using lines north of Lake Erie. Headquarters for the Blue Line were located in Detroit. The Great Western eventually contributed eight hundred cars to the pool. The first year of operations was a resounding success, with 91,500 tons shipped east and 55,400 tons shipped west. Each car averaged 30,000 miles annually, a figure sure to please any traffic manager. The most important line to the Great Western was the Erie and North Shore Line, which began in 1872 as a co-operative of the Erie, Great Western, Detroit and Milwaukee, and Wabash roads. In 1876, the Erie and Milwaukee, Commercial Express, and Diamond Lines would be absorbed by the Erie and North Shore Line.

Other lines of similar ilk emerged over the years. Eventually, the Great Western was to participate in seven pseudo-private lines: Blue Line, Milwaukee Line, Michigan Line, Hoosac Tunnel Line, Erie & North Shore Line, Erie & Milwaukee Line, and Saginaw Valley Line. Cars contributed by the Great Western to these seven pools would number some 2,385 cars by July 31, 1881!

PASSENGER CARS

Early in its existence, the Great Western Railway would allow local consortiums to manufacture cars in its newly built car shops in Hamilton. One known example of this is the manufacture of passenger cars for the railway in 1854 by Brainard, Williams, Fisher and Company. No details are available regarding these cars except for the types and quantity of each. Over the one year period, twenty-five eight-wheeled passenger cars, four eight-wheeled express and mail cars, eight eight-wheeled baggage cars, and twenty eight-wheeled emigrant cars were produced. With time, the railway began producing its own passenger cars.

Table 4-8 provides details of the passenger car numbering schemes for the Grand Trunk Railway's Great Western and Detroit, Grand Haven, and Milwaukee divisions. Table 4-9 lists those Grand Trunk Railway passenger cars transferred over from the Great Western in the 1882 amalgamation and still on the roster in January 1896. Table 4-10 lists those Grand Trunk Railway passenger cars transferred over from the Great Western in the 1882 amalgamation and still on the roster in 1901 (and beyond). This table also provides more details regarding the physical characteristics of the cars themselves. These tables were adapted from G. Lepkey and B. West eds. *Canadian National Railways: An Annotated Historical Roster of Passenger Equipment 1867–1992* (Ottawa: Bytown Railway Society, 1995). Unfortunately, Great Western numbering data are not available for these units nor is the key linking the 1896 and 1901 Grand Trunk numbering schemes in the latter two tables.

Further analysis of the data in the latter two tables provided the following results. From tables 4-9 and 4-10, it appears that 176 Great Western passenger cars were transferred to the Grand Trunk in 1882 (142 built by the Great Western, twenty-three built by William Hamilton and Sons [St. Lawrence Foundry] [SLF], nine built by Crossen Car Manufacturing, and two built by Pullman). Of these, 165 cars were still on the roster in January 1896 (131 Great Western-built and thirty-four built by other manufacturers). Cars on the roster in 1901 numbered 101 (ninety-two built by the Great Western and nine built by other manufacturers [two by Crossen, seven by Hamilton [SLF]). One can compare these numbers to those found in table 4-6 (latest pre-amalgamation data from 1881). These suggest that minimal attrition occurred in the numbers of Great Western passenger cars kept on the Grand Trunk roster until January 1896, almost fourteen years after amalgamation of the two roads. Even in 1901 the percentage of retained Great Western units compared with January 1896 was 61 percent.

Around 1862, seventy passenger cars were fitted with new lamps, which burned the new Canadian Enniskillen "Earth Oil" from the Petrolia "Oil Patch" (i.e., kerosene). Although it was an expensive retrofit, savings compared with the old system of candles was 90 percent. Each new lamp equalled twelve candles in illumination capacity.

Several notable passenger cars were built in the Hamilton car shops of the Great Western. The sleeping car *Mayflower*, which was built in 1867 and operated on the pooled Chicago–Rochester (New York) run, burned in 1875. Another sleeping car, *Viceroy*, was built in either 1865 or 1867 and also operated in pooled long-distance service. It was equipped with two eight-wheeled trucks, which were swapped out for standard six-wheeled trucks in August 1874. Seating fifty-six passengers, this car weighed 37.5 tons and cost $20,000. Great Western car number 95 was a second-class coach (also known as a Drovers Car) built prior to 1882 (hence, its build location could have been either Hamilton or London). The term "Drovers Car" arose from the use of passenger coaches by drovers (individuals driving cattle or sheep) who would accompany their precious cargo to the slaughter houses, assuring that the latter were adequately fed and watered during the journey and that they were paid in full upon delivery of their cargo. Among this group of known Hamilton home-builds is a combination car (combine) which was built before 1870 and became Grand Trunk car number 823 followed by number 953 (latter in March 1915).

Some notable passenger cars were built/rebuilt by the Great Western in its London shops, which opened late in 1874. The dining cars *Continental* (GTR #787) and *International* (GTR #788) were rebuilt in 1876 and 1880, respectively, to the designs of J.D. McIlwain, master car builder on site, receiving much acclaim. Even after the amalgamation with the Grand Trunk Railway in 1882, three Great Western-built passenger cars (parlour-buffet cars *London* [GTR #783] and *Clifton*[GTR #784], and dining car *Windsor* [GTR #789]) built in 1883 were written up extensively in the lay press and contemporary railway trade journals. Another example included the official car which became the *Algonquin* of the Grand Trunk (rebuilt in 1876). Unfortunately, the Great Western car numbers for all of these cars are unknown.

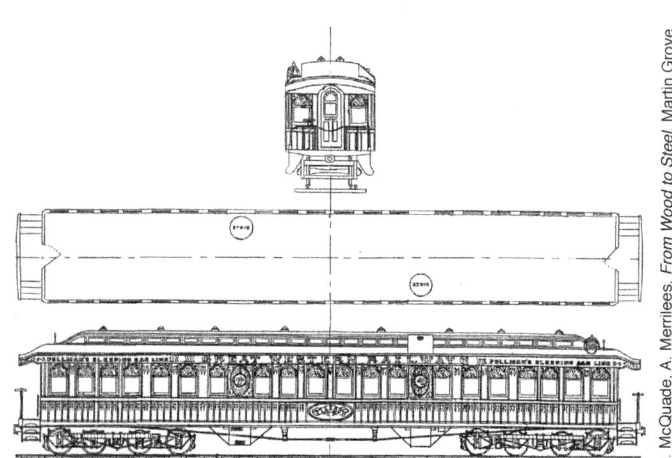

R. McQuade, A. Merrilees, *From Wood to Steel*, Martin Grove Press, 2003.

Line drawing of Great Western sleeping car *Viceroy*. Owned by Pullman's Palace Car Company, it was built in the Great Western Hamilton car shops in 1867.

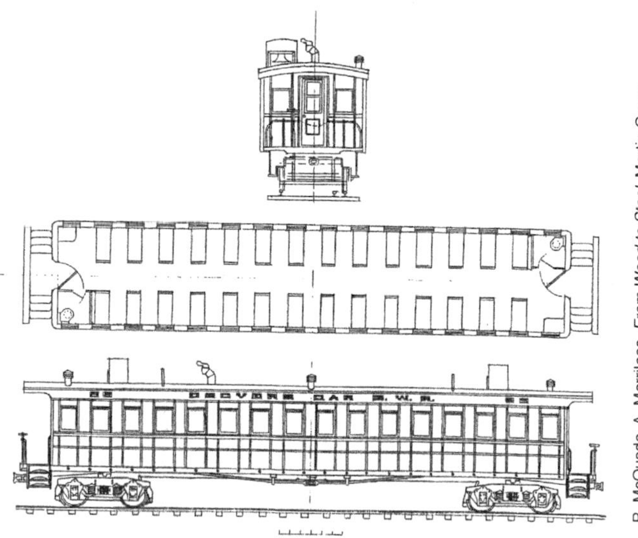

R. McQuade, A. Merrilees, *From Wood to Steel*, Martin Grove Press, 2003.

Line drawing of elliptical-roof second-class Great Western passenger coach #95 (manufacturer and date of manufacture are unknown).

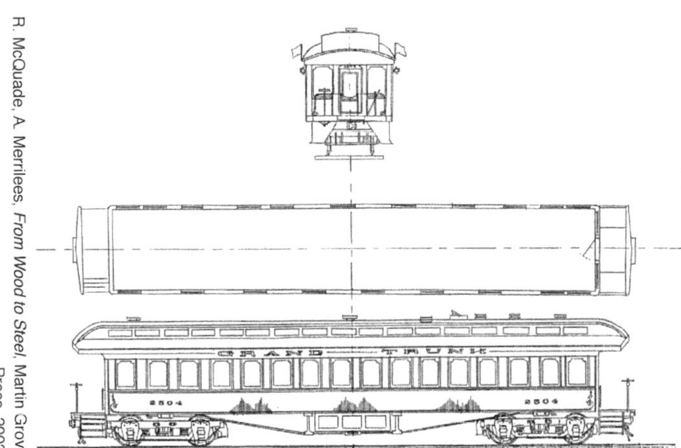

R. McQuade, A. Merrilees, *From Wood to Steel*, Martin Grove Press, 2003.

Line drawing of Grand Trunk parlour-buffet car #2504, a former Great Western passenger car built in its London shops in 1883. Formerly known as GTR #784 (*Clifton*), it would be renumbered to GTP #4101 (August 1909) and CN #45 (September 1923) and scrapped in June 1956.

All of these home-built cars were all-wood, with underframes reinforced with steel truss rods and queen posts, wood sides, and open platform ends.

The Great Western built five open section hotel cars for Pullman in 1865 (*Viceroy* and *Victoria*) and June through August 1867 (*Niagara*, *St. Lawrence*, and *President*) in the Hamilton shops. *Niagara* and *St. Lawrence* were built to Pullman plan 7, *President* and *Viceroy* were built to plan 13 (12 open section drawing room), and *Victoria* was built to a plan as yet unknown. After 1875 *Niagara* was renamed *Olympus* and was subsequently sold in January 1891 to L.M. Crawford. Before 1875, *St. Lawrence* was renamed *Helvetica* and was later sold in January 1891 to F.E. Griswold. Before 1875 *President* was renamed *Marathon* and was later sold in January 1891 to J.S. McMahan. Last, before 1875 *Viceroy* was renamed *Algeria*. It was stored in September 1888 and sold in January 1891.

The Great Western placed orders in 1872 with James Hamilton and Sons (St. Lawrence Foundry) for seventeen second-class coaches and six combination second-class coach-mail cars. All twenty-three cars appear to have survived until January 1896 (table 4-9) and at least seven cars until 1901 (table 4-10). However, the six combine cars appear to have either been converted to mail/smoking cars prior to January 1896 or the entries in the Lepkey and West text (i.e., as second-class mail coach cars) were made in error. It is impossible to verify the accuracy of either statement at this time. It appears that two of the combines (as second-class coach-mail cars) survived into the 1920s as Grand Trunk Railway cars numbers 303 and 341. At that time, both cars were listed as being of all-wood construction, with wooden end platforms, Baker heaters and oil lamps, and riding on two four-wheeled trucks fitted with cast-iron wheels and "quick action" brakes. Grand Trunk #303 measured forty-nine feet ten inches in length over the sills and weighed 50,700 pounds. In the 1920 inventory no construction data were provided for Grand Trunk #341, but it had a length over the sills of forty-nine feet eight inches and a weight of 51,400 pounds.

Crossen Car Manufacturing of Cobourg is listed as having produced passenger cars for the Great Western. However, available data are inconsistent. Data from the Andrew Merrilees fonds in Library and Archives Canada suggest that Crossen produced nineteen passenger cars for the railway. Grand Trunk Railway cars numbers 670–678 (nine cars) were first-class coaches produced in

1882 for the Great Western. These were renumbered to 1654, 1658–1661 (only five cars) (RG-31, A-010, V57). Grand Trunk car #346 was a second-class coach-mail combination car produced in 1882 (no renumbering). Renumbered Grand Trunk car numbers 1671–1678, 1807 (nine cars) were first-class coaches produced in 1883 (RG-31, A10, 3-ring binder). Despite production dates of 1882 and 1883, all nineteen cars were considered by Merrilees to be Great Western cars.

In contrast, West and Lepkey, in their history of *Canadian National Railways Passenger Equipment 1867–1992*, list Grand Trunk cars numbers 1674–1678 as Crossen-built but not for the Great Western, while they list Grand Trunk numbers 1671–1673 as not Crossen-built but built by/for the Great Western. Assuming that West and Lepkey are correct, Crossen built eleven cars for the Great Western (Merrilees' list minus numbers 1671–1678), with nine and two cars being mentioned in the 1896 (table 4-9) and 1901 (table 4-10) lists, respectively.

Which list should one believe? Messrs. Ted Rafuse and Don McQueen (electronic communications, April 24, 2013 and March 10, 2014, respectively) suspect that West and Lepkey had access to a greater number of equipment portfolios than did Merrilees and it is here that car histories are found. While these records tend to be accurate, there is no guarantee of accuracy. West and Lepkey likely surpassed Merrilees in the number and quality of source materials used. Both datasets have been provided to the reader since there are discrepancies between them. It is impossible to verify the accuracy of both datasets at this time.

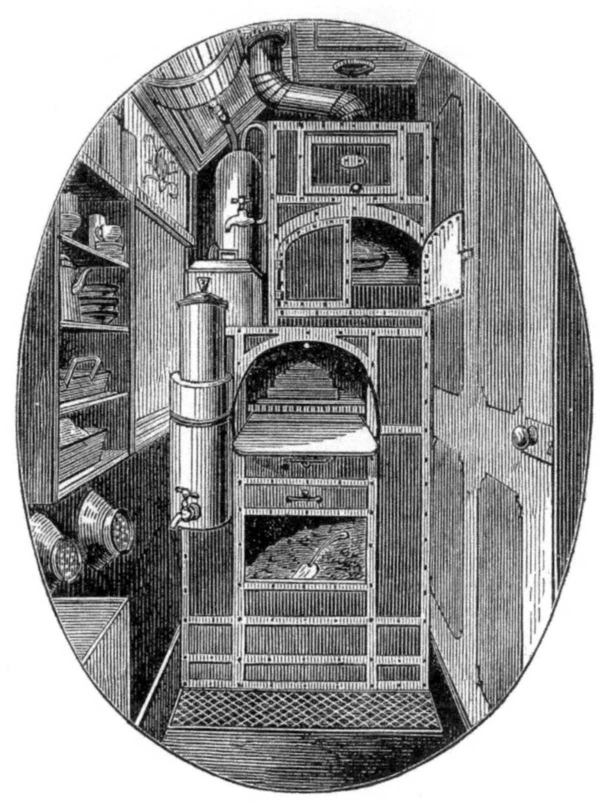

The diminutive kitchen of Pullman hotel cars was still capable of serving first-class meals.

Hotel cars were produced when a small kitchen was added to a palace sleeping or coach car. In 1866 and 1867 several new cars of this type were built for the Great Western, Michigan Central, and Burlington roads. A tiny kitchen was placed in the centre of the car. It served the two ends, which were outfitted like a standard open-section sleeper except that small folding tables were installed during the day between the seats. These could be used for writing or dining. At night they were stored in a

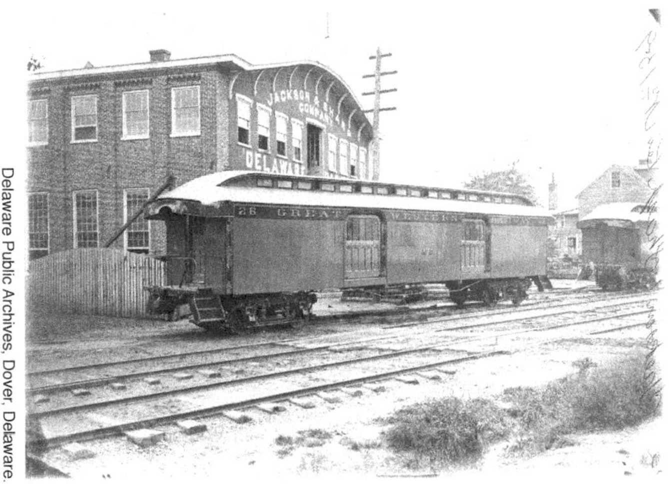

Delaware Public Archives, Dover, Delaware.

A Jackson and Sharp builder's photograph of Great Western baggage-express #26 in 1872.

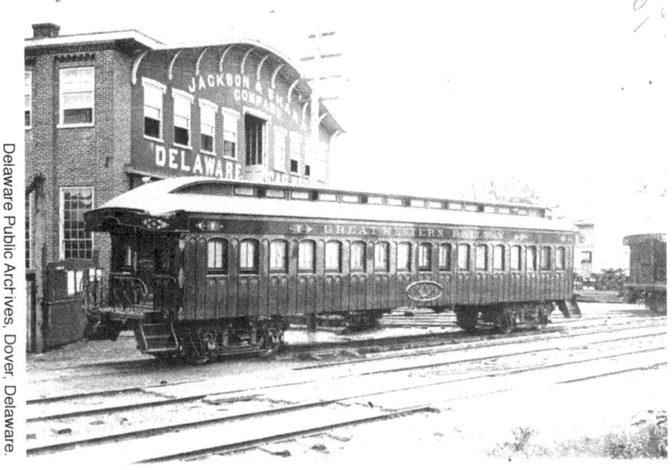

Delaware Public Archives, Dover, Delaware.

A Jackson and Sharp builder's photograph of Great Western coach #85 in 1872.

closet. Hotel cars slept thirty, but could seat and feed as many as forty passengers. Food was prepared and served by a staff of four or five crewmen. The menus in hotel cars were surprisingly varied considering the kitchen size of only three feet by six feet (eighteen square feet). Built-in cabinets adjacent to the kitchen stored 133 food items, liquor, one thousand napkins, one hundred fifty tablecloths, china, flatware, and glassware sufficient for a long-distance journey. According to Porter (1888), the Great Western produced the first "hotel car," which was named *President* and entered service in 1867.

Jackson and Sharp produced two known passenger cars for the Great Western (#85, a coach, and #26, a baggage-express) in 1872. No other details are available.

Taunton Car Company produced two parlour cars for Pullman (*Leo* and *Mars*), which were assigned to the Suspension Bridge to Hamilton run on the Great Western Railway as early as 1871. The sixty-two-foot-long bodies were divided into five compartments: a central compartment (drawing room) seating twenty; two state rooms, each seating six; and two end compartments, which could be used as smokers (no capacity provided). In the end compartments there were well-cushioned easy chairs upholstered in Turkey Morocco. Moveable chairs and settees in the drawing room and one stateroom were upholstered in velvet plush. Interior woodwork was gilded and rosewood veneer. The windows were huge by the standards of the era, being of French glass, twenty-four inches by forty-eight inches. Partitions between compartments were easily closed. Patrons could pass from one end of the car to the other without entering any of the compartments, by using a side passage. Lastly, each car also had a cupola, wine cellar, and park and kitchen garden. At three cents per mile, first-class luxury was also affordable.

In addition, on April 25, 1871, two sixty-five-foot-long Pullman Palace cars, costing $25,000 each, were delivered by Taunton to the Great Western. No details are available regarding these latter cars.

It has been frequently claimed that the Great Western Railway invented the sleeping car in Hamilton and first produced it in the Hamilton shops in 1858. Another claim is that Mr. George M. Pullman, the inventor of the Pullman sleeping car, visited the Great Western in Hamilton and observed the Great Western model, later copying its design in the U.S. Both claims cannot be supported by available evidence. The following are the facts surrounding this issue which can be verified as true.

Three sleeping cars built in the Great Western Hamilton shops entered service in November 1858. They had been designed by the car superintendent of the road, Mr. Samuel Sharp. Several months prior to this event, the Grand Trunk Railway had introduced sleeping cars, on June 22, 1858. These cars had been produced in the Pointe St. Charles shops in Montreal. Both of these Canadian events had been antedated by the introduction of sleeping car services on several U.S. railways, including the Illinois Central and the Chicago and Alton as early as 1856. Thus, the Great Western sleeping cars were neither the first sleeping cars in North America nor even the first in Canada.

These early Great Western sleeping cars were quite different from those later versions that would be built in the Hamilton shops under Pullman patents. The 1858 cars had a partition dividing the car lengthwise into two parts: one for gentlemen and one for ladies and children. Thus, families would be split up, at least at night. Against the partitions were three tiers of berths, six in a row. Thus, each car could hold thirty-six individuals (assuming one individual per berth). The space between the berths and windows was wide enough to allow a row of single seats next to the windows.

Berths were equipped with springs and carpet-covered horsehair mattresses. Pillows, quilts, and silk damask curtains were also provided. Cars had a black walnut interior, suggesting a higher quality of interior woodwork. There was only a single washroom for thirty-six passengers! These sleeper cars were built for the Albany–Chicago run via the Suspension Bridge at Niagara Falls.

In 1862 the Great Western reported that it had finished a new sleeping car, being a conversion of the 1860 Royal saloon car used by the Prince of Wales during his tour of southern Ontario on Great Western rails. The outside appearance had not been altered. The new ventilation system developed by Sharpe was incorporated in the car. Ventilators at the ends of the car admitted air while exhaust ports over each berth provided air a means to escape, all without the slightest draft. Forty-four passengers could be accommodated, during the day or night. Polished solid-walnut partitions divided the car into eleven compartments, with four berths in each. Beds were spring-stuffed and covered with moquette. Compartments were enclosed by damask curtains to promote "complete privacy." There were two washrooms, one for ladies and one for gentlemen, at the diagonal corners of the car. The trucks were kept the same as they were during the tour of the Prince of Wales, built upon the compensating double lateral motion principle, which dampened the transmission of vibration into the car and oscillatory (i.e., back and forth) motion.

In January 1867 Pullman sleepers came into use in a pooled service with the Great Western, Michigan Central, and New York Central lines. Since at that time there were no Pullman shops to build his cars, Pullman licensed various custom car builders and some of the railways utilizing his cars to build sleeping cars to his designs. Several were built in the Great Western Hamilton shops, the first being completed on May 10, 1867. These were placed in a pooled service between Chicago and Rochester (the Great Western line was utilized for the segment of Windsor to the Suspension Bridge at Niagara Falls). These cars were unique since they utilized special eight-wheeled trucks. These were of Allen's centre-bearing swing design, an invention of C.F. Allen, master mechanic of the Chicago, Burlington and Quincy shops in Aurora, Illinois. These trucks were first used on Pullman cars built by and operated on that road. These trucks were rigid, providing sixteen wheels upon the rails, under each car. However, in 1875 the New York Central ruled them to be too rigid and would not allow them on the road. Thus, interchange of cars equipped with these trucks was forbidden. As a result, these trucks were removed and replaced by conventional six-wheeled trucks. After the 1876 expiration of the Pullman contract, the Great Western contracted with Wagner Sleeping Car Company for these services.

On August 25, 1879, the Great Western completed an elegant official car (#43) at the London car shops. It was inspected that day by F. Broughton, the general manager. The car had five compartments: parlour-saloon, two bedrooms, dining room, and a kitchen. A large wooden table surrounded by cushioned leather chairs dominated the parlour-saloon. The bedrooms contained a total of twelve bunk beds (not your usual official or business car). The dining room seated twelve. The interior was finished largely in oak with walnut panels. Unlike the case with other roads, it was only named *Official Car*.

Table 4-11 provides summary information on Great Western passenger cars described in the preceding text but not specifically available in tables 4-9 and 4-10, including those units leased to the railway by Pullman. Table 4-12 provides a summary of Detroit, Grand Haven, and Milwaukee passenger cars transferred over to the Grand Trunk in the 1882 amalgamation and still on the roster in 1901 and beyond (adapted from Lepkey and West, 1995). Fourteen cars built by the railway were still on the Grand Trunk roster in 1901 and beyond. Using data from table 4-7, the retention rate to 1901 was 35 percent as compared with data from 1882, much lower than the 61 percent retention figure for Great Western cars.

The Long and Varied Life of Great Western 4-4-0 #219

Great Western 4-4-0 #219, being the oldest Kingston-built locomotive acquired by the Canadian National Railways (CNR) from the Grand Trunk, was granted a temporary reprieve from the scrapper's torch for special uses during 1926 and 1927. Pleas from Huntsville representatives resulted in the removal of the locomotive from the scrap line and its restoration to operating condition, including a diamond stack, as GTR #2194. The train, comprising #2194 plus three repainted passenger cars, proceeded under its own power to Toronto in March 1926.

In May/June 1926 the locomotive was modified by the substitution of a balloon stack (done in the Toronto shops) and relettering/renumbering to "Toronto and

Nipissing Rly. 269." The train proceeded to Huntsville for the town's "Old Huntsville Days" celebration from July 31 to August 6, 1926. This coincided with the fortieth anniversary of the opening of the line from Gravenhurst to North Bay.

The locomotive was probably converted back to GTR #2194 during late 1926 or early 1927 after returning to Stratford. Retaining the balloon stack, it reverted back to the 1910 style of GTR markings. The locomotive was converted again in 1927 in order to pose next to the first CNR 4-8-4 (#6100) in a photo shoot as the latter was being readied in Toronto for a trip to the Baltimore & Ohio Railroad Centenary Exhibition held in August/September 1927. It was lettered "Trevithick" on the cab sides and "G.T.R. No. 269" in nineteenth-century letter font on the tender sides.

The locomotive was held for possible reuse but never did return to special or regular service. On October 14, 1929, the locomotive met its fate in Stratford.

TABLE 4-1. GREAT WESTERN BROAD GAUGE POWER

Original		GWR 1862			New	Delivery		Specifications		
Name	#	Renumbering(#)	Builder	C/N	Date	Date	Comments	Cylinders	Drivers	Disposition
4-4-0										
Hercules	1	23	Schen.	23[a]	11/52	7/53	Standard-gauged 2/73	16x22	72	Off roster by '82
Samson	2	26	Schen.	24[a]	11/52	/53		16x22	72	Scrapped '63
Canada	3	24	Lowell	107	/51	5/53	Rebuilt 6/61	16x22	72	Scrapped by '73
Niagara	4	27	Lowell	108	/51	5/53		16x22	72	Scrapped '61/62
Hamilton	5	25	Lowell	114	/53	5/53	Rebuilt 12/61	16x22	72	Scrapped by '73
London	6	28	Lowell	113	/53	5/53		16x22	72	Scrapped '61/62
Oxford	-	-	Schen.							Wrecked 3/57
Middlesex	7	1	Schen.	54[a]		10/53	Rebuilt c. '65	15x22	66	Scrapped c. '75
Lightning	8	2	Schen.	55[a]		10/53	Rebuilt c. '65	15x22	66	Sold c. '71[b]

Detroit	9	3	Schen.	58[a]		10/53	Rebuilt c. '65	15x22	66	Sold '73[c]
Lincoln	10	4	Schen.	59[a]		10/53	Rebuilt c. '65	15x22	66	Scrapped c. '75
Windsor	11	5	Schen.	82[a]		10/53	Rebuilt c. '65	15x22	66	Sold '72[b]
Chatham	12	6	Schen.	83[a]		10/53	Rebuilt c. '65	15x22	66	Scrapped c. '75
Paris	13	7	Schen.	90[a]		12/53	Rebuilt c. '65	15x22	66	Scrapped c. '75
Woodstock[c]	14	8	Schen.	91[a]		12/53	Rebuilt c. '65	15x22	66	Scrapped c. '75
Essex	15	11	Lowell	123	3/53	1/54		14x22	66	Scrapped '67/68
Kent	16	12	Lowell	124	3/53	1/54		14x22	66	Scrapped '67/68
Elgin	17	13	Lowell	125	3/53	1/54		14x22	66	Scrapped '67/68
Norfolk	18	14	Lowell	126	3/53	1/54		14x22	66	Scrapped '67/68
Brant	19	15	Lowell	127	3/53	1/54		14x22	66	Scrapped '67/68
Wentworth	20	16	Lowell	128	3/53	1/54		14x22	66	Scrapped '67/68
Ontario	21	86	Globe (Souther)			9/53	Rebuilt 6/61[d]	13x20	54	Rebuilt '70 to 0-4-4T
Erie	22	87	Globe (Souther)			9/53	[d]	13x20	54	Rebuilt '71 to 0-4-4T
St. Clair	23	91	Globe (Souther)			10/53	Rebuilt '65	13x20	54[e]	Sold '70
Huron	24	92	Globe (Souther)			10/53	Rebuilt 12/62	13x20	54[e]	Rebuilt '70 to 0-4-4T
Superior	25	88	Globe (Souther)			10/53	Rebuilt 6/62	13x20	54	Rebuilt '70 to 0-4-4T
St. Lawrence	26	90	Globe (Souther)			11/53	[d]	13x20	54[e]	Rebuilt '70 to 0-4-4T
Reindeer	27	44	Amos.	128	12/53	12/53		16x22	72	Off roster '69/70

4-4-0										
Welland	55	9	Schen.	97		7/54		15x22	66	Scrapped c. ’75
St. Catharines	56	10	Schen.	99		8/54		15x22	66	Scrapped c. ’75
0-6-0										
Lion	57	66	Slaughter			12/55		16x24	60	Scrapped ’73
Lioness	58	67[h]	Slaughter			12/55	Standard-gauged ’73	16x24	60	
Tiger	59	68	Slaughter			12/55		16x24	60	Scrapped ’73
Tigress	60	69	Slaughter			3/56		16x24	60	Scrapped ’73
Leopard	61	70[h]	Slaughter			3/56	Standard-gauged ’73	16x24	60	
Panther	62	71[h]	Slaughter			2/56	Standard-gauged ’73	16x24	60	
Vulcan	63	72	Slaughter			1/56		16x24	60	Scrapped ’73
Etna	64	73[h]	Slaughter			3/56	Standard-gauged ’73	16x24	60	
Stromboli	65	74[h]	Slaughter			5/56	Standard-gauged ’73	16x24	60	
Styx	66	75[h]	Slaughter			3/56	Standard-gauged ’73	16x24	60	
2-4-0										
Gem[g]	67	38	Fairbairn			2/56	Rebuilt c. ’60	16x24	72	Retired by ’73
Ruby[g]	68	39	Fairbairn			3/56	Rebuilt c. ’60	16x24	72	Retired by ’73
Emerald[g]	69	40	Fairbairn			8/56	Rebuilt c. ’60	16x24	72	Retired by ’73
Sapphire[g]	70	41	Fairbairn			4/56	Rebuilt c. ’60	16x24	72	Retired by ’73

2-2-2										
Mazeppa[g]	71	29	Jones			1/56	Rebuilt c. '60	16x24	66	Retired by '73
Medea[g]	72	31	Jones			1/56	Rebuilt c. '60	16x24	66	Retired by '73
Medusa[g]	73	30	Jones			1/56	Rebuilt c. '60	16x24	66	Retired by '73
2-4-0										
Ajax[g]	74	53	PBB&J	21		11/55	Rebuilt c. '60	16x24	66	Retired by '73
Titan[g]	75	54	PBB&J	22		12/55	Rebuilt c. '60	16x24	66	Sold 2/71[i]
Minos[g,i]	76	55	PBB&J	23		11/55	Rebuilt c. '60	16x24	66	Sold c. '73[i]
0-6-0										
Castor	77	76[h]	Slaughter			12/56	Standard-gauged '73	16x24	60	
Pollux	78	77[h]	Slaughter			11/56	Standard-gauged '73	16x24	60	
Erebus	79	78	Slaughter	992		10/56		16x24	60	Retired by '73
Cyclops	80	79	Slaughter	993		10/56		16x24	60	Retired by '73
Ixion	81	80	Slaughter	994		10/56		16x24	60	Retired by '73
2-4-0										
Ariel	82	50	Stephenson	989		10/56	[j]	16x24	72	Sold in '73[j]
Oberon	83	51	Stephenson	990		12/56	[j]	16x24	72	
Prospero	84	52	Stephenson	991		10/56	[j]	16x24	72	Sold in '73[j]
Diadem[g]	85	42	Fairbairn			1/57	Rebuilt c. '60	16x24	72	Retired by '73
Diamond[g]	86	43	Fairbairn			4/57	Rebuilt c. '60	16x24	72	Retired by '73

0-6-0										
Achilles	87	56	Gunn	4		8/57	Rebuilt in '70	16x22	60	Retired by '73
Bacchus	88	57	Gunn	5		9/57	Rebuilt in '70	16x22	60	Retired by '73
Geo. Stephenson	89	81	GWR-Ham.	1		1/60		16x24	60	Sold in ‘73[k]
Scotia	90	82	GWR-Ham.	2		1/61		16x24	60	Retired by '73
Erin	91	83	GWR-Ham.	3		2/61		16x24	60	Retired by '73
Sarnia	92	84	GWR-Ham.	4		12/61		16x24	60	Sold in '73[k]
Saxon	93	85	GWR-Ham.	5		1/62		16x24	60	Sold in '73[k]
4-4-0										
London		2nd 28	GWR-Ham.	6		3/62				Retired by '73
Niagara		2nd 27	GWR-Ham.	7		1/63				Retired by '73
Samson		2nd 26	GWR-Ham.	8		6/63				Sold to Northern
?		94	GWR-Ham.	9		6/63				Retired by '73
Essex		2nd 11	GWR-Ham.	10		10/67		16x24	60	Sold in '71[l]
Kent		2nd 12	GWR-Ham.	11		11/67		16x24	60	Sold in '71[l]
Elgin		2nd 13	GWR-Ham.	12		12/67		16x24	60	Sold in '71[l]
Brackstone Baker		2nd 14	GWR-Ham.	13		7/67		16x24	60	Sold in '71[l]
Brant		2nd 15	GWR-Ham.	14		3/68		16x24	60	Sold in '71[l]
Wentworth		2nd 16	GWR-Ham.	15		4/68		16x24	60	Sold in '71[l]
Stag		2nd 47	GWR-Ham.	16		'68		16x22	69	Sold in '72[m]
Elk		2nd 45	GWR-Ham.	17		'69		16x22	69	Sold in '72[m]
Antelope		2nd 48	GWR-Ham.	18		'69		16x22	69	Sold in '72[m]

Greyhound		2nd 49	GWR-Ham.	19		'69		16x22	69	Sold in '72[m]
Reindeer		2nd 44	GWR-Ham.	20		'69		16x22	69	Sold in '72[m]
Gazelle		2nd 46	GWR-Ham.	21		'69		16x22	69	Sold in '72[m]
Victoria		95	CE&MCo.	68		5/68		16x24	69	Sold in '71[l]
Albert		96	CE&MCo.	69		5/68		16x24	69	Sold in '71[l]
Prince Alfred		97	CE&MCo.	70		5/68		16x24	69	Sold in '71[l]
Prince Arthur		98	CE&MCo.	71		5/68		16x24	69	Sold in '71[l]
Prince Leopold		99	CE&MCo.	72		5/68		16x24	69	Sold in '71[l]

[a] Listing does not agree with R&LHS Schenectady records.

[b] #2 *Lightning* was sold to the Windsor & Annapolis; #5 *Windsor* was sold to the Northern, where it was #35.

[c] *Woodstock* renamed *Dakin* in 1864; #3 *Detroit* was sold to the Hamilton & Northwestern, where it was #13 *Col. McGivern.*

[d] #s 86, 87, 89, 90 were converted to standard gauge in 1870; possibly renumbered to #s 301–304, but there is no proof.

[e] #s 89–93 were rebuilt to 15x20-56 or 60; #s 91, 93 were sold to the Northern, where they were #s 4, 5.

[f] #s 17–22 were rebuilt to 16x24-72; possibly renumbered to #s 155–165 in 1872 but there is no proof.

[g] #s 41–46, 67–76, and 85 and 86 were rebuilt into 4-4-0s in 1859–60.

[h] Thirteen locomotives in series 58–77 were possibly renumbered in 1873 to #s 352–370, 388–392 (even), but there is no proof.

[i] #55 was renamed *Adam Brown* in 1870. #s 54, 55 were sold to the Wellington, Grey and Bruce.

[j] #s 82–84 were rebuilt to 16x24-50; #s 50, 52 were sold to the Midland, becoming members of its #19–23 series.

[k] #s 81, 84, 85 were sold to the Midland, becoming their #s 21–23 (?).

[l] #s 11–16 and 95–99 became GTR #s 341–351.

[m] #s 44–49 were sold to the Northern, becoming members of its #30 series (specifically, #s 30–34, 36).

Abbreviations: GWR = Great Western Railway; C/N = construction number; Schen. = Schenectady; Amos. = Amoskeag; PBB&J = Peto, Brassey, Betts & Jackson; Ham. = Hamilton; c. = circa; R&LHS = Railway & Locomotive Historical Society; CE&MCo. = Canadian Engine & Machine Company (Kingston)

TABLE 4-2. GREAT WESTERN STANDARD GAUGE PASSENGER POWER

GWR	**GTR Renumberings (#)**				**GTR**					**Final Specs**		
#	1882	1898	1904	1910	Class	Builder	C/N	Date	Reblt.	Cylinders	Drivers	Disposition
4-4-0												
101	701(707)[a]	378	--	--	--	Rhode Is.	205	8/70	11/86	17x24	69	Scrapped 9/04
103	702	171	137	--	N	Rhode Is.	206	8/70		16x24	70	Scrapped 6/06
105	703	340	340	2131	J3	Rhode Is.	207	8/70	12/89	17x24	69	Scrapped 1/21
107	704	341	341	2132	J3	Rhode Is.	208	9/70		17x24	63	Scrapped 3/15
109	705	322	322	(2130)	J3	Rhode Is.	209	9/70		17x24	69	Scrapped 7/10
111	706	323	323	--	J3	Rhode Is.	210	9/70	8/92	17x24	69	Scrapped 9/09
113	707	--	--	--	--	Rhode Is.	234	12/70		16x24	69	Wrecked 2/88
115	708	172	142	--	N	Rhode Is.	235	12/70		16x24	69	Scrapped 6/06
117	709	313	313	2129	J3	Rhode Is.	236	12/70	/93	17x24	70	Scrapped 3/25[b]
119	710	359	302	2124	J3	Rhode Is.	237	12/70	10/85	17x24	63	Scrapped 1/16
121	711	305	305	2127	J3	Rhode Is.	238	12/70	7/90	17x24	63	Scrapped 3/19
123	712	360	303	2125	J3	Rhode Is.	239	12/70	11/85	17x24	69	Scrapped 9/25[b]
125	713	516	350	2133	J3	Rhode Is.	240	12/70		17x24	70	Scrapped 5/19
127	714	513	343	2136	J3	Rhode Is.	258	4/71		17x24	63	Scrapped 3/25[b]
129	715(77)[c]	164	293	2134	J3	Rhode Is.	259	4/71	12/84	17x24	69	Scrapped 10/20
131	716	149	149	--	N	Rhode Is.	278	5/71		16x24	69	Scrapped 11/04

133	717	514	348	2137	J3	Rhode Is.	279	5/71		17x24	69	Scrapped 7/15
135	718	150	150	--	N	Rhode Is.	287	6/71		16x24	69	Scrapped 9/08
137	719	151	151	--	N	Rhode Is.	288	6/71		16x24	69	Scrapped 9/06
139	720	354	354	--	J3	Rhode Is.	289	7/71	6/86	17x24	69	Scrapped 9/09
141	721	152	152	--	N	Rhode Is.	290	7/71		16x24	70	Scrapped 9/09
143	722	160	--	--	--	GWR-Ham.	27	5/71		16x24	69	Scrapped 9/00
145	723	161	--	--	--	GWR-Ham.	28	6/71		16x24	69	SS 5/98
147	724	162	--	--	--	GWR-Ham.	29	7/71		16x24	69	Scrapped 10/00
149	725	163	--	--	--	GWR-Ham.	30	9/71		16x24	69	Scrapped 8/00
151	726	164	--	--	--	GWR-Ham.	31	11/71		16x24	69	Scrapped 10/99
153	727	165	165	--	N1	GWR-Ham.	32	11/71		16x24	69	Scrapped '04

155–165 (odd numbers): possibly from #s 17–22 when converted from broad gauge in 1872. see table 4-1. If still active in 1882, they would have been GTR #s 728–733, but no such record has been found.

167	734	343	359	2063	J4	CE&MCo.[d]	147	6/72	1/88	17x24	63	Scrapped 5/15
169	735	518	367	2065	J4	CE&MCo.[d]	145	7/72		17x24	69	Scrapped 2/17
171	736	132	--	--	--	CE&MCo.[d]	149	7/72		16x24	69	Scrapped 11/01
173	737	133	155	--	N1	CE&MCo.[d]	150	8/72		16x24	69	Sold 3/07[e]
175	738	134	156	1985	N1	CE&MCo.[d]	151	8/72		16x24	69	Scrapped 9/11

177	739	135	157	1986	N1	CE&MCo.[d]	152	9/72		16x24	70	Scrapped 4/11
179	740	507	366	2064	J4	CE&MCo.[d]	153	9/72		17x24	69	Scrapped 9/14
181	741	342	358	2062	J4	CE&MCo.[d]	154	9/72	1/89	17x24	63	Scrapped 11/16
183	742	357	357	--	J4	CE&MCo.[d]	155	10/72	2/86	17x24	63	Scrapped 9/08
185	743	158	158	--	N1	CE&MCo.[d]	156	10/72		16x24	70	Scrapped 6/06
187	744	159	159	1987	N1	CE&MCo.[d]	157	11/72		16x24	69	Scrapped 7/12
189	745	508	336	2148	J3	Rhode Is.	433	9/72	[f]	17x24	69	Scrapped 6/14
191	746	367	309	2143	J3	Rhode Is.	434	10/72	8/84[f]	17x24	73.5(?)	Scrapped 5/25[g]
193	747	509	337	2149	J3	Rhode Is.	435	10/72	[f]	17x24	69	Scrapped 4/18
195	748	368	310	2144	J3	Rhode Is.	436	10/72	8/84[f]	17x24	69	Scrapped 5/21
197	749	344	344	2153	J3	Rhode Is.	437	10/72	6/88[f]	17x24	69	Scrapped 2/14
199	750	314	314	2145	J3	Rhode Is.	438	10/72	/93[f]	17x24	69	Scrapped 9/14
201	751	355	355	2154	J3	Rhode Is.	439	11/72	10/86[f]	17x24	69	Scrapped 1/16
203	752	286	298	2139	J3	Rhode Is.	440	11/72	1/85[f]	17x24	73.5(?)	Scrapped 4/23[g]
205	753	356	356	2168	J3	Rhode Is.	632	11/73	4/86[f]	17x24	69	Scrapped 3/19
207	754	369	311	--	J3	Rhode Is.	633	11/73	3/83[f]	17x24	73.5(?)	Scrapped 5/09
209 (ex 266)	755	345	345	2166	J3	(Rhode Is.	500	4/73)	9/88[f]	17x24	70	Scrapped 3/25[g]
211 (ex 138)	756	370	312	2128	J3	(Rhode Is.	244	12/70)	4/83[f]	17x24	69	Scrapped 10/22

213 (ex 120)	757	47	--	--	--	(Rhode Is.	220	10/70)	1/88[f]	16x24	68	Scrapped 7/03
215(?)	See note[h]											
217(?)	See note [h]											
219[i]	758	521	402	2194	H9	CL&E Co.	231	2/83		18x24	69	Scrapped 10/29[g]
221[i]	759	522	403	--	H9	CL&E Co.	232	2/83		18x24	69	Scrapped 9/08
Dummy (4-wheeled)												
1	--	--	--	--	Dummy	BLW	?	5/78		10x12	42	Off roster by '82
2	760	--	--	--	Dummy	BLW	?	5/78		10x12	42	Sold 10/92[j]

[a] #701 changed 11/90 to #707.

[b] #s 2125, 2129 changed in 1923 to CNR #s 248, 249 (class B-10-a); #2136 changed in 1923 to CNR #136 (class A-14-a).

[c] #715 changed in 1898 to #77 and then in 12/02 to #164.

[d] #s167–187 construction numbers: #147–157, missing in CE&MCo. records, have been reconstructed using other sources.

[e] #155 sold to J.B. Smith & Sons.

[f] #s 189–221 were all 16x22-66 as built; #s 219, 221 were 17x24-73.5.

[g] #s 2139, 2143, 2166 were changed in 1923 to CNR #s (250), 251, 252 (class B-10-a); # 2194 was changed in 1923 to CNR #269 (class B-13-a).

[h] #s 215, 217 possibly converted from #100–120 series, then back to 2nd #266 and 2nd #352 (freight).

[i] CL&E Co. construction list shows built as #s 220, 221. Originally 17x24-73.5.

[j] #760 sold to J.B. Smith.

Abbreviations: GWR = Great Western Railway; GTR = Grand Trunk Railway; C/N = construction number; NB = newly (re) built; Spec = specifications; Is. = Island; Ham. = Hamilton; CE&M Co. = Canadian Engine and Machine Company (Kingston); CL&E Co. = Canadian Locomotive and Engine Company (Kingston); BLW = Baldwin Locomotive Works; CNR = Canadian National Railways; SS = Sold for scrap

TABLE 4-3. GREAT WESTERN STANDARD GAUGE FREIGHT POWER

GWR	GTR Renumberings (#)					GTR					Final Specs		
#	1882	1898	12/02	1904	1910	Class	Builder	C/N	Date	Reblt.	Cylinders	Drivers	Disposition
4-4-0													
102 138	775	324	--	324	--	J3	Rhode Is.[a]		9/70	10/84	17x24	63	Scrapped 4/08
104 174	793	63-154	--	119	1975	N	Rhode Is.[a]		9/70	--	16x24	63	Scrapped 5/18[b]
106 266	839	372	--	361	--	J4	Rhode Is.[a]		[c]	1/83	17x24	63	Scrapped 6/07
108 352	882	373	--	362	--	J4	Rhode Is.[a]		[c]	1/83	17x24	63	Scrapped 6/06
110	761	887-44	--	--	--	--	Rhode Is.[a]		9/70	--	16x24	62	Scrapped 9/00[b]
112	762	361	--	304	2126	J3	Rhode Is.[a]		9/70	10/85	17x24	63	Scrapped 2/17
114	763	48-131	--	131	(1976)	N	Rhode Is.[a]		10/70	3/88	17x24	63	Scrapped 1/10[b]
116	764	30	--	--	--	--	Rhode Is.[a]		10/70	11/88	16x24	62	Scrapped 5/03
118	765	49	--	--	--	--	Rhode Is.[a]		10/70	2/88	16x24	57	Scrapped 11/02
120 213[d]							Rhode Is.[a]		10/70				
122[e]	767	176	--	--	--	--	GWR-Ham.	22	8/70		16x24	62	Scrapped 9/00
124[e]	768	177	--	--	--	--	GWR-Ham.	23	8/70		16x24	62	Scrapped 8/99
126[e]	769	178	--	--	--	--	GWR-Ham.	24	9/70		16x24	62	SS 5/98
128[e]	770	179	--	--	--	--	GWR-Ham.	25	9/70		16x24	62	SS 5/98
130[e]	771	180	--	--	--	--	GWR-Ham.	26	9/70		16x24	62	SS 6/98

132	772	69	156	123	--	N	Rhode Is.	241	12/70	11/85	16x24	63	Scrapped 7/09
134	773	371	371	360	2067	J4	Rhode Is.	242	[c]	1/83	17x24	63	Scrapped 12/24[f]
136	774	51	139	139	--	N	Rhode Is.	243	12/70	2/88	16x24	63	Scrapped 6/06
138[g]	See #211 in table 4-2						Rhode Is.	244	12/70				
140	776	173	173	145	--	N	Rhode Is.	245	12/70		16x24	63	Scrapped 10/09
142	777	34	119	292	2123	J3	Rhode Is.	246	12/70	/92	17x24	69	Scrapped 2/25[h]
144	778	31	113	113	--	N	Rhode Is.	247	12/70	4/80	16x24	58	Scrapped 6/06
146	779	174	174	146	--	N	Rhode Is.	248	12/70		16x24	63	Scrapped 6/06
148	[g]	--	--	--	--	--	Rhode Is.	249	12/70		16x24	54	Off roster by '72
150	781	52	--	--	--	--	Rhode Is.	280	5/71	1/88	16x24	62	Scrapped 8/02
152	782	386	386	396	--	J4	Rhode Is.	281	[i]	7/81	17x24	63	Scrapped 4/08
154	783	287	287	299	--	J3	Rhode Is.	282	5/71	8/86	17x24	63	Scrapped 11/06
156	784	53	--	--	--	--	Rhode Is.	283	6/71	10/88	16x24	57	Scrapped 8/02
158	785	35	35	--	--	--	Rhode Is.	291	6/71		16x24	62	Scrapped 5/03
160	786	153	153	153	(1978)	N	Rhode Is.	292	6/71		16x24	63	Scrapped 1/10
162	787	--	--	--	--	--	Rhode Is.	293	6/71		16x24	57	SS 1/98
164	788	80	168	--	--	--	Rhode Is.	294	6/71	4/83	16x24	57	Scrapped 8/04

166	789	70	159	127	1977	N	Rhode Is.	312	9/71	2/85	16x24	63	Sold 7/12[j]
168	790	515	515	349	--	J3	Rhode Is.	313	9/71	1/90	17x24	63	Scrapped 9/08
170	791	155	--	--	--	--	Rhode Is.	325	11/71		16x24	57	Scrapped 6/00
172	792	156	--	--	--	--	Rhode Is.	326	11/71		16x24	62	Sold 6/01[j]
174[g]							Rhode Is.	327	11/71		16x24	57	Sold to Welland Railway (#5 in ?1873 then #1 after 1882) then back to GWR as #354 (? date)
176	794	157	157	125	--	N	Rhode Is.	328	12/71		16x24	63	Scrapped 7/09
178	795	288	288	300	2135	J3	Rhode Is.	329	12/71	9/95	17x24	63	Scrapped 12/18
180	796	351	351	351	2138	J3	Rhode Is.	330	12/71	12/87	17x24	63	Scrapped 1/14
182	797	158	158	126	--	N	Rhode Is.	331	12/71		16x24	63	Scrapped 7/09
184	798	346	346	346	--	J3	Rhode Is.	332	12/71	3/88	17x24	63	Scrapped 7/09
186	799	159	--	--	--	--	Rhode Is.	333	12/71		16x24	57	Scrapped 11/02
188	800	54	--	--	--	--	Rhode Is.	334	1/72	4/88	16x24	62	Sold 9/01[j]
190	801	510	510	338	2150	J3	Rhode Is.	335	1/72		17x24	63	Scrapped 9/23[h]
192	802	138	138	138	--	N	Rhode Is.	336	1/72		16x24	63	Scrapped 10/08
194	803	347	347	347	--	J3	Rhode Is.	423	8/72	3/88	17x24	63	Scrapped 6/06

196	804	511	511	339	2151	J3	Rhode Is.	424	8/72		17x24	63	Scrapped 11/16
198	805	139	--	--	--	--	Rhode Is.	425	9/72		16x24	57	Scrapped 3/00
200	806	315	315	315	2146	J3	Rhode Is.	426	9/72	3/83	17x24	63	Scrapped 12/21
202	807	140	--	--	--	--	Rhode Is.	427	9/72		16x24	57	Sold 4/02 [k]
204	808	141	141	141	--	N	Rhode Is.	428	9/72		16x24	58	Scrapped 10/07
206	809	55	140	140	--	N	Rhode Is.	429	9/72	10/88	16x24	58	Scrapped 11/06
208	810	306	306	306	2141	J3	Rhode Is.	445	9/72	3/83	17x24	63	Scrapped 7/16
210	811	512	512	342	2152	J3	Rhode Is.	446	9/72	4/83	17x24	63	Scrapped 12/13
212	812	395	395	318	2147	J3	Rhode Is.	447	9/72	5/80	17x24	63	Scrapped 9/13
214	813	32	116[k]	1501	1979	N	Rhode Is.	448	11/72	1/82	16x24	63	Scrapped 6/12[k]
216	814	33	117	117	--	N	Rhode Is.	449	11/72	10/85	16x24	63	Sold 6/05[k]
218	815	66	--	--	--	--	Rhode Is.	450	11/72	3/86	16x24	62	Scrapped 6/02
220	816	56	143	143	(1980)	N	Rhode Is.	451	11/72	1/88	16x24	63	Scrapped 9/10
222	817	289	289	301	2140	J3	Rhode Is.	456	11/72		17x24	63	Scrapped 2/13
224	818	142	142	--	--	--	Rhode Is.	457	11/72		16x24	62	Scrapped 10/03
226	819	362	362	307	2142	J3	Rhode Is.	458	11/72	12/85	17x24	63	Scrapped 9/13
228	820	67	--	--	--	--	Rhode Is.	459	11/72	3/86	16x24	57	Scrapped 10/99
230	821	143	--	--	--	--	Rhode Is.	460	12/72		16x24	57	Scrapped 8/99
232	822	57	--	--	--	--	Rhode Is.	461	12/72	2/88	16x24	57	Scrapped 11/02

234	823	71	160	128	--	N	Rhode Is.	462	12/72	7/85	16x24	63	Scrapped 6/06
236	824	--	--	--	--	--	Rhode Is.	467	12/72		16x24	57	SS 1/98
238	825	145	145	--	--	--	Rhode Is.	468	12/72		16x24	62	Scrapped 4/03
240	826	146	146	--	--	--	Rhode Is.	469	12/72		16x24	57	Scrapped 5/03
242	827	147	--	--	--	--	Rhode Is.	470	12/72		16x24	57	Scrapped 11/02
244	828	--	--	--	--	--	Rhode Is.	471	12/72	2/87	See class K		Rebuilt into 0-4-2T
246	829	--	--	--	--	--	Rhode Is.	472	12/72	9/85	See class K		Rebuilt into 0-4-2T
248 (2nd)	830	148	--	--	--	--	Rhode Is.	473	12/72		16x24	57	Scrapped 11/99
148	780	175	175	154	--	N	Rhode Is.	491	1/73		16x24	58	Scrapped 6/06
250	831	103	--	--	--	--	Rhode Is.	492	1/73		16x24	62	Scrapped 11/02
252	832	23	--	--	--	--	Rhode Is.	493	3/73	2/83	16x24	62	Scrapped 11/02
254	833	104	--	--	--	--	Rhode Is.	494	3/73		16x24	62	Scrapped 8/99
256	834	105	--	--	--	--	Rhode Is.	495	3/73		16x24	62	Scrapped 8/00
258	835	352	352	352	--	J3	Rhode Is.	496	3/73	11/87	17x24	63	Scrapped 9/08
260	836	106	--	--	--	--	Rhode Is.	497	3/73		16x24	57	Scrapped 8/00
262	837	24	106	112	--	N	Rhode Is.	498	3/73	5/88	16x24	63	Scrapped 6/06
264	838	498	498	329	2160	J3	Rhode Is.	499	4/73		17x24	63	Sold 3/25[m]
266[l]							Rhode Is.	500	4/73				

268	840	499	499	330	2161	J3	Rhode Is.	501	4/73	2/86	17x24	63	Scrapped 11/16
270	841	107	--	--	--	--	Rhode Is.	502	4/73		16x24	57	Scrapped 9/00
272	842	72	161	--	--	--	Rhode Is.	503	4/73	11/85	16x24	57	Scrapped 11/04
274	843	58	144	144	--	N	Rhode Is.	504	4/73	9/88	16x24	58	Scrapped 6/06
276	844	500	500	331	2169	J3	Rhode Is.	508	4/73		17x24	63	Scrapped 3/25[m]
278	845	108	108	--	--	--	Rhode Is.	509	5/73		16x24	62	Scrapped 3/03
280	846	64	--	--	--	--	Rhode Is.	510	5/73	12/87	16x24	57	Scrapped 8/02
282	847	316	316	316	2158	J3	Rhode Is.	511	5/73	3/86	17x24	63	Scrapped 4/18
284	848	317	317	317	2159	J3	Rhode Is.	512	5/73	6/80	17x24	63	Scrapped 4/18
286	849	82	169	135	--	N	Rhode Is.	513	5/73	1/82	16x24	63	Sold 1/07[n]
288	850	109	109	115	--	N	Rhode Is.	514	5/73		16x24	58	Sold 10/05[n]
290	851	110	--	--	--	--	Rhode Is.	515	5/73		16x24	57	Scrapped 10/00
292	852	26	110	118	--	N	Rhode Is.	516	5/73	9/84	16x24	58	Sold 11/05[n]
294	853	59	--	--	--	--	Rhode Is.	517	5/73	3/88	16x24	57	Sold 3/03
296	854	73	162	129	--	N	Rhode Is.	518	5/73	4/85	16x24	63	Scrapped 9/09
298	855	111	111	111	--	N	Rhode Is.	519	5/73		16x24	58	Scrapped 4/05
300	856	78	167	134	--	N	Rhode Is.	520.5	5/73	10/84	16x24	58	Sold 11/06[n]
302	857	112	--	--	--	--	Rhode Is.	555	9/73		16x24	57	Scrapped 11/02

304	858	60	--	--	--	--	Rhode Is.	556	9/73	3/88	16x24	57	Sold 8/02
306	859	113	--	--	--	--	Rhode Is.	557	9/73		16x24	57	Scrapped 6/00
308	860	68	155	121	1981	N	Rhode Is.	558	9/73	1/86	16x24	63	Scrapped 4/11
310	861	501	501	332	2162	J3	Rhode Is.	559	9/73	4/90	17x24	63	Scrapped 10/16
312	862	84	170	136	--	N	Rhode Is.	560	9/73	12/81	16x24	63	Scrapped 6/06
314	863	114	114	114	--	N	Rhode Is.	561	9/73		16x24	63	Scrapped 6/06
316	864	290	290	290	2155	J3	Rhode Is.	562	9/73	/95	17x24	63	Scrapped 9/23[o]
318	865	74	--	--	--	--	Rhode Is.	563	9/73	12/85	16x24	62	Sold 7/02[P]
320	866	85	176	--	--	--	Rhode Is.	564	9/73	7/80	16x24	57	Scrapped 11/03
322	867	115	115	291	2156	J3	Rhode Is.	565	10/73		17x24	63	Scrapped 1/13
324	868	502	502	333	2163	J3	Rhode Is.	566	10/73		17x24	63	Scrapped 4/11
326	869	36	120	120	--	N	Rhode Is.	567	10/73		16x24	63	Scrapped 9/08
328	870	116	--	--	--	--	Rhode Is.	568	10/73		16x24	57	Scrapped 9/00
330	871	46	130	130	1982	N	Rhode Is.	569	10/73	1/89	16x24	63	Sold 7/12[P]
332	872	81	--	--	--	--	Rhode Is.	570	10/73	2/83	16x24	62	Scrapped 11/02
334	873	117	--	--	--	--	Rhode Is.	571	10/73		16x24	57	Scrapped 5/00
336	874	503	503	334	2164	J3	Rhode Is.	572	10/73		17x24	63	Scrapped 11/13
338	875	65	--	--	--	--	Rhode Is.	573	10/73	11/87	16x24	62	Sold 4/02[P]

340	876	118	118	--	--	--	Rhode Is.	574	10/73		16x24	62	Sold 9/04
342	877	119	--	--	--	--	Rhode Is.	575	10/73		16x24	57	Scrapped 11/00
344	878	120	--	--	--	--	Rhode Is.	576	10/73		16x24	57	SS 6/98
346	879	504	504	335	2165	J3	Rhode Is.	577	10/73	1/85	17x24	63	Scrapped 8/14
348	880	25	107	--	--	--	Rhode Is.	578	10/73	2/85	16x24	62	Scrapped 9/03
350	881	517	517	353	2167	J3	Rhode Is.	579	10/73		17x24	63	Scrapped 7/14

352–370 (even): Possibly these #s were first assigned to ten of the thirteen Slaughter 0-6-0 freight engines converted in 1873 from broad-gauge series #58–77. See table 4-1. Further, it is possible that a few years later four remaining engines in this group were renumbered to 2nd #s 102, 104, 106, and 108, thus clearing the #352–370 series so that all Rhode Island locos could be grouped together, including those which follow. This is all pure conjecture (there is no proof).

352 (2nd): See #102–120 series above

354 (2nd), 356 (2nd), 358 (2nd), 360 (2nd): see Welland #s 2–5 in reference material (Edson and Corley, 1982).

362 (2nd), 364 (2nd), 366 (2nd), 368 (2nd), 370 (2nd): possibly renumbered from the #376–386 series below. See also [q].

372	892	61	147	147	--	N	Rhode Is.	624	10/73	4/88	16x24	58	Scrapped 9/06
374	893	62	148	148	--	N	Rhode Is.	625	10/73	3/88	16x24	58	Scrapped 10/08
376[q]	887	--	--	--	--	--	Rhode Is.	626	10/73		16x24	57	Scrapped 12/92
378[q]	888	37	121	--	--	--	Rhode Is.	627	11/73		16x24	62	Scrapped 6/04
380[q]	889	363	363	308	2157	J3	Rhode Is.	628	11/73	10/85	17x24	63	Scrapped 5/13
382[q]	890	79	--	--	--	--	Rhode Is.	629	11/73	10/84	16x24	57	Scrapped 11/02

384[q]	891	75	163	133	--	N	Rhode Is.	630	11/73	10/85	16x24	58	Scrapped 6/06
386[q]	766	50	132	132	--	N	BLW	2209	9/70	5/88	14x24	45	Sold 6/97

388, 390, 392: possibly these #s were first assigned to the Slaughter 0-6-0 freight engines converted in 1875 from broad gauge series #58–77, see table 4-1. Conceivably, one or more of these later became the 2nd #s 102, 104, 106, or 108. This, again, is pure conjecture (there is no proof).

0-4-4T Switchers[r]

86-301-401[t] Rebuilt from 4-4-0 in ’70
87-302-402[t] Rebuilt from 4-4-0 in ’70
88-303-403[u] Rebuilt from 4-4-0 in ’70
89-304-404 Rebuilt from 4-4-0 in ’70
90-305-405 Rebuilt from 4-4-0 in ’70
92-306-406[u] Rebuilt from 4-4-0 in ’70

0-4-0T Switchers[r]

91-307-407[u] BLW C/N 2209, built 9/70, 14x24 cylinders 45 drivers, Sold 6/97

0-4-2T Switchers[r,s]

308-408	903	--	--	--	--		BLW	2941	10/72		14x24	45	Sold 6/97
309-409	904	610	7	--	2543	F8	BLW	2943	10/72		14x24	45	Sold 7/23[v]
310-410	905	611	8	--	2541	F8	BLW	2953	11/72		14x24	45	Sold 5/12[w]
311-411	906	612	9	--	2542	F8	BLW	2954	11/72		14x24	45	Sold 5/12[w]
312-412	907	--	--	--	--		BLW	2959	11/72		14x24	45	Sold 6/97

313-413	908	--	--	--	--		BLW	2961	11/72		14x24	45	Sold 6/97
314-414	909	--	--	--	--		BLW	3060	1/73		14x24	45	Sold 6/97
315-415-393	894	606	--	--	--		BLW	3065	1/73		14x24	45	Sold 10/00[w]
316-416-394	895	607	--	--	--		BLW	3073	1/73		14x24	45	Sold 10/98[w]
317-417-395	896	608	--	--	--		BLW	3078	1/73		14x24	45	Sold 12/00[w]
418-396	897	--	--	--	--		BLW	3349	8/73		14x24	45	Sold 5/97
419-397	898	--	--	--	--		BLW	3353	8/73		14x24	45	Sold 5/97[x]
420-398	899	--	--	--	--		BLW	3358	8/73		14x24	45	Sold 9/97[x]
421-399	900	609	6	--	2544	F8	BLW	3374	8/73		14x24	45	Sold 2/25[v]
422-400	901	--	--	--	--	--	GWR-Ham.	--	9/73	9/83	14x24	45	Sold 6/97

[a] #s 102–120 (even numbers) were built as Rhode Is. C/N 211–220. First renumbering within this framework is guesswork.

[b] #761 was changed in 10/94 to #887, #63 was changed in 1902 to #154. #48 was changed in 1902 to #131.

[c] GTR records show (re)built by CL&E Co. 1/83; CL&E Co. records show that only boilers were rebuilt.

[d] 2nd #120 (ex #386). See later in this table and under Welland Railway in reference material (Edson and Corley, 1982).

[e] Some sources list these with original #s 122–126.

[f] #2067 was changed to CNR #129 (class A-11-a) in 1923.

[g] For the 2nd #s 138 and 174 (ex #102 series), see earlier in this table. For the 2nd #148 (new 1/73), see later in this table.

[h] #s 2123, 2150 were changed to CNR #s 135, 137 (class A-14-a) in 1923.

[i] GTR record shows #782 was built by the GWR in 7/81; it is assumed that this is the date of rebuilding.

[j] #1977 sold to North Shore Railway & Navigation Co.; #156 sold to Rock Lake Mining Co.; #54 sold to Brompton Paper.

[k] #116 was changed to #1501 in 1908 then to #1979; #140 was sold to Ontario Smelting Works and #117 to the Lotbiniere & Megantic.

[l] 1st #266 was renumbered #209. 2nd #266 renumbered from #102 series. See earlier in this table.

[m] #s 2160, 2169 were changed to CNR #s 139, 140 (class A-14-a) in 1923.

[n] #135 sold to Atlantic & Superior, #115 to Phoenix Bridge Co., and #s 118, 134 to Quebec Railway, Light, & Power, becoming their #s 1 and 4.

[o] #2155 was changed to CNR #138 (class A-14-a) in 1923.

[p] #74 sold to Sun Portland Cement Co., #1982 sold to North Shore Railway & Navigation Co., and #65 sold to National Portland Cement Co.

[q] #s 376–386 (even) were possibly renumbered to 2nd #s 362, 364, 366, 368, 370, 120 but this is conjecture (there is no proof).

[r] All pre-1882 renumbering on the GWR is pure speculation.

[s] Supplied as 0-4-0Ts from BLW. Rebuilt into 0-4-2Ts and coal burners after 1874. GTR #s 6 and 7 rebuilt back to 0-4-0Ts between 6/01 and 6/05, perhaps when renumbered in 1902.

[t] #s 86 and 87 were named *Geo. Smith* and *Wm. Weir*, respectively.

[u] #s 88, 91, 92 later named *George Smith*, *John Fildes*, *Gilson Homan*.

[v] #s 2543 and 2544 were changed to CNR #s 36 and 37 (class X-6-a) in 1923, then sold to Knox Bros. and L. Dussault Ltd., followed by Harbour Commissioners of Montreal.

[w] #s 2541 and 2542 were sold to F.H. McGuigan Construction Co.; #s 606 and 608 were sold to Hamilton Steel & Iron Co.; #607 was sold to the LE&DR.

[x] #898 was sold to M.J. Hogan and #899 to Onderdonk.

Abbreviations: GWR = Great Western Railway; GTR = Grand Trunk Railway; C/N = construction number; NB = newly (re) built; Spec = specifications; Is. = Island; Ham. = Hamilton; BLW = Baldwin Locomotive Works; CLC = Canadian Locomotive Co.; CNR = Canadian National Railways; LE&DR = Lake Erie & Detroit River Railway; SS = Sold for scrap; CL&E = Canadian Locomotive & Engine

TABLE 4-4. GREAT WESTERN RAILWAY LOCOMOTIVES ACQUIRED BY CANADIAN NATIONAL RAILWAYS

CNR Class	CNR Road Number	Quantity	Builder	Build Dates	Heritage	Disposition
4-4-0						
A-11-a	129	1	Rhode Island	1870	GWR→GTR[a]	Sc. 12/24
A-14-a	135-140	6	Rhode Island	1870–1873	GWR→GTR[b]	Sc. 9/23-3/25
B-10-a	248-252	5	Rhode Island	1870–1873	GWR→GTR[c]	Sc. 4/23–9/25
B-13-a	269	1	CL&ECo.	1883	GWR→GTR[d]	Sc. 10/29
0-4-0T						
X-6-a	36, 37	2	Baldwin	1872–1873	GWR→GTR[e]	So. 7/23[f], 2/25[g]

[a]GWR #134 → GTR #2067.

[b]GWR #s 142, 127, 190, 316, 264, and 276, respectively → GTR #s 2123, 2136, 2150, 2155, 2160, and 2169, respectively.

[c]GWR #s 123, 117, 107, 191, and 209, respectively → GTR #s 2125, 2129, 2132, 2143, and 2166, respectively.

[d]GWR #219 → GTR #2194.

[e]GWR #309 → #409 and #421 → #399, respectively → GTR #2543 and #2544, respectively

[f]Sold to Knox Bros.

[g]Sold to L. Dussault Ltd.

Abbreviations: CL&E Co. = Canadian Locomotive & Engine Company (Kingston); CNR = Canadian National Railways; GTR = Grand Trunk Railway; GWR = Great Western Railway; Sc. = scrapped; So. = sold

TABLE 4-5. DETROIT, GRAND HAVEN AND MILWAUKEE RAILWAY LOCOMOTIVES

Original		**Renumberings**									**Final Specs**		
Name	#	DGH& M '81	GTR '98	GTR '10	GTR Class	Type	Builder	C/N	Date	Re-build	Cylinders	Drivers	Disposition
Sherman Stevens						?	BLW		1838				
General Cass	1					4-4-0	Boston	570	9/55		15x22	60	
Shubael Connant	2					4-4-0	Boston	571	10/55		15x22	60	
Henry N. Walker	3					4-4-0	Boston	580	12/55		15x22	60	
Nelson P. Stewart	4					4-4-0	Boston	581	12/55		15x22	60	
Genesee	5					4-4-0	Boston	593	6/56		15x22	60	
Oakland	6					4-4-0	Boston	594	6/56		15x22	60	
Shiawassee	7					4-4-0	Boston	599	7/56		15x22	60	
Clinton	8					4-4-0	Boston	600	7/56		15x22	60	Off roster by 12/81
Owasso	9					4-4-0	Boston		'56		15x22		Off roster by 12/81
St. Johns	10					4-4-0	Boston		'56		15x22		Off roster by '83
Higham	11					4-4-0	Brice & Neilson			10/67			Off roster by '83
Milwaukee	12					4-4-0	Breeze, Knee			1/64			Off roster by '83
Ontario	13	[a]				4-4-0	Boston			12/71	16x22		
?	14					4-4-0	?		?				Off roster by 1/70
Ottawa	15					4-4-0	Boston		6/58		15x22		
Kent	16	[a]				4-4-0	Brice & Neilson		6/58	6/71	15x22		
St. Clair	17	[a]				4-4-0	Boston		9/58	10/68	16x22		
Erie	18	[a]				4-4-0	Boston		10/58	10/70	16x22		

Michigan	19					4-4-0	Boston		11/58		16x22		
Huron	20					4-4-0	Boston		11/58		16x22		
Superior	21					4-4-0	Boston		11/58		16x22		
Grand Rapids	22					4-4-0	Boston		11/58		16x22		
Lyons	23					4-4-0	Boston		11/58		16x22		
Pewamo	24	[a]				4-4-0	Boston		12/58	8/68	16x22		
?		224				4-4-0	?		?	'71	16.5x22	63	SS12/97
Royal Oak	25					4-4-0	Boston		12/58		16x22		
Washington	26					4-4-0	Boston		12/58		16x22		
Livingston	27					4-4-0	Boston		12/58		16x22		
Lansing	28					4-4-0	Boston		1/59		16x22		
Boston	29					4-4-0	Boston		1/59		16x22		
Detroit	30					0-4-0T	BLW	991	2/61		11x16	40	
Ionia	31	[b]				4-4-0	BLW	1445	1/66		16x24	60	
Montcalm	32					4-4-0	BLW	1447	1/66		16x24	60	
Pontiac	33					0-4-0T	BLW	1427	11/65		14x22	54	
Ovid	34	[b]				0-4-0T	BLW	1694	1/68		14x22	54	
Ada	14	[b]				0-4-0T	BLW	2052	1/70		14x24	44	
Grand Haven	35	213	1203	2612	F2[c]	2-6-0	Dickson	198	10/76		18x24	57	Scrapped 4/13
Holly	36	214	1271	2611	F2[c]	2-6-0	Dickson	199	10/76		18x24	57	Scrapped 8/12
Vernon	37	215	1204	2363	E5	2-6-0	Dickson	200	10/76		18x24	57	Scrapped 1/13
Corunna	38	216	(1205)		E5	2-6-0	Dickson	201	10/76		18x24	57	Scrapped 9/04
	39	205	1003			4-4-0	Rhode Is	768	6/79		16x24	61	Scrapped 9/04
	40	206	1004			4-4-0	Rhode Is	769	6/79		16x24	61	Scrapped 7/02

	41	207				4-4-0	Rhode Is	770	6/79		16x24	61	Scrapped 12/97
	42	208				4-4-0	Rhode Is	771	7/79		16x24	61	SS 12/97
	43	209	1005[d]		N	4-4-0	Rhode Is	772	7/79		16x24	61	Scrapped 9/07
	44	210	1006			4-4-0	Rhode Is	773	7/79		16x24	61	Scrapped 10/01
	45	211				4-4-0	Rhode Is	935	1/81		16x24	61	SS 12/97
	46	212	1007			4-4-0	Rhode Is	936	1/81		16x24	61	Scrapped 10/01
		223	1052	2104		4-4-0	BLW	?	'73	'97	17x24	60	Scrapped 3/15
	(ex-GTR 235)	232	1053	2105		4-4-0	BLW	3463	'73	'97	17x24	60	Scrapped 11/14
	(ex-GTR 236)	233				4-4-0	BLW	3464	'73		17x24	60	Scrapped 8/95
	(ex-GTR 237)	234	1054	2106		4-4-0	BLW	3466	'73		17x24	60	Scrapped 6/12
	(ex-GTR 238)												
	re207	72	1027	(re '07 1161)		4-4-0	BLW	3468	11/73		17x24	60	Scrapped 11/08
	(ex-GTR 239)	235	1055			4-4-0	BLW	3470	11/73		17x24	60	Scrapped 9/08
	(ex-GTR 240)	236	1056			4-4-0	BLW	3471	11/73		17x24	60	Scrapped 11/04
	(ex-GTR 241)	237	1057	2107		4-4-0	BLW	3472	11/73	'95	17x24	60	Scrapped 11/15

	(ex-GTR 242)	238	1058			4-4-0	BLW	3473	11/73		17x24	60	Scrapped 10/01
	(ex-GTR 243)	239	1059			4-4-0	BLW	3474	11/73		17x24	60	Scrapped 6/07
	(ex-GTR 244)	240	1060			4-4-0	BLW	3478	11/73		17x24	60	Scrapped 11/09
	(2nd 8)	217	1251	(re '02 1251)		0-4-2T	BLW	5940	12/81		14x24	44	Scrapped 10/09
	(2nd 9)	218	1252	(re '02 1252)		0-4-2T	BLW	5941	12/81		14x24	44	Scrapped 10/09
	(2nd 10)	202	1019	(re '06 1034)		4-4-0	Hinkley	1565	1/83		17x24	63	Scrapped 6/06
	(2nd 11)	203	1020	2190		4-4-0	Hinkley	1566	1/83		17x24	63	Scrapped 8/20
	(2nd 12)	204	1021	2191		4-4-0	Hinkley	1567	1/83		17x24	63	Scrapped 5/11
		200	1017			4-4-0	Hinkley	1571	1/83		17x24	63	Scrapped 10/01
		201	1018	2192		4-4-0	Hinkley	1573	1/83		17x24	63	Scrapped 8/26

[a] Many of these early engines, particularly those rebuilt after 1867, were renumbered in 1883 to the #219–233 series, but details are unknown, except that #s 220, 229, 230 were scrapped 8/95; #s 225 and 226 were scrapped 9/95; #s 227 and 228 were scrapped 10/95; and #s 219, 221, 222, and 231 were scrapped 11/95.

[b] Several of these engines were renumbered in 1883 to the #219–231 series.

[c] #s 2611, 2612 were converted 0-6-0 switchers.

[d] #1005 was renumbered in 5/06 to #1022 and in 1907 to #1156.

Abbreviations: DGH&M = Detroit, Grand Haven and Milwaukee Railway; GTR = Grand Trunk Railway; C/N = Construction Number; Re = renumbered; Boston = Boston Locomotive Works; Breeze Knee = Breeze, Kneeland & Company; BLW = Baldwin Locomotive Works; Rhode Is. = Rhode Island Locomotive Works; Dickson = Dickson Manufacturing Co.; Hinkley = Hinkley Locomotive Co.; SS = Sold for scrap; Specs = Specifications

TABLE 4-6. GREAT WESTERN RAILWAY ROLLING STOCK ROSTER (1871-81) EXPRESSED AS NUMBER OF UNITS

	1871[a]	1872[b]	1873[b]	1874[b]	1875[b]	1876[b]	1880[b]	1881[b]
Passenger cars (include 1st and 2nd class coaches, dining cars)	129	129	154	159	159	162 (98/61/3)[c]	165 (105/57/3)[c]	165 (105/57/3)[c]
Baggage-mail[d]	41	41	43	43	43	43	38	39
Freight cars	1794	2334	3699	4331	4551	4551	4751	4877
Express/merchandise box						772	753	878
Blue Line box						800	805	809
Milwaukee Line box						80(100)[e]	207	206
Michigan Line box						350	236	184
Hoosac Tunnel Line box						--	125	136
Long Star box						600	546	520
Erie & North Shore Line box						220	220	220
Erie & Milwaukee Line box						--	196	260
Saginaw Valley Line box						50	--	--
Cattle						535	413	463
Flat (incl. timber)						855[f]	794	910
Coal flat (gondolas)						100	172	182
Auxiliary						12	13	13
Oil tank						75	96	96
Service cars (construction, gravel, snow ploughs, others)	167	207	222	225	225	225	225	225

[a] August 1.

[b] July 31.

[c] First- and second-class coaches/baggage-mail/diners.

[d] Includes passenger coach-style and box car-style units

[e] ( ) Refers to combination.

[f] Sum of flat cars and 4-wheel timber trucks.

TABLE 4-7. DETROIT AND MILWAUKEE/DETROIT, GRAND HAVEN AND MILWAUKEE RAILWAY ROLLING STOCK ROSTER (1868-82) EXPRESSED AS NUMBER OF UNITS

	1868	1872	1875	1877	1878	1880	1881	1882
Passenger cars (include 1st- and 2nd-class coaches, dining cars, emigrant/colonist cars)	29	20/10/7[a]	28/7[b]	28	30	28	28	29
Baggage-mail-express	20	20	20	9	9	16	16	11
Freight cars								
Box	333	330[c]	323	295	324	324	324	369
Flat	187	188	151	138	104	124	124	198
Stock (cattle)				29		26	26	48
Coal								18
Other	5			3				
Auxiliary		1						
Service cars (construction, gravel, snow ploughs, etc.)		3			20	4	4	12

[a] 8-wheeled/12-wheeled/emigrant

[b] First-class/emigrant

[c] Box + stock (cattle)

TABLE 4-8. PASSENGER CAR NUMBERING SCHEMES ON THE GRAND TRUNK RAILWAY'S GREAT WESTERN AND DETROIT, GRAND HAVEN, AND MILWAUKEE DIVISIONS FOR 1890 AND 1897

Types of Cars	1890	1897	
	DGH&M (#)	DGH&M (#)	GW (#)
Parlor	1205, 1206	1205, 1206	781–784
First-Class	1200–1228	1200–1230	601–800
Excursion	1215–1217, 1227, 1241–1244	1215–1217, 1241–1244	---
Second-Class	---	---	801–869
Colonist	---	---	870–876
Dining	---	---	787–789
Combination	1251–1260	1251–1260	---
BM&E	1261–1277	1261–1278	---
Postal	---	---	888–900
Baggage	---	---	901–964
Pay	1204	1204	---
Official	1210	---	---

Abbreviations: DGH&M = Detroit, Grand Haven, and Milwaukee; GW = Great Western; BM&E = baggage, mail, and express

TABLE 4-9. GRAND TRUNK RAILWAY PASSENGER EQUIPMENT FROM THE GREAT WESTERN RAILWAY, TRANSFERRED OVER IN THE 1882 AMALGAMATION, AND ON ROSTER IN JANUARY 1896

GTR Car #	Date Built (mo./yr.)	Builder	Length (feet)	Capacity	Status[a] (1/96)
Combination First-Class/Baggage Cars					
601	?/?	GWR	45	34	IS/M
602	?/?	GWR	45	45	IS/G
603	?/?	GWR	44	44	IS/G
604	?/?	GWR	46	28	IS/G
605	?/?	GWR	44	32	IS/G
606	?/?	GWR	44	36	IS/G
607	?/?	GWR	47	36	IS/M
608	?/?	GWR	47	28	IS/G
609	?/?	GWR	46	36	IS/G
610	?/?	GWR	46	32	IS/G
611	?/?	GWR	46	36	IS/G
612	?/?	GWR	47	32	IS/G
613	?/?	GWR	48	50	IS/M
First-Class Cars[b,c]					
614	?/?	GWR	44	51	IS/G
615	?/?	GWR	45	51	IS/B
616	?/?	GWR	47	56	IS/G
617	?/?	GWR	45	51	IS/M
622	?/?	GWR	47	56	IS/G
624	?/?	GWR	47	56	IS/G
625	Smoker ?/?	GWR	50	53	IS/G
626	?/?	GWR	47	51	OS/U
627	?/?	GWR	46	56	IS/G
628	?/?	GWR	47	50	IS/G
629	?/?	GWR	--	--	OR
630	?/?	GWR	49	55	IS/G

631	?/?	GWR	47	50	IS/G
632	?/71	GWR	49	54	IS/G
635	?/?	GWR	52	54	IS/G
636	FC/Smoker ?/?	GWR	44	52	IS/M
638	?/?	GWR	49	54	IS/G
639	?/?	GWR	49	54	IS/G
640	?/?	GWR	49	56	IS/G
641	?/?	GWR	50	52	OS/U
642	?/?	GWR	49	56	IS/M
643	?/?	GWR	49	54	IS/G
644	SC/Smoker ?/?	GWR	47	56	IS/G
645	?/?	GWR	51	56	IS/G
646	?/?	GWR	46	52	IS/G
647	?/?	GWR	50	60	IS/G
648	?/?	GWR	51	60	IS/G
670	?/82	Crossen	50	63	IS/M
671	?/82	Crossen	50	64	IS/M
672	?/82	Crossen	50	64	IS/G
673	?/82	Crossen	50	64	IS/G
674	?/82	Crossen	50	64	IS/G
675	?/82	Crossen	50	58	IS/G
676	?/82	Crossen	50	64	IS/G
677	?/82	Crossen	50	64	IS/G
678	?/82	Crossen	50	64	IS/M
679	?/?	GWR	49	59	IS/G
680	?/?	GWR	49	60	IS/G
681	?/?	GWR	49	60	IS/G
682	?/?	GWR	49	55	IS/M
683	?/?	GWR	49	55	OS/U
684	?/?	GWR	49	59	IS/G
685	?/?	GWR	49	55	IS/M
686	?/?	GWR	49	55	IS/G

687	?/?	GWR	49	59	IS/G
688	?/?	GWR	49	55	IS/G
689	?/?	GWR	49	59	IS/G
690	?/?	GWR	49	62	IS/M
691	?/?	GWR	49	60	IS/B
692	?/?	GWR	49	55	IS/G
693	?/?	GWR	49	55	IS/B
695	?/?	GWR	49	58	IS/G
696	SC ?/?	GWR	49	59	IS/G
697	?/?	GWR	49	59	IS/G
698	?/82	GWR	49	59	IS/G
699	?/82	GWR	49	59	IS/G
700	?/82	GWR	49	59	IS/G
701	?/82	GWR	49	59	IS/G
702	?/82	GWR	49	60	IS/M
703	?/82	GWR	49	59	IS/G
704	?/82	GWR	49	64	IS/G
705	?/82	GWR	46	60	IS/M
706	?/82	GWR	46	60	IS/G
707	?/82	GWR	49	62	IS/G
708	?/82	GWR	49	64	IS/G
709	?/82	GWR	49	64	IS/G
710	?/82	GWR	55	64	IS/G
711	?/82	GWR	49	64	IS/G
712	SC/Smoker ?/82	GWR	49	64	IS/G
713	?/82	GWR	49	64	IS/M
714	?/82	GWR	49	64	IS/G
715	?/82	GWR	55	64	IS/G
Smoking Cars					
761	?/76	GWR	44	45	IS/G
762	?/76	GWR	44	45	IS/G
763	?/77	GWR	44	23	IS/G

764	?/77	GWR	44	25	IS/G
Parlour Cars					
782	?/82	GWR	49	34	IS/G, re GTR 2506 *Toronto*
783	?/83	GWR	55	34	IS/M, re GTR 2503 (7/01) *London*
784	?/83	GWR	55	34	IS/M, re GTR 2504 *Clifton*
Dining Cars					
787	?/76 (GWR rebuilt)	Pullman Detroit, 4/72	63	40	--, re GTR 2801(1) (7/01) *Continental*, 6-wheeled trucks
788	?/80 (GWR rebuilt	Pullman Detroit, 6/77	63	40	--, re *International*➔ GTP *Prince Rupert* (1) (4/08), 6-wheeled trucks
789	?/83	GWR	56	36	--, re GTR 2800 *Windsor*, 6-wheeled trucks
Business Car					
798	?/?	GWR	49	--	IS/G, re GTR *International*
First-Class Car					
799	?/?	GWR	49	56	IS/G
Second-Class Cars[d]					
801	?/?	GWR	40	52	IS/B
802	?/?	GWR	40	54	IS/B
803	?/?	GWR	40	54	IS/B
804	?/?	GWR	40	54	IS/B
805	?/?	GWR	40	53	IS/B
806	?/?	GWR	40	52	IS/B
807	?/72	Hamilton (SLF)	40	52	IS/B
808	?/?	Hamilton (SLF)	40	52	IS/B
809	?/?	Hamilton (SLF)	40	50	IS/B
810	?/?	Hamilton (SLF)	40	52	IS/B
811	?/?	Hamilton (SLF)	40	52	IS/B
812	?/?	Hamilton (SLF)	40	52	IS/B
813	?/?	Hamilton (SLF)	40	52	IS/B
814	?/?	Hamilton (SLF)	40	54	IS/B
815	?/?	Hamilton (SLF)	40	52	IS/B

817	?/72	Hamilton (SLF)	40	54	IS/B
818	?/72	Hamilton (SLF)	40	52	IS/B
819	?/72	Hamilton (SLF)	40	52	IS/B
820	?/72	Hamilton (SLF)	40	52	IS/B
821	?/?	GWR	46	52	IS/G
822	?/?	GWR	44	52	IS/G
823	?/?	GWR	44	56	IS/G
824	?/?	GWR	44	56	IS/G
825	?/72	Hamilton (SLF)	44	56	OS/U
826	?/72	Hamilton (SLF)	44	52	OS/W
827	?/72	Hamilton (SLF)	45	52	IS/G
829	?/72	Hamilton (SLF)	45	57	IS/G
832	?/?	GWR	44	50	IS/G
838	?/?	GWR	34	36	IS/M
839	?/?	GWR	46	52	IS/M
840	?/?	GWR	44	56	IS/G, re GTR 1010
841	?/?	GWR	45	52	IS/M
842	?/?	GWR	49	60	IS/M
843	?/?	GWR	49	59	IS/G
844	?/?	GWR	44	50	IS/G
Colonist Cars					
870	?/?	GWR	--	48	IS/G
871	?/?	GWR	--	48	IS/G
872	?/?	GWR	--	48	OS/W
873	?/?	GWR	--	56	IS/G
874	?/?	GWR	--	56	OS/U
Combination Mail/Smoking Cars					
892	?/?	GWR	50	28	IS/G
893	?/?	GWR	49	26	IS/G
894	?/?	GWR	50	26	IS/G
895	?/72	Hamilton (SLF)	50	26	IS/M
896	?/72	Hamilton (SLF)	50	28	IS/G

897	?/72	Hamilton (SLF)	50	30	IS/G
898	?/72	Hamilton (SLF)	50	28	IS/M
899	?/72	Hamilton (SLF)	50	28	IS/G
900	?/72	Hamilton (SLF)	50	30	IS/G
Mail/Baggage & Express Cars					
901	?/?	GWR	36	--	IS/B, Baggage-express
904	?/?	GWR	50	--	IS/M, Mail-baggage-express
905	?/?	GWR	43	--	IS/G, Mail-baggage-express
907	?/70	GWR	53	--	IS/G, Mail-baggage-express
910	?/?	GWR	42	--	IS/M, Baggage-express
911	?/?	GWR	53	--	IS/G, Mail-baggage-express
912	?/83	GWR	50	--	IS/G, Baggage-express
913	?/?	GWR	52	--	IS/M, Mail-baggage-express
914	?/?	GWR	50	--	IS/G, Mail-baggage-express
915	?/?	GWR	56	--	IS/G, Baggage-express
916	?/?	GWR	52	--	IS/G, Mail-baggage-express
917	?/?	GWR	50	--	IS/G, Mail-baggage-express
918	?/?	GWR	36	--	IS/G, Baggage-express
919	?/?	GWR	36	--	IS/M, Baggage-express
920	?/?	GWR	35	--	IS/M, Baggage-express
922	?/?	GWR	40	--	IS/G, Baggage-express
934	?/73	GWR	45	--	IS/G, Baggage-express
935	?/83	GWR	50	--	IS/M, Baggage-express
941	?/82	GWR	33	--	IS/M, Baggage-express

[a] IS/G = in service, good condition; IS/M = in service, medium condition; IS/B = in service, bad condition; OS/U = out of service, undergoing heavy repairs; OS/W = out of service awaiting heavy repairs; U = disposition unknown.

[b] Some exceptions noted.

[c] Following first-class cars were off the roster by 1/96: #s 618-621, 623, 629, 633, 634.

[d] Following second-class cars were off the roster by 1/96: #s 816, 828, 837.

Abbreviations: GTR = Grand Trunk Railway, GWR = Great Western Railway, FC = first-class, SC = second-class, SLF = St. Lawrence Foundry

TABLE 4-10. GRAND TRUNK RAILWAY PASSENGER EQUIPMENT BUILT BY GREAT WESTERN RAILWAY AND ON ROSTER AFTER 1901

GTR #	Month/Year Built[a]	GTR/CN Renumbering(s) and Month/Year Date(s)[b]	Comments[b]
Mail/Baggage Cars			
101	?/82	CN 7758 (9/24)	B4FN (2 DPS), RUF 10/20; 50 feet/56 feet 8 inches
102	?/78	CN 7761 (1/24)	B4FN (2 DPS), RUF 10/20; 51 feet 5 inches/52 feet 8 inches
114	?/70	GTR 92598 (4/13)	O4FN (3 DPS), OS. F; 53 feet 10 inches/60 feet 3 inches
119	?/?	CN 7740 (12/23)	O4FN (2 DPS), RUF (8/19); 49 feet 8 inches/56 feet 4 inches
Combination Mail/Second-Class Coaches			
303[c]	?/72	GTR 142 (ND)	O4RN (1 DPS), capacity 30, 49 feet 10 inches/ 56 feet 6 inches ➔ B4FN, RUF 10/20, 49 feet 10 inches/53 feet
326	?/?	CN 7400 (2) (4/24)	O4 (1 DPS), capacity 24; 49 feet 4 inches/56 feet
327	?/?	GTR 94288 (6/15)	O4RN (1 DPS), capacity 30; 49 feet 9 inches/56 feet 5 inches
328	?/?	GTR 152 (6/22)	O4RN (1 DPS), capacity 30, 51 feet 5 inches/58 feet ➔ B4FW (2 DPS), RUF, 49 feet 10 inches/58 feet (6/22)
339	?/?	GTR 92837 (2/12)	O4RN (1 DPS), capacity 24; 49 feet 2 inches/55 feet 10 inches
340	?/?	GTR 157 (6/22)	O4RN/RW (1 DPS), capacity 28; 49 feet 10 inches/56 feet 6 inches ➔ B4RN (2 DPS), TRW, RUF (6/22)
341[c]	?/?	? GTR 159 (ND)	O4RN/RW (1 DPS), capacity 28, 49 feet 8 inches/56 feet 4 inches; rebuilt RWF (12/23)
346[d]	?/?		O4RN (1 DPS), capacity 24; 49 feet 9 inches/57 feet
Express Car			
430	?/?		B4 (1 DPS); 39 feet 11 inches/41 feet 7 inches
Baggage Cars			
503	?/?	GTR 92668 (8/13)	O4FN (2 DPS), OS, F; 36 feet/42 feet 8 inches
505	?/?	GTR 92613 (5/13)	O4FN (1 DPS) OS, FA; 35 feet 10 inches/42 feet 6 inches
530	?/73	CN 8047 (1) (6/24)	B4 (2 DPS), 44 feet 9 inches/46 feet 9 inches
572	?/83	CN 8059 (1) (10/23)	B4 (2 DPS); 49 feet 10 inches/51 feet 6 inches

573	?/?	CN 8062 (1) (6/25)	B4FN (2 DPS); 49 feet 9 inches/51 feet 5 inches
577	?/?	CN 8066 (1) (12/23)	B4 (2 DPS); 49 feet 9 inches/57 feet 8 inches
578	?/?		Destroyed Moorfield, ON (2/5/08)
579	?/?	CN 8067 (1) (4/24)	B4 (1 DPS); 49 feet 9 inches/51 feet 5 inches
580	?/?	CN 8197 (1) (9/23)	B4 (2 DPS); 50 feet/51 feet 8 inches
582	?/83	CN 8068 (1) (11/27)	B4 (2 DPS); 49 feet 8inches/50 feet 4 inches
588	?/76	GTW 8041 (12/26)	B6FN (2 DPS); 56 feet 4 inches/59 feet
621	?/?	CN 8211 (10/24)	B4FN (2 DPS); 55 feet 11 inches/58 feet 11 inches
Combination Baggage/Second-Class Cars			
800(1)	?/?	GTR 940 (4/14)	O4RN (1 DPS), capacity 30; 49 feet 5 inches/56 feet 1 inch
823(1)	?/?	GTR 953 (3/15)	O4RN (1 DPS), SF elliptical head roof, capacity 32; 49 feet 3 inches/55 feet 11 inches
834(1)	?/?	GTR 962 (10/15)	O4RN (1 DPS), OS elliptical head roof, no UD, capacity 32; 44 feet 5 inches/51 feet 1 inch
837(1)	?/?	GTR 92679 (3/14)	O4RN (1 DPS), OS elliptical head roof; 46 feet 8 inches/52 feet 8 inches
838(1)	?/?		O4RN (1 DPS), OS elliptical head roof, cupola for van; 46 feet 7 inches/53 feet 3 inches
841(1)	?/?	GTR 964 (2/16)	O4RN (1 DPS), OS elliptical head roof, capacity 24; 46 feet/54 feet 2 inches
842(1)	?/?	GTR 965 (9/14)	O4RN (1 DPS), capacity 20; 49 feet 5 inches/56 feet 3 inches
843(1)	?/?		O4RN (1 DPS); 49 feet 3 inches/55 feet 11 inches
851(1)	?/?	GTR 970 (9/14)	O4RN, capacity 22; 44 feet 6 inches/51 feet 2 inches
Second-Class Coaches			
1005	?/76	GTR 92343 (5/23)	O4, capacity 56; 43 feet 9 inches/59 feet 5 inches
1008	?/56	GTP 500 (6/06)	
1009	?/?	GTR 92689 (7/14)	O4, capacity 60; 44 feet 4 inches/51 feet 10 inches
1010	?/56	Ex-GTR 840 GW Division Old Series ➔ GTP 302 (6/06)	TRW, O4FN
1013	?/?	GTP 511 (7/06)	
1014	?/?	GTP 512 (7/06)	
1019	?/?	GTR 92794 (9/10)	OS ends
1022	?/?	GTP 507 (7/06)	

1023	?/75	GTP 505 (7/06)	TRW, O4FN
1024	?/?	GTP 513 (8/06)	OS ends
1034	?/76	GTR 1313(2)(3/12)	O4RN, capacity 36/20 smokers; 43 feet/50 feet 4 inches
First-Class Coaches[e]			
1519[f]	?/70	GTR 94139 (9/10)	
1535[f]	?/?		Sold to Toronto and York Radial Rwy. (#302)
1549[f]	?/?	GTR 94127 (1/08)	
1563(1)[f]	?/?	GTP 533 (4/07)	
1577[f]	?/?		
1578[f]	?/?		
1580[f]	?/83	GTP 539 (5/07)	
1581[f]	?/?	GTR 94336 (7/16)	O4, capacity 64; 49 feet 4 inches/56 feet
1582[f]	?/?	GTR 92828 (5/14)	O4, capacity 64; 49 feet 5 inches/55 feet 8 inches
1583[f]	?/?		O4, capacity 60; 49 feet 5 inches/55 feet 7 inches
1584[f]	?/?	GTR 94678 (6/17)	O4, capacity 62; 49 feet 2 inches/55 feet 8 inches
1585[f]	?/?	GTR 94337 (7/16)	O4, capacity 64; 49 feet 3 inches/55 feet 11 inches
1586[f]	?/?	GTR 92721 (9/18)	O4 (side ventilators), capacity 64; 49 feet 5 inches/56 feet 1 inch
1587[f]	?/?	GTR 94679 (6/17)	TRW, O4RN, capacity 64; 49 feet 5 inches/56 feet 1 inch
1588[f]	?/81	GTW 94452 (9/17)	O4, capacity 64; 49 feet 5 inches/56 feet 1 inch
1589[f]	?/?	GTR 2987 (3/17)	O4 (hurricane roof), capacity 64; 49 feet 6 inches/56 feet 1 inch
1590[f]	?/?	GTR 94482 (5/17)	Capacity 64; 49 feet 3 inches/55 feet 8 inches
1592[f]	?/?	GTR 94072 (1/21)	O4, capacity 58; 49 feet 4 inches/56 feet
1593[f]	?/?	GTR 94672 (8/17)	O4, capacity 64; 49 feet 3 inches/55 feet 11 inches
1594[f]	?/82	GTR 94646 (7/17)	O4, capacity 68; 49 feet 4 inches/56 feet
1595[f]	?/82	GTR 94698 (?/?)	O4, capacity 62; 49 feet 1 inch/55 feet 9 inches
1597[f]	?/82	GTR 92836 (6/11)	
1599[f]	?/?	GTR 94675 (6/17)	O4, capacity 64; 49 feet 4 inches/55 feet 2 inches
1616[f]	?/?	GTR 92761 (10/15)	O4, capacity 62; 49 feet 4 inches/56 feet
1631[f]	?/77	GTR 92716 (7/18)	O4, capacity 56; 43 feet 9 inches/50 feet 10 inches
1632[f]	?/77		O4, capacity 56; 43 feet 10 inches/50 feet 6 inches
1654[d,f]	?/82	GTR 94270 (11/18)	O4, capacity 58; 47 feet/53 feet 8 inches
1658[d,f]	?/82	GTR 94745 (9/17)	O4, capacity 64; 49 feet 2 inches/56 feet 3 inches
1659[d,f]	?/82	CN 3107 (10/23)	O4, capacity 62; 49 feet 10 inches/56 feet 6 inches

1660[d,f]	?/82	CN 3108 (3/24)	O4, capacity 62; 49 feet 9 inches/56 feet 5 inches
1661[d,f]	?/82	GTR 94674 (9/17)	O4, capacity 64; 49 feet 11 inches/56 feet 9 inches
1662[f]	?/82	GTR 94251 (8/19)	O4, capacity 62; 49 feet 2 inches/55 feet 5 inches
1666[f]	?/70	GTP 529 (4/07)	OS elliptical head roof
1671[f]	?/83		Burned Point Levis, PQ, 12/11
1672[f]	?/83	CN 3150 (11/24)	O4, capacity 62; 50 feet 7 inches/57 feet 6 inches
1673[f]	?/83	CN 3151 (9/23)	O4, capacity 66; 50 feet 6 inches/57 feet 4 inches
1679[f]	?/83	CN 3113 (?/?)	
1694[f]	?/?	GTR 94070 (?/?)	O4, capacity 64; 49 feet 6 inches/56 feet 2 inches
1695[f]	?/82	CN 3117 (9/23)	O4, capacity 64; 49 feet 2 inches/55 feet 8 inches
1696[f]	?/82	GTR 92722 (9/18)	O4, capacity 64; 49 feet 3 inches/56 feet 1 inch
1697[f]	?/83	CN 3133 (6/24)	O4, capacity 64; 49 feet 3 inches/56 feet 1 inch
1789[g]	?/82	CN 3211(1) (?/24)	O4, capacity 66; 55 feet 4 inches/62 feet 1 inch
First-Class Coaches with Smoking Room[e]			
1803[g]	?/82	GTR 92914 (9/22)	O4, capacity 36/24 smokers; 49 feet 4 inches/56 feet 9 inches
1806[g]	?/76	GTP 538 (5/07)	
1807[d,g]	?/83	GTR 92795 (9/10)	OS roof
1808[g]	?/82	GTR 92765 (10/18)	O4, capacity 36/26 smokers; 49 feet 4 inches/56 feet
1809[g]	?/82		Destroyed Brantford, ON (6/15/10)
1832[g]	?/?		O4, OS elliptical head roof, capacity 39/20 smokers; 52 feet 5 inches/59 feet 1 inch
1833[g]	?/?	GTR 94024 (1/08)	OS elliptical head roof
1834[g]	?/?	CN 3248 (11/24)	O4, capacity 44/20 smokers; 49 feet 4 inches/56 feet
Parlour-Buffet Cars			
782 (*Toronto*)	?/82	GTR 2506 (?/?)	capacity 34; 49 feet
783 (*London*)	?/83	GTR 2503 (7/01)	capacity 34; 55 feet
784 (*Clifton*)	?/83	GTR 2504 (7/01)	capacity 34; 55 feet
Dining Cars			
787 (*Continental*)	4/72	GTR 2901(1) (7/01) ➔ GTR *Algonquin* (7/08)	Built 4/72 (Pullman Detroit shops); 63feet/?, 6-wheeled trucks, capacity 40; rebuilt in ?/83, 62 feet 10 inches/69 feet 10 inches in 7/08
788 (*International*)	6/77	GTR *International* (?/?) ➔ GTP *Prince Rupert* (1) (4/08)	Built 6/77 (Pullman Detroit shops), rebuilt ?/80 (GWR London), rebuilt ?/89 after St. George, ON wreck; 63 feet/?, 6-wheeled trucks, capacity 40
789 (*Windsor*)	?/83	GTR 2800 (?/?)	56 feet/?, capacity 36

[a] Only cars with build dates up to and including 1883 have been included.
[b] Data have been presented up to and including the second renumbering (into GTR/GTP/CN rosters). Only the earliest physical descriptors are presented so as to provide data closest to those of the cars under Great Western ownership.
[c] William Hamilton and Sons (St. Lawrence Foundry) was the builder of these cars.
[d] Crossen Car Manufacturing of Cobourg was the builder of these cars.
[e] These first-class coaches had open platforms.
[f] These first-class coaches had dry toilets only (GTR #s 1500–1724).
[g] These first-class coaches had water-flushed toilets/wash stands (GTR #s 1724 and higher).

Abbreviations: TRW = all-wood car with underframe reinforced with steel truss rods and queen posts; O6FN = open-platform, 6-wheeled trucks, flat top narrow (single) windows; B4FN = blind end, 4-wheeled trucks, flat top narrow (single) windows; RUF = reinforced underframe; DPS = door(s) per side; ____/_____ = length over end sills/length overall; O4FN = open-platform, 4-wheeled trucks, flat top narrow (single) windows; O4 = open-platform, 4-wheeled trucks; O4RN = open-platform, 4-wheeled trucks, narrow (single) windows with arch tops/transoms; B4FW = blind end, 4-wheeled trucks, flat top wide (double) windows; RW = wide (double) windows with arch tops/transoms; B4RN = blind end, 4-wheeled trucks, narrow (single) windows with arch top/transoms; B4 = blind end, 4-wheeled trucks; OS = old style GWR (Merrilees designation, probably like old style flat arch roof); FA = flat arch roof; B6FN = blind end, 6-wheeled trucks, flat top narrow (single) windows; ND = No data; GTR = Grand Trunk Railway; GTP = Grand Trunk Pacific Railway; CN = Canadian National Railways

TABLE 4-11. DETAILS OF GREAT WESTERN PASSENGER CARS NOT SPECIFICALLY INCLUDED IN TABLES 4-8 AND 4-9

GWR #	Car Description	Builder/Date	Comments
95	second-class coach	GWR/before 1882	no details available
?	hotel car *President*	GWR-H/1867	no details available
?	3 sleeping cars	GWR-H/11-58	designed by Samuel Sharp, GWR Car Superintendent
?	2 second-class coaches	BWF/8-54	no details available
26	baggage-express car	J-S/1872	no details available
85	coach	J-S/1872	no details available
?	parlour cars *Leo* and *Mars*	Tau/pre-1872	built for Pullman and assigned to GWR as early as 1871
?	2 palace cars ?	Tau/pre-1872	built for Pullman and assigned to GWR on 4/25/71
?	sleeping car *Mayflower*	GWR-H/1867	built for Pullman and assigned to GWR in 1867. burned 1875
?	sleeping car *Viceroy*	GWR-H/1865	built for Pullman and assigned to GWR after built. 8-wheeled trucks changed to 6-wheeled trucks in 8/74. Before 1875, name changed to *Algeria*. Stored 9/88, sold 1/91
?	sleeping car *Niagara*	GWR-H/6-67	built for Pullman. After 1875, renamed *Olympus*. Sold 1/91
?	sleeping car *Victoria*	GWR-H/1865	built for Pullman. Disposition unknown
?	sleeping car *St. Lawrence*	GWR-H/7-67	built for Pullman. Before 1875, renamed *Helvetica*. Sold 1/91
?	sleeping car *President*	GWR-H/8-1-67	built for Pullman. Before 1875, renamed *Marathon*. Sold 1/91

Abbreviations: GWR = Great Western Railway; H = Hamilton; BWF = Brainard, Williams, Fisher and Company; J-S = Jackson and Sharp; Tau = Taunton

TABLE 4-12. GRAND TRUNK RAILWAY PASSENGER EQUIPMENT BUILT BY THE DETROIT, GRAND HAVEN, AND MILWAUKEE (DETROIT AND MILWAUKEE) RAILWAY AND ON ROSTER FROM 1901 ONWARD

GTR #	Month/Year Built[a]	GTR/GTW Renumbering(s) and Month/Year Date(s)[b]	Comments[b]
Express Cars			
435	?/?	GTW 8450 (10/23)	B4FN (1 DPS); 43 feet/45 feet 8 inches
439	?/?	GTW 8452 (11/23)	B4FN (1 DPS); 47 feet 3 inches/50 feet 3 inches
Baggage Cars			
600	?/?	GTW 8004 (11/24)	O4FN (2 DPS); 49 feet 11 inches/52 feet 10 inches
601	?/?	GTW 8005 (3/24)	B4FN (2 DPS); 50 feet 11 inches/50 feet 9 inches
619	?/?	GTW 8040 (6/25)	B6FN (2 DPS); 54 feet 10 inches/57 feet 9 inches
First-Class Coaches			
1605	?/81		sold to DBCW (3/18/11)
1607	?/?	GTW 92856 (6/10)	
1608	?/?	GTW 92855 (1/10)	
1609	?/?	GTW 92823 (8/12)	O4, capacity 54; 42 feet 3 inches/49 feet 3 inches
1610	?/?	GTW 94123 (2/08)	
1611	?/?		sold to DBCW (3/18/11)
1612	?/?	GTW 92857 (6/10)	
1647	?/81	GTR 130 (7/12)	O4, capacity 66; 50 feet/57 feet ➔ B4 (2 DPS); 49 feet 11 inches /52 feet 7 inches (7/12)
1775	?/83	GTR 92087 (3/21)	O4, capacity 64; 50 feet 10 inches/57 feet 6 inches

[a] Only cars with Detroit, Grand Haven, and Milwaukee or Detroit and Milwaukee build dates up to and including 1883 have been presented. #1647 was built by Pullman.

[b] Data have been presented up to and including the second renumbering (into GTR/GTW car rosters). Only the earliest physical descriptors are presented so as to provide data closest to those of the cars under Detroit, Grand Haven, and Milwaukee ownership.

Abbreviations: GTR = Grand Trunk Railway; GTW = Grand Trunk Western Railway; B4FN = Blind end, 4-wheeled trucks, flat top narrow (single) windows; DPS = door(s) per side; O4FN = open-platform, 4-wheeled trucks, flat top narrow (single) windows; B6FN = blind end, 6-wheeled trucks, flat top narrow (single) windows; DBCW = Detroit, Bay City, and Western Railroad; O4 = open-platform, 4-wheeled trucks; __/__ = length over end sills/length overall

CHAPTER 5

MARITIME OPERATIONS

In light of the incompatible gauges of the Great Western Railway (five feet six inches) and U.S. railways in the Detroit area (four feet eight and a half inches), the first cross-river connections comprised small break-bulk ships (*Ottawa*, *Windsor*, *Transit*) built in 1853 or 1856 (see table 5-1).

The *Ottawa*, a Detroit-built sidewheeler, is said to have been a freight-only vessel. The *Windsor*, another Detroit-built sidewheeler, is known to have carried freight and passengers. The screw (propeller)-driven *Transit* was a general-purpose vessel.

In 1856 the railway bought or leased the *Globe*, a ten-year-old propeller vessel (see table 5-1). Unfortunately, it capsized at the Michigan Central wharf in Detroit on March 9, 1858, while loading cattle. It was salvaged, repaired, and resumed its duties. In 1857 the railway began operating the *Union*, a 163-foot-long sidewheeler of 1,190 tons, reported to have an iron-sheathed hull (see table 5-1). She became the Great Western's principal ship, since she was larger and more powerful than the others. Passenger accommodations were comfortable and the restaurant was said to be excellent. Upon her arrival, the *Transit* was assigned to hauling cattle.

Starting on June 18, 1855, the Great Western steamers *America* (captained by John Masson) and *Canada* (captained by G.E. Willoughby), which cost the railway $360,000, and the leased steamer *Europa* began serving Hamilton, Toronto, and Oswego, New York (see table 5-1). The two routes were Hamilton-to-Oswego and Oswego-to-Hamilton, both with intermediate stops in Toronto, with a scheduled time between the two principal ports of about twelve and a half hours. These routes were run daily except Sundays. Unfortunately, the Great Western lost $60,000 over the first six months of operations before suspending service for the winter. The directors of the Great Western blamed the competition of the steamers of the Huron and Ontario Railroad Company for the poor results. The Huron and Ontario received its charter in 1836 to build a railway from Burlington Bay to Goderich. The railway was never built, but the charter's authorization to operate steamers apparently was exercised. In 1856 *Canada* and *America* (but not *Europa*) ran between Hamilton, Brockville, Prescott, Cape Vincent, and Ogdensburg (latter two in New York State), and by August 31 had accumulated a deficit of $25,000. In addition, because these ships drew some traffic from the Grand Trunk and competing lines across New York State, they likely stimulated retaliatory rate cutting. Hemorrhaging red ink, the railway was happy to sell these ships in 1857 to the Detroit and Milwaukee, even for the modest sum of $180,000 in Detroit and Milwaukee stock. In 1858 the Detroit and Milwaukee sold both ships to eastern U.S. interests (see table 5-1).

Under threat by U.S. standard-gauge roads to begin transfer of standard-gauge U.S. cars as soon as possible, the Great Western began, in the middle 1860s, the conversion from broad to standard gauge by installation of a third rail to accommodate standard-gauge rolling stock. At this time, the break-bulk ships began to become expendable and the railway ordered its first railway car ferry, the *Great Western*. She was a product of the Clyde shipyard of Barclay Curle and Company of Glasgow, Scotland. Assembled there, she was subsequently disassembled for transit (in 10,878 pieces!) to Windsor, where she was reassembled at the shipyard of Henry Jenkings located in Sandwich East, just east of Walkerville. The engines to power her sidewheels were built at Dundas (Hamilton) by the firm of Gartshore while her boilers were built in the Hamilton shops of the Great Western. The *Great Western* was launched amid much fanfare on September 6, 1866. Completed with a long tubular housing covering her main deck, she had pilot houses fore (at the front or bow) and aft (at the rear or stern) and was nominally double-ended. However, for unknown reasons, she only had cars loaded or discharged from her bow. Details of this vessel can be found in table 5-1.

January 1, 1867, saw the initiation of mixed-gauge service on the rail lines of the Great Western and cross-river service with the *Great Western.* June 1, 1867, saw the initiation of interchange of standard-gauge rolling stock with the Michigan Central at Detroit.

To facilitate mixed-gauge interchange, the *Great Western* had two tracks on her deck, both laid to dual gauges. By the standards of the day, with a length of two hundred twenty feet, she was considered monstrous, the largest steel or iron vessel on the Great Lakes and, with one exception, the largest vessel of any kind (wood, steel, or iron) on the Lakes. The publicity accorded the *Great Western* was in marked contrast to that received by the *International,* the Grand Trunk railway car ferry which antedated her. Indeed, the *Great Western* was erroneously declared by some authorities to have been the first Great Lakes car ferry.

Between 1872 and 1874 the Great Western completed the conversion to standard gauge, completing the elimination of all barriers to interchange with U.S.

railroads. As a result, cross-border traffic expanded greatly, requiring the purchase of three additional car ferries during this period (for details of all, see table 5-1). The first was a combination passenger and car ferry intended for the Sarnia–Port Huron cross-river traffic called the *Transit* (not to be confused with the break-bulk ship of the same name). This vessel replaced the passenger break-bulk ship called the *Florence.* The latter vessel may have also occasionally ferried railway equipment on barges (newspaper accounts of her activities are ambiguous). The *Transit* was designed to carry passengers in cabins around the tracks on her main deck. She had two standard-gauge tracks, each one capable of holding five freight cars. She is believed to have had only a single forward pilot house, twin stacks, and an enclosed car deck. She was propeller-driven (twin screws) and her hull was of wood (white oak).

In 1873 a new slip dock for ferry boats was built just outside the older slip dock in Windsor in order to speed up the exchange of cars. With two docks available, one ferry would no longer have to wait if the other dock was occupied by another ferry. The Michigan Central was said to be doing the same thing in Detroit at its dock.

The *Transit* was launched at 1530 hours on July 9, 1872, at the Jenkings Yard. At that time, her boilers and engines were in place and her tracks and cabins were yet to be added. Her total cost was approximately $85,000. Before the vessel was even completed, the Great Western had decided to use her at the Windsor–Detroit crossing. Trial runs were made on September 7, 1872, and on September 12 she was reported to be at her slip in Windsor, ready for work.

The Great Western ordered a smaller car ferry for the Sarnia–Port Huron crossing once it was decided to use the *Transit* at the Windsor–Detroit crossing. In July 1872 a contract was signed with the Port Huron Dry Dock Company to build a 142-foot-long single-screw ferry capable of handling only four freight cars. Reportedly, she also had passenger accommodations. With the keel laid in August 1872, work on the *Saginaw* progressed over the fall and winter. She was launched by March 1873 and subsequently had her engines installed. Ready for service by May, the Great Western decided to shift her to the Windsor–Detroit crossing, presumably due to a deluge of cross-river traffic there. Arriving in Detroit about June 1, the *Saginaw* ferried rail cars across the Detroit River over the summer and fall. In November she returned to Port Huron and entered service. Subsequently, she would occasionally be sent to Windsor to relieve the larger Great Western car ferries. Her small size — being the smallest car ferry to serve on the Great Lakes and only bigger than the St. Lawrence River car ferries — was a handicap from the start.

Both of the new propeller car ferries (*Transit, Saginaw*) quickly showed themselves to be failures during winter operations. In January 1873 the ice was so heavy that only the *Great Western* was able to get through it. On January 7, 1873, the railway announced its plans to order a new car ferry, a sidewheeler of greater size and capacity than the *Great Western.* The railway stated in no uncertain terms that the propeller arrangement was unsatisfactory in ice, which was an interesting comment considering the almost universal poor experiences by others with sidewheeler vessels in ice. In fact, virtually all subsequent Great Lakes car ferries would be screw-driven, often with screws at both ends of the vessels to aid in ice clearance. Contracts were signed in April 1873 with the Jenkings Yard for the hull and Gilbert's Canada Engine Works of Montreal for the engines. The *Michigan* was to be a double-tracked car ferry, capable of carrying eighteen freight cars at a time. With a gross tonnage of 1,344, she was expected to be the largest ship on North American fresh water. She was to have a wooden hull sheathed with 3/16-inch-thick iron plates for six feet below the water line. Her rudders were to be submerged two feet to avoid sheet ice.

Construction began in late spring and, by July, her wooden framing (aka "hog bracing") was reported in place. She had pilot houses fore and aft, like the *Great Western,* and twin stacks outboard of the hog bracing. Old prints and photographs indicate that she had an enclosed car deck, like previous Great Western car ferries.

The *Michigan* was scheduled for a Thursday, December 18, 1873, launching at 1330 hours. After christening with a bottle of brandy, her stays were removed but she moved not an inch. Railway officers, having guests watching from the *Union,* were highly embarrassed, but could do nothing. The *Transit* put a line on the *Michigan* but could not tow her off. For two days, the ship defied all efforts to launch her. On December 20, shortly before noon, she finally gave way to a battery of wedges and jack screws and slid into the water. Towed to the Great Western berth for her fitting-out, she was ready for service by February 1874.

With arrival of the *Michigan,* the Great Western made several changes in its trans-river services. Captain C.W. Stone, commodore of the fleet, transferred to the *Michigan* and Captain Mason (late of the Canada Southern's *Transfer*) was brought in to replace him on the *Great Western,* the latter now sporting pure-white upper works and a black hull, an "immense improvement" on her previous garb. At this time, the passenger and break-bulk ships were discontinued. Previously, only freight cars had been ferried across regularly, but the *Michigan* was expected to ferry Great Western passenger trains, in addition to making eight or nine trips per day with freight cars.

Burton Collection, Detroit Public Library.

A view of the 1880 Detroit waterfront at the Michigan Central freight yard, illustrating the car ferry slip containing the Great Western sidewheeler *Michigan*. The car ferry appears to have been emptied and is awaiting a fresh load of freight cars destined for Canada. In only three years, the Michigan Central would have its own car ferry fleet plying the waters of the upper Detroit River.

In March 1875 there were more changes in supervisory personnel of the trans-river services. Captain Sullivan, new superintendent of Great Western rail ferries, took over the helm of the ferry *Michigan.* Captain Stone, who had brought out the ferry *Michigan* and had commanded her since, took the helm of the *Great Western.* Captain Aldred stayed with the ferry *Transit.*

The *Michigan* proved to be another winter failure. Expensive ($230,000), she was an inferior ice-breaker. Her wooden hull was weak and no match for the pack ice of the Detroit River. Nonetheless, she remained in service with her three running mates as long as the Great Western was an independent railway.

In mid-December 1876 a devastating early ice blockade occurred in the Detroit River. The passenger ferries *Victoria* and *Fortune* crossed with extreme difficulty while the *Great Western* and *Transit* car ferries, each laden with passenger cars of eastbound passengers, floundered helplessly about until noon, when the *Great Western* had finally made its way back to Detroit. The *Transit* remained helpless for hours with ice piled high under the guards. Finally, the *Michigan* got up steam and opened a channel to the Michigan Central slip.

A plan was developed in early 1877 by Captain Sullivan, commodore of the Great Western fleet, to keep the river clear of ice between Windsor and Detroit. The plan was approved by managers Broughton and Muir of the Great Western engineering staff. The scheme consisted of a series of booms and scows chained together, with attachments made so as to maintain control and the five scows were secured by heavy anchors. The plan was to stretch the line across the river some distance above the Great Western slip docks as soon as ice began to form, a section two hundred feet long so adjusted that, in the event of vessels desiring to pass upstream or downstream, it could be readily swung open. By catching and holding thin ice that first flowed downstream from Lake St. Clair, it was hoped that this would form a solid band of ice that should resist the ice pressures seen later in the winter. It was decided to go forward with this plan during the next winter (1877–78). No evidence could be found that this plan was ever implemented. In any case, it would unlikely have met with success.

In spring 1882, the *Great Western* was sent to dry dock for an extensive rebuilding. She emerged in mid-September with her deck housing removed. Thereafter, she operated with an open deck, like all subsequent Detroit River car ferries. The change lowered her gross tonnage from 1,252 to 1,080.

On August 12, 1882, the *Great Western*, *Transit*, *Saginaw*, and *Michigan* passed into the hands of the Grand Trunk Railway.

Of interest, Captain Oliver Maisonville was the captain during the first railway car transfers across both the Detroit and St. Clair Rivers. He had a fifty-seven-year career sailing the Great Lakes and piloted the *Great Western* for many years. He died on April 8, 1901, at his home in Sandwich East Township at the age of eighty-eight years (*Railway and Shipping World*, #38, May 1901).

DETROIT AND MILWAUKEE BREAK-BULK LINE

The break-bulk line directly across Lake Michigan to Milwaukee, at first from Grand Haven and later on from Muskegon, was the first trans-Great Lakes railway shipping line to be established and its successor was the last to succumb. Grand Haven-Milwaukee steamer service was inaugurated by the Wards' pioneering operations in the mid-1840s followed by Clement's in the early 1850s. However, of greatest interest to readers of this book are the subsequent maritime operations of the Detroit and Milwaukee Railway from 1858 until May 1, 1869.

The cross-lake break-bulk line to be described was integral to the success of the railway and began with the building of two ocean-type sidewheel paddle steamers, the *Detroit* and *Milwaukee* (see table 5-2). Unfortunately, the financial troubles of the railway during the panic of 1857 slowed their construction. In addition, they brought on the entrance of a new owner of the railway, the Great Western Railway of Canada, which completed the line to Grand Haven in late summer 1858.

Between the time at which the Detroit and Milwaukee reached Grand Rapids (mid-summer 1858, being located forty miles upstream on the Grand River from Grand Haven) and the completion of the railway's own steamships (late summer 1859), leased steamers would have to carry passengers and freight. The propeller *Michigan* provided winter service, while the sidewheelers *Forester*, *Cleveland*, *City of Cleveland*, and *Gazelle* provided summer services.

As announced in the *Detroit Tribune* newspaper in early September 1853, the Detroit and Milwaukee would soon be building two 1,800-ton sidewheelers costing about $200,000 each. They were to be built along the lines of transatlantic steamers of the era, with all of their staterooms and public rooms in the hull, no superstructure beyond the pilothouse, and a minimum of topside spars and rigging. It was reported that the railway would finance one ship and the citizens of Milwaukee the other, unless a Detroit resident — presumably Eber Ward — undertook to build it. After all, Ward, reputed to be the wealthiest man in Michigan, had already invested $35,000 in the railway project. Since the steamer line was integral to the railway, the ships were intended to operate an average of 355 days annually.

By November 1853 more specific details of the ships became available. The maritime component of the railway was organized by Captain Lewis H. Cotton, former master of the large sidewheeler *Western World*. There is some controversy in terms of the identity of the ships' designer. The names F.N. Jones and H.O. Perry have both been mentioned in this regard. There are several indications that the designer was changed over the course of construction. The ships were to have wooden hulls with extensive iron bracing and what were called "Bishop's arches." As built, they did not have any external arches for bracing. Originally projected to be 325 feet long by forty feet wide by fourteen feet deep, with guards only in the immediate vicinity of the paddle wheels, the ships emerged as two hundred forty-seven feet long by thirty-four feet wide. The design was based on contemporary ocean sidewheelers of the American Collins Line and British Cunard Line. The *Detroit* and *Milwaukee* were the only large ships on the Great Lakes of this design, but there were several revenue cutters and other small federal vessels of this design on the Lakes.

The hull in this design was to have two saloons, one being one hundred feet forward of the engine and the other being one hundred fifty feet rearward. Luggage, mail, and light freight were to be carried on both sides of the engine.

The hull was not equipped with holds for hauling bulk products. Projected to have three masts, they emerged with two in a brigantine rig (i.e., foremast being square-rigged). Both ships had black hulls with gold trim and stacks with black tops, resulting in a strikingly handsome appearance.

From the beginning, the ships were intended to have beam engines, although not the ones with which they emerged. Captain Cotton had incorporated the projected Milwaukee–Grand Haven line separately as the Wisconsin and Michigan Transit Company, although the railway had a community of ownership with it. In mid-1852 Cotton reorganized the projected break-bulk line as the Lake Michigan Transportation Company, still with a community of interest with the railway. Before the 1857 season, Cotton bought two Canadian sidewheelers that had been running unprofitably on Lake Ontario for the Great Western Railway: the *Canada* and *America* (see earlier in this chapter).

The Great Western was more than happy to sell the ships since their operation had led to annual losses of up to $60,000. In addition, they had drawn traffic from the Grand Trunk and competing railways across New York State, stimulating retaliatory rate-cutting. Even for the modest sum of $180,000 in Detroit and Milwaukee stock (which was eventually to be worthless), the Great Western lost no time in selling them.

Cotton intended to remove their beam engines for installation in the *Detroit* and *Milwaukee,* followed by their scrapping in Hamilton. While this was the plan, it was expected that the new sidewheelers would be built by Ward at Newport, Michigan. Instead, in November 1858, Cotton placed the order for the ships with Mason and Bidwell of Buffalo and the order for new engines with Shepard Iron Works of Buffalo. No reason for this change in plans has been discovered, but the two Canadian engines may have been judged too small for the projected ships, even after they had been scaled down in size. Shepard's products were typical coal-burning beam engines but huge, with sixty-inch-diameter cylinders and a twelve-foot stroke, said to be as large as a two-storey house when completed. In the end, the engines were not removed from *Canada* and *America.* Filled with "free" Great Western coal, they were sailed to the Atlantic Coast and sold by the Detroit and Milwaukee.

Since the ships were intended to operate year around, how they would break ice was of prime importance. By this time, it had been well-established that sidewheelers were impotent in anything but the mildest ice conditions. They were poorly manoeuvrable and their wheels fractured in thick sheet ice. These ships were built with frames running to the tops of the bulwarks, and bulwarks being integrated into the hull, to produce unusually great strength. They were equipped with sharply pointed, iron-sheathed bows to slice the ice. Unfortunately, as we now know, this was the wrong configuration for ice-breaking. This was very early in the ice-breaking "game," such that all designs in that era were experimental.

By the time that Cotton reorganized his maritime service as the Lake Michigan Transit Company on August 4, 1859, the Detroit and Milwaukee Railway had come under control of the Great Western (see chapter 3). W.K. Muir, superintendent of the Great Western, became superintendent of the maritime operations as well.

Finally, on August 29 and 30, 1859, the *Detroit* and *Milwaukee* went into service, while the leased ships were returned to their owners. Early in operation, freight was far more important than passengers and, in October 1859, it was announced that the saloons would be moved from lower to upper decks to free up additional space for freight. The modifications made to the *Detroit* while in dry dock in early winter 1859–60 included installation of a superstructure (saloon and thirty new staterooms — first-class accommodation), revision of below-deck space to second-class accommodation, and changes in gangways and staircases.

The inaugural winter season with the *Detroit* and *Milwaukee* confirmed the widely held opinions about sidewheelers in ice conditions. Due to the *Detroit* being in dry dock for extensive modifications as just reviewed, it fell upon the *Milwaukee* to demonstrate her ice-breaking skills in late December to early January, as well as February to early March, in and near Chicago. These skills were virtually non-existent, proving the error in her (and her sister's) configuration. Never again would they be entered into winter service by the railway.

Overall, these ships were at least moderately successful, with large passenger capacities, strong hulls, and dependable machinery. However, they were time-consuming and expensive to load (with freight) and were incapable of winter operations, a prime necessity in a year around maritime-railway joint operation. Designed with sharp bows heavily metal-plated, they were intended to fracture ice so that the ship could follow through the fragments. Their impracticality in such conditions was manifest by January 1860. Thus, the railway was forced to lay up these expensive vessels each fall and lease winter replacements for the cross-lake winter services.

In the winter of 1859–60, the propellers *Wisconsin* and *Cuyahoga* were chartered. The *Cuyahoga* lost about six weeks in January and early February with boiler troubles. In the spring, the *Detroit* and *Milwaukee* returned. As previously discussed, over the winter the *Detroit* had received a new upper cabin that was inconsistent with the original plan of having both passenger and freight compartments entirely within the hull.

Interruptions in cross-lake service in February 1860 caused the railway to reduce the number of daily trains to Grand Haven to one, precipitating placement of the railway into receivership. Eventually, operations continued as planned with morning and evening departures from Milwaukee, each ship providing one daily round trip. When traffic fell, service was cut to a single trip in each direction daily.

The line's basic trip was the evening departure from Milwaukee. When only one of the ships was being used, it made a day return from Grand Haven. At other times — as early as the 1865 season — each of the ships made a single overnight crossing daily. Since a round trip with an overnight sailing from Wisconsin was the reverse of the daily round trips offered by most of the fruit-hauling ship lines, this line stood apart from other cross-lake lines. The ships connected closely with the schedules of the day and night passenger trains at Grand Haven.

Toward the end of the usual navigation season, when passenger loads were light, management ignored its schedule and ran the ships as needed to handle accumulated freight. In 1860 the two ships ran on schedule until early December and then were ordered to handle a deluge of freight before winter truly set in. Over the winter of

1860–61, the propeller *Wabash Valley* was chartered, an attractive ship due to the grain hold below her cargo deck. The propeller *Quincy* was also chartered that winter.

The Detroit and Milwaukee had a glut of traffic in the spring of 1861 that could not be relieved until the opening of inter-lake traffic through the Straits (of Mackinac). *Quincy* was kept on well into April, mainly to transport eastbound shipments of pork, butter, and flour. The line also chartered the *Ottawa*, *Robert H. Foss*, and the twin propeller *Edith* in April. Winter storms had built up the sandbar off Grand Haven, restricting ships entering the harbour mouth to a draft of eight and a half feet or less. When the *Detroit* came out in mid-April, she could only carry passengers and had to unload them on a harbour tug that acted as a lighter because she could not clear the sandbar. For the 1861 season, the *Milwaukee* had been equipped with above-deck cabin accommodations similar to those installed previously on the *Detroit*. The bar trapped the *Milwaukee* in the harbour until approximately May 20. It must have been noticed by now by the line's management that propellers of standard type were far more suited to the local conditions than were the ocean-type sidewheelers.

The railway made the decision that winter operations required three propeller ships. For the winter of 1861–62, the railway again chartered the *Quincy* and added the inter-lake propellers *Niagara* and *Ogdensburg*. Since inter-lake lines could not operate when the Straits were blocked with ice, they were a ready source of ships for off-season use. The *Niagara* made it through the winter and spring, but in May was found to have been sold to Canadian owners in the previous year and therefore to be illegal in U.S. domestic trade. The two sidewheelers emerged on May 24–25, 1862, and, fortunately, no problems were reported during their 1862 operating season. The *Detroit* operated until December 9, 1862, when she was laid up in Grand Haven. It had been a banner year for freight traffic and the backlog kept the *Milwaukee* operating until at least December 18, 1862. The railway built additional storage facilities in Grand Haven and for the winter chartered four propellers: *Racine*, *Pittsburgh*, *Susquehanna*, and *Potomac*.

The *Detroit* came out for the 1863 season on March 18, followed by the *Milwaukee* on March 23. Of note, the 1863 season was significant for an exceptionally high level of shipping of live sheep, apparently for slaughter in Milwaukee. In early August both ships had carried over 3,000 sheep during the preceding four weeks, 1,180 by the *Milwaukee* on August 7 alone.

For winter 1864–65, the railway drew upon the Grand Trunk's Chicago and Sarnia Propeller Line for its winter replacement ships. These included the *S.D. Caldwell* and *Gov. Cashman*. The *Caldwell* was one of the few twin-propeller vessels of the era. She was one of the fastest propellers on the Great Lakes and her twin propellers had the added benefit of clearing sand that had built up in channels during storms. She was also chartered the next winter (1865–66).

The arrangements for the winter of 1866–67 were hastened by an accident involving the *Milwaukee*, which foreshadowed the type of accident that would end her career. On November 7, 1866 ("the gales of November"), the *Milwaukee* was inbound to Grand Haven when she hit a sandbar, spun around, and grounded in four feet of water. The only significant damage was a bent gallows

Milwaukee Public Library, Milwaukee, Wisconsin.

This is an advertising piece that might have hung on the walls of Detroit and Milwaukee and Great Western stations and travel agencies, showing an immaculate version of the ships *Detroit* and *Milwaukee*, immense in comparison with the tiny sailing vessel in the foreground. Notice the railway routes radiating from one port-of-call (Milwaukee) and the smaller number radiating out from the other port-of-call (Grand Haven), although the latter includes the all-important Detroit and Milwaukee/Great Western Railways.

frame on the beam engine. After being pumped out, the *Detroit* (after discharging her passengers and freight) pulled her free. The railway at first chartered the *G.J. Truesdell* to replace her then chartered the *Gov. Cashman* and *S.D. Caldwell* once again as winter boats.

It appears that the railway had finally given up on the sidewheelers by this time. It had been unable to interest the federal government in them for use in the Civil War. The railway may have been intending to showcase them when it sent first the *Detroit*, and second the *Milwaukee*, to Detroit for dry docking at the end of the 1866 season. This trip produced a disaster in which the *Milwaukee*, barely embarked on her return trip, collided with the downbound Lake Superior propeller *Lac La Belle*, sinking her after nearly cutting her in two. This accident demonstrated the menace of sharp metal-enclosed bows in a collision. The *Milwaukee* was returned to the Detroit shipyard and spent the winter there.

The *Milwaukee* emerged for the 1867 season, but her working days on the break-bulk line were numbered. She served until October 9, 1868, when, approaching Grand Haven in a typical autumnal storm at the end of an overnight eastbound crossing, she hit the ever-present sandbar, drifted off, grounded, and was pummelled to pieces by wave action that afternoon. The railway chartered the *City of Fremont* as a winter replacement for the *Milwaukee*. Finally, with the last straw being broken, the railway gave up on its maritime operations and contracted with Nathan Engelmann, who was the established operator of the Milwaukee-Ludington-Manistee line together with a long line connecting the major east coast Lake Michigan ports from St. Joseph to the ports on Grand Traverse Bay. Engelmann would provide the break-bulk shipping services needed by the railway for five years.

The *Detroit* did not last much longer, running only until November 27, 1869. Withdrawal of the Detroit and Milwaukee from maritime services coincided with changes in the port of Grand Haven itself. In 1858 the Detroit and Milwaukee Railway had built a wharf for the ocean sidewheelers on the north bank of the Grand River, opposite Grand Haven. This terminal required a ferry connection with the town. This north shore approach was also chronically troubled with wind-driven sand and snow. Early in 1869 the railway worked out an agreement with the town council and the Michigan Lake Shore Railroad (a predecessor of the Pere Marquette Railroad) for the two roads to enter town via a joint bridge over the Grand River. The new Detroit and Milwaukee Railway terminal was built at the foot of Washington Street in central Grand Haven. The new location was in use by late 1869 or early 1870, and the north shore line was abandoned.

In its early years, the railway hauled a substantial volume of wheat, especially during the winter after the normal shipping season was closed. Break-bulk service with grain products was labour-intensive and time-consuming, since the grain had to be bagged or moved by shovel and wheelbarrow. In Milwaukee this problem had been at least partially solved by the creation of steam-powered grain elevators. Engelmann felt that Grand Haven needed an elevator as well, so he formed the Grand Haven Elevator Company and built a 35,000-bushel elevator on the railway's new dock in 1871. A spectacular fire in July 1875, followed by the burning of the rebuilt elevator in 1886, combined with the ascendency of Minneapolis as the king of the flour industry, eventually left grain traffic on the Detroit and Milwaukee in tatters.

Engelmann's luck in shipping proved no better than it had been with grain elevators. On October 1, 1872, one ship foundered, leaving six dead. With the ship being insured for only 50 percent of its value, the railway had to take $9,000 in Engelmann notes and endorse another $10,000 note so that he could buy a replacement ship. The railway also took out insurance policies on his three operating boats.

On September 15, 1873, another Engelmann ship foundered, claiming twenty-one lives. By this time, railway executives were frustrated by Engelmann's bad luck and the expense and service disruptions that his misfortunes brought. They shopped around for a replacement shipping line, but none was interested or able to meet their requirements. Reluctantly, the relationship with Engelmann was continued, only to have another ship founder on January 3, 1874, to their horror. With these losses it would now be impossible to secure insurance coverage. Over the next year things seemed to settle down, when suddenly, on April 9, 1875, Engelmann, for reasons only known to himself, sold one of his ships and the railway contract to the Northwest Transportation Company. The latter line, owned by R.J. Hackett and E.M. Peck of Cleveland, was well-respected and had much better luck than had Engelmann. In fact, the business relationship continued even after bankruptcy in 1878 forced the railway to reorganize as the Detroit, Grand Haven and Milwaukee Railway, still under Great Western control. And so it continued until 1882, when the Great Western Railway was taken over by the Grand Trunk Railway.

The Detroit and Milwaukee Railway did not have the best of luck with their small roster of cross-lake ships. Unfortunately, the same could be said of their luck with the harbour at Grand Haven and its facilities.

In 1857 Robert Higham, the railway's engineer, travelled to Grand Haven to evaluate the harbour. After renting a steam tug and making depth soundings, he pronounced that even the shallowest spot at the mouth of the Grand River would allow a draft of eleven and a half feet. Failing to recognize the dramatic fluctuations in the lake level and that storms build sandbars, he declared his delight with the findings.

With time, the harbour at Grand Haven did not reflect Higham's optimistic appraisal. Sandbars were building at the harbour mouth and ships drawing more than seven feet of water were endangered. In June 1859 the railway contracted with Samuel C. Ridley to build a two-thousand-foot breakwater on the south side of the Grand River at a cost of $200,000! The railway had to bear this expense because President Franklin Pierce had vetoed the funding bill for Great Lakes harbour improvements for reasons that are too complicated to detail herein.

Ridley drove three rows of piles into the lake bed, stacked brush between the rows, and capped the pier with stone. The pier was fifteen feet wide at the shoreline and twenty-four feet wide at the end, where a forty-foot lighthouse was erected. When the pier was nearly completed, a November storm washed away one hundred fifty feet of piling and wrecked the pile-driver.

Despite construction of a pier, problems with sandbars continued. During the severe winter of 1860–61, an ice buildup closed the harbour for most of February. When the heavy snowfall melted, the Grand River overflowed, undercutting a dune. Sand from the collapsing dune created a bar, closing the harbour and halting traffic for another three months. The Detroit and Milwaukee Railway hired a dredge to clear the channel and lengthened the breakwater. Unfortunately, a year later, the line's engineer had to report that instead of correcting the problem, the extension, built at a cost of $50,000, was actually helping to build sandbars and another breakwater would be needed on the north side of the river.

Following these improvements, stockholders must have thought that the problems at Grand Haven were behind them, but such was not the case. In May 1866 sparks from the *Detroit* fell on the pier, starting a fire that burned everything, including the lighthouse, down to the waterline. Adding insult to injury, no sooner had repairs been completed than the U.S. Corps of Engineers reported that the railway's pier did not conform to plans that had been developed by the government and were an engineer's nightmare. The south pier was in the wrong place, built at the wrong angle, and was too long. The pier was not only being undermined, but it was also contributing to formation of sandbars by diverting the normal flow of the river.

Moreover, most of the sand clogging the channel was coming from the railway's own dock. The dock was rebuilt in 1866 on a bend in the river. A huge, moving dune above the depot (Dewey Hill) had encroached upon the dock, so it was repositioned on piles, which were again filled in with brush. Too much space was left between the pilings, so sand escaped and made its way into the mouth of the Grand River. Despite additional construction and improvements throughout the nineteenth century, the Grand Haven breakwater in 1900 still retained its odd angle and sandbars still continued to plague navigation. It is no wonder that the Grand Trunk moved the Michigan port-of-call to Muskegon, but why successor Grand Trunk Western waited until 1933 to do so is unknown.

One interesting sidelight to close out this chapter: The steamer *Detroit* initiated railway post office (R.P.O.) services in a railway-owned ship, beginning in 1860. Trains would pick up mail while steaming west through Michigan, load it aboard the *Detroit* at Grand Haven, and the mail would be sorted during the six-hour lake crossing. It should be noted that the term "Travelling Post Office" or T.P.O., rather than R.P.O., would soon become the terminology used to signify postal cancellations in marine vessels.

TABLE 5-1. BREAK-BULK SHIPS AND RAILWAY CAR FERRIES USED BY THE GREAT WESTERN RAILWAY ON THE DETROIT AND ST. CLAIR RIVERS AND LAKE ONTARIO

Break-Bulk Ships	
Ottawa	
Registration:	USA (18922)
Dimensions:	120 feet long x 30.3 feet wide x 9.7 feet deep
Hull Material:	Wood
Propulsion:	Steam sidewheeler
Builder:	Joseph Jenkings, Detroit (1853)
Engines:	ND
Boilers:	ND
Gross Tonnage:	316.6
Disposition:	The ship was converted to a steam propeller before June 7, 1866 (dimensions: 122 feet long x 30.2 feet wide x 9.3 feet deep, 220.1 tons). In 1868 her tonnage was noted to be 578 (District of Milwaukee). Sometime between 1868 and 1870 she was reduced to a barge of 258 tons. Her registration was surrendered on December 31, 1870 (endorsed as "out of commission").
Incidents:	Collision of steamers *Tibbitts* and *Ottawa* near Brockport in the St. Lawrence River on July 24, 1855. *Ottawa* sank. About the close of season in 1872 a tow of barges, including the *Ottawa*, was ensnared in the ice near Middle Bass Island in Lake Erie. The *Ottawa* sank, becoming a total loss, soon after her entombment in ice.
Owners	**Dates**
G.B. Russel	1853–66
A.H. Adams	1866–73

Alpena Public Library, Alpena, Michigan.

Sidewheeler *Ottawa*.

Transit	
Registration:	Canada (ND)
Dimensions:	ND
Hull Material:	Wood
Propulsion:	Steam propeller
Builder:	Jenkings, Windsor (1854)
Engines:	ND
Boilers:	ND
Gross Tonnage:	500
Disposition:	In 1880 the *Transit* underwent extensive repairs. Initially, the only repairs intended were to her bulwarks but when it was found that escaping steam had rotted her arches, which up to that time had been encased, it proved necessary to replace them entirely. These repairs occurred at Detroit Dry Dock at a cost of $3,000 and were completed the week of July 2.

Windsor	
Registration:	U.S. (62523)
Dimensions:	104 feet long x 30 feet wide x 10.1 feet deep (remeasured in 1865: 111.8 feet x 30 feet x 9.9 feet)
Hull Material:	Wood
Propulsion:	Steam sidewheeler
Builder:	J.S. Jenkings, Detroit (1856)
Engines:	ND
Boilers:	ND
Gross Tonnage:	223.1 (old style)
Disposition:	Laid telegraph cable across Detroit River via Belle Isle in 1857. Rebuilt in 1864 and 1868. Converted into an unpowered barge by J. Dean Jr. in Detroit in 1871. Rigged as a two-masted schooner on August 25, 1876. Rebuilt in 1892. Wrecked on Lake Michigan on September 30, 1893, near Cona Island (Green Bay, Wisconsin).
Incidents:	In July 1858 collided with tug *Uncle Ben* in Detroit River. On September 17, 1859, collided with steamer *John Martin* opposite Great Western wharf. On April 26, 1866, cargo exploded and ship burned followed by docks and wharves (twenty-eight lives lost, ship's machinery was transferred to 1870s steamer *Hope*). Sunk in Benton Harbor, Michigan, in November 1870. Collided with schooner *Lookout* at Manitowoc, Wisconsin, in May 1883.
Owners	**Dates**
George B. Russell	1856–58
Detroit and Milwaukee Railroad/ Railway	1858–63

Lake Michigan Transit Co.	1863–71
J. Dean et al	1871–73
L.W. Nuttal et al	1873–75
Gifford and Co.	1875–76
Thomas S. Ruddock et al	1876–81
Dewitt C. Palmer et al	1881–_8?
Charles H. Ruddock et al	188? –93

Alpena Public Library, Alpena, Michigan.

Sidewheeler *Windsor*.

Globe	
Registration:	U.S. (39339)
Dimensions:	143.9 feet long x 24 feet wide x 9.7 feet deep
Hull Material:	Wood
Propulsion:	Steam sidewheeler
Builder:	S.H. Hubbell, Maumee City, Ohio (1846)
Engines:	Cuyahoga Steam Furnace, Cleveland was source. No other details are available.
Boilers:	ND
Gross Tonnage:	313
Disposition:	When built, the ship had twenty-six state rooms with double berths, on the upper deck. There was also a gentlemen's cabin more than one hundred feet long and two steerage cabins, having in total thirty double berths. The *Globe* was converted, during the process of an extensive overhaul, into a propeller with two new engines, at the Buffalo Works. These two engines were attached to one shaft with a 10.5 foot wheel. The date for this work is controversial, with support for both 1856 and 1860. Converted, yet again, this time into an unpowered barge in 1868 (208.3 tons gross, 142 feet long x 24 feet wide x 8 feet deep). Registration for the vessel was surrendered at Port Huron on July 17, 1878.

Incidents:	On September 12, 1846, the *Globe* crashed into the dock of J.L. Hurd & Co., Detroit, causing considerable damage to the dock and the stern of the vessel. On September 19, 1846, the ship was struck by lightning off Ashtabula, Ohio. Although it passed through the pilot house, engine room, and firemen's room, no damage was done to the ship or anyone on board. On May 23, 1856, the *Globe* broke some part of her machinery about fifteen miles from Erie, Pennsylvania, and required a tow into Erie for repairs (tow was provided by the *Ohio*). Sunk in the last week of October 1856 while trying to make Milwaukee Harbor in one of the most violent gales ever experienced on Lake Michigan. The ship was subsequently raised but after preliminary repairs, it still leaked badly. Decision was made to leave it in Milwaukee until the opening of navigation in 1857, at which point it would proceed to another port for repairs. During the second week of August 1863, fire overtook the *Globe* near the Charity Islands in Saginaw Bay and it burned to the water line. It subsequently sank in four fathoms (twenty-four feet) of water. During this season, the ship had been extensively repaired as well as had received a new boiler. In June 1867 Spalding and coworkers were able to salvage the vessel and its almost new boiler. The *Globe* was converted the next year into an unpowered barge. On August 21, 1873, the barge *Globe* arrived in Buffalo from Kelley's Island. A portion of the *Globe*'s bulwarks, rail, and stanchion were gone on the port side. The litany of bad luck for the *Globe* finally ended on October 21, 1873, when it was dashed to pieces in the shallow waters off Point Pelee, along with its tow vessel and two other barges. It was a total loss.
Owners	**Dates**
Sheldon McKnight	1853–59
G.B. Russel	1859–61
John P. Ward	1861–62
John G. Williams	1862–63
Ballentine, Crawford & Co.	1867–73

Bowling Green State University, Bowling Green, Ohio.

Sidewheeler *Globe*.

Union	
Registration:	Canada (ND)
Dimensions:	163 feet long x 33 feet wide x 10.8 feet deep
Hull Material:	Wood (iron-sheathed)
Propulsion:	Steam sidewheeler
Builder:	J. & S. Jenkings, Windsor (1857)
Engine:	Inclined compound, 2 cylinders
Boilers:	ND
Gross Tonnage:	1,190/999 (old style)
Disposition:	Owned by Great Western Railway for its entire existence. For most of its working life it worked the cross-border traffic between Windsor and Detroit. In 1874 it was transferred to work the Sarnia–Port Huron cross-border traffic. It was reported lost, with its machinery being removed, on December 9, 1874. It was laid up for 1875 and on June 16, 1876, the hull was burned in Port Huron. In April 1877 the burned hull was transferred to the lower Port Huron dry dock where it was recaulked. No further details are available.

Alpena Public Library, Alpena, Michigan.

Sidewheeler *Union*.

America	
Registration:	Canada (ND) then U.S. (ND)
Dimensions:	285.5 feet long x 38.3 feet wide x 14 feet deep
Hull Material:	Wood
Propulsion:	Steam sidewheeler

Builder:	Niagara Dock Co. (Edwards), Niagara, Ontario (1854)
Engines:	70-inch cylinder x 12-foot stroke, 1,000 horsepower, built by West Point Foundry Company, New York
Boilers:	2
Gross Tonnage:	1,683
Disposition:	Under the ownership of Peter Hargous, the ship was rebuilt in Sneeden's Shipyard in New York City in 1858 (guards were narrowed three feet, main deck was built up, and additional framing was added to the hull). The ship was admitted to U.S. registry by a special Act of Congress, January 19, 1859. Under the ownership of Marshall Roberts, the ship was under frequent charter to the U.S. Army Quartermaster-General between March 1861 and September 1862. Upon purchase by the People's Line in 1862, the ship was rebuilt completely. The ship departed for the Pacific Ocean via Cape Horn in November 1863. The end came on March 11, 1869, at a refuelling stop at San Juan, Nicaragua, when she burned to the waterline while bound from Panama to San Francisco. The crew was rescued by the French frigate *Du Chayla.* With so many owners, it is surprising that the ship only changed names twice: to *Coat Zacoalas* from 1859–62 and back to *America* in 1862 with the ownership change.
Owners	**Dates**
Great Western Railway	1854–57
Detroit and Milwaukee Railroad/ Railway	1857–58
Peter Hargous	1858–60
Marshall O. Roberts	1860–62
People's Line	1862–64
Central American Transit Co.	1864–66
North American Steamship Co.	1866–68
Pacific Mail Steamship Co.	1868–69

Canada	
Registration:	Canada (ND) then U.S. (ND)
Dimensions:	279 feet long x 36 feet wide x 13.5 feet deep
Hull Material:	Wood
Propulsion:	Steam sidewheeler
Builder:	Niagara Dock Co. (Edwards), Niagara (1854)
Engines:	70-inch cylinder x 12-foot stroke, 1,000 horsepower, built by West Point Foundry Company, New York

Boilers:	2
Gross Tonnage:	453 (old style)
Disposition:	After N.P. Stewart assumed ownership in 1858, ship was transferred to Sneeden's yard in New York City for fitting for high seas use. It was subsequently used on the Atlantic Ocean, chartered by the U.S. War Department to transport artillery and munitions. On January 27, 1859, it was renamed *Mississippi* (2,026 tons). Under P. Hargous' ownership, the ship operated between New Orleans and Mexican ports. After another ownership transfer, it was used in the Rio Plata trade. Bound from Montevideo, Uruguay to China, the ship foundered in a gale on August 30, 1862, in the Atlantic Ocean. Crew and passengers were rescued.
Owners	**Dates**
Great Western Railway	1854–57
Detroit and Milwaukee Railroad/ Railway	1857–58
N.P. Stewart	1858–59
Peter Hargous	1859–62
N.P. Stewart and G. Savary	1862

Alpena Public Library, Alpena, Michigan.

Sidewheeler *Canada*.

Europa	
Registration:	Canada (ND)
Dimensions:	233.6 feet long x 27.5 feet wide x 13 feet deep
Hull Material:	Wood

Propulsion:	Steam sidewheeler
Builder:	E. Harrison and Company, Hamilton (1854)
Engine:	Vertical beam (walking beam)
Boilers:	ND
Gross Tonnage:	341 (old style)
Disposition:	Could carry 200 cabin passengers. Chartered to the Great Western Railway for the 1855 shipping season. Sailed for the Independent Express Line during the 1856 season. Chartered to the Upper Canada Royal Mail Steamers during the late 1857 season. Chartered to the American Line Steamers during the 1858 season ("a poor one"). Scrapped in 1867.
Incidents:	Ship grounded on Snake Island Shoal (eastern end of Lake Ontario) on June 25, 1855, without damage. A fender broke at Gananoque, killing a man, on October 16, 1855. Ship collided with the schooner *T.Y. Avery* at Oswego, NY, on October 1, 1856. Sank at the wharf in Toronto on April 1, 1858, presumably due to holes chewed through the hull by rats. This implied carelessness on the part of the watchmen supervising the ship in winter quarters.
Owners	**Dates**
M.W. Browne et al	1854–56
J. Coleman	1856–57
Thomas Patton	1857–57
R. Bull	1857–61
Sincennes, MacNaughton and Company	1861–63
The Richelieu Company	1863–67

Car Ferries	
Great Western	
Registration:	Canada (80576)
Dimensions:	220 feet long x 40.2 feet wide x 13 feet deep
Hull Material:	Iron
Propulsion:	Steam sidewheeler
Builder:	Henry Jenkings, Windsor (1866). H. Jenkings was sent by the Great Western over to Glasgow to supervise construction of the vessel. Assembled there, it was subsequently disassembled for shipping to Canada (in 10,878 pieces!).
Engines:	2 single cylinder, horizontal, 42-inch piston diameter x 96-inch stroke, 1,360 horsepower, built by Gartshore, Dundas, Ontario

Boilers:	4 Scotch from Great Western Hamilton shops (reboilered with 4 Scotch, 9.5 feet x 14 feet, 65 pounds/square inch, built by Grand Trunk, Montreal , 1888)
Capacity:	2 tracks, 12 cars
Gross Tonnage:	1,252 (reduced to 1,080 in 1882 rebuilding)
Disposition:	In 1882 her tonnage was reduced (to 1,080 tons gross, 662 tons net), probably by removal of most of her superstructure. In 1923 she was reduced to an unpowered sand barge (220 feet long x 40.2 feet wide x 10 feet deep, 973 tons gross and net).
Owners	**Dates**
Great Western Railway	1866–82
Grand Trunk Railway	1882–1923
Essex Transit Co.	1923–32
Wallaceburg Sand & Gravel	1932–39
Pine Ridge Navigation Co.	1939–41
United Towing & Salvage	1941–66

Windsor Community Museum.

View of the car ferry *Great Western* at the dock, illustrating the fully enclosed nature of early trans-river car ferries. After personnel became aware of the wind tunnel phenomena with these enclosures during high winds, these enclosures were removed, leaving the open ferries characteristic of the Grand Trunk and Canadian National eras.

Transit	
Registration:	Canada (ND)
Dimensions:	168 feet long x 39.1 feet wide x 14.6 feet deep
Hull Material:	Wood
Propulsion:	Steam propeller
Builder:	Henry Jenkings, Windsor (1872)

Engines:	Four cylinders, details unknown
Boilers:	ND
Capacity:	2 tracks, 10 cars
Gross Tonnage:	1,057
Disposition:	Laid up, 1884; burned at Windsor on March 4, 1889.

Bowling Green State University, Bowling Green, Ohio.

Propeller Car Ferry *Transit*.

Saginaw	
Registration:	Canada (69524)
Dimensions:	142 feet long x 25.5 feet wide x 10.4 feet deep
Hull Material:	Wood
Propulsion:	Steam propeller
Builder:	Port Huron Dry Dock Co., Port Huron (1873)
Engines:	Double, high-pressure, non-condensing, 20-inch x 20-inch piston diameters x 30-inch stroke, 90 revolutions/minute, 520 horsepower, built by E.E. Gilbert & Sons, Montreal
Boilers:	2 fire box, 6.5 feet x 15 feet, built by Buhl Iron Works, Detroit, 1886, 85 pounds/square inch. Earlier boilers unknown.
Capacity:	1 track (?), 4 cars
Gross Tonnage:	365 (net 242)
Disposition:	Steamer *Saginaw* underwent a thorough overhaul in mid-1879 (redecked throughout and new and larger boilers installed). Barge *Sarnia* and steamer *Amerique* took her place during her overhaul. *Saginaw* was dry docked for repairs and repainting before going into service for the Grand Trunk (April 1883). Laid up 1884. Was offered for sale in Detroit (April 1885). Rebuilt as wrecking steamer for Isaac Watt and Great Lakes Towing Co. Probably used as a rafting tug on Georgian Bay by E.A. Booth. Broken up in 1940.

Owners	Dates
Great Western and Grand Trunk Rwys	1873–88/90
Isaac Watt Wrecking Co.	1888/90–1901
Great Lakes Towing Co.	1902–08
E.A. Booth	1909–38

Alpena Public Library, Alpena, Michigan.

Propeller Car Ferry *Saginaw*, shown here in her later form as a rather odd-looking tug.

Michigan	
Registration:	Canada (ND) then U.S. (91847)
Dimensions:	265 feet long x 38.4 feet wide x 14.2 feet deep
Hull Material:	Wood
Propulsion:	Steam sidewheeler
Builder:	Jenkings Bros., Windsor (1873)
Engine:	Double, horizontal, low pressure 50-inch x 50-inch piston diameters x 108-inch stroke, 1,360 horsepower, built by E.E. Gilbert & Sons, Montreal, 1872
Boilers:	ND
Capacity:	2 tracks, 18 cars
Gross Tonnage:	1,344
Disposition:	Engines and part of superstructure were placed in the *Lansdowne* (Grand Trunk car ferry). Hull sold to F.W. Gilchrist for use as a barge (U.S. Reg. 91847). First enrollment under U.S. registration occurred in 1886 as a barge (271.2 feet long x 41.7 feet wide x 15.5 feet deep, 1,291 tons gross, 1,228 tons net). Foundered off Point Sable, Lake Superior, September 2, 1893, while taking iron ore from Marquette, Michigan, to Ashtabula. Crew was rescued by the propeller steamer *City of Naples*.

Bowling Green State University, Bowling Green, Ohio.

Sidewheeler Car Ferry *Michigan*.

TABLE 5-2. BREAK-BULK SHIPS OWNED BY THE DETROIT AND MILWAUKEE RAILROAD/RAILWAY AND USED ON THE GRAND HAVEN-MILWAUKEE ROUTE ACROSS LAKE MICHIGAN

Detroit and *Milwaukee*	
Registration:	U.S. (16619 — *Milwaukee*) (6198 — *Detroit*)
Dimensions:	247 feet long x 34 feet wide x 17.4 feet deep
Hull Material:	Wood
Propulsion:	Steam sidewheeler
Builder:	Mason and Bidwell, Buffalo (1859)
Engine:	Beam condensing, 60-inch piston diameter x 144-inch stroke, 1,050 horsepower, built by Sheperd Iron Works, Buffalo (1859)
Boilers:	2, 10 feet x 23.5 feet, built by Shepherd Iron Works, Buffalo (1859)
Gross Tonnage:	1,100
Disposition:	These vessels were built as oceangoing vessels to provide an extra measure of safety for passengers. Construction was under the superintendence of Julius Movius, Esq. of the Great Western and Detroit and Milwaukee. The gentlemen's cabin and dining room on the lower deck seated 100 in comfort. There were 14 state rooms in the ladies cabin, all furnished with a double bed and berth. Besides officer's rooms on the upper deck, there were ten commodious state rooms. On the *Detroit*, thirty additional state rooms were added to her upper decks by Shearer and Brothers at the insistence of Detroit and Milwaukee personnel during the winter of 1859–60. *Milwaukee* was lost on October 9, 1868 while trying to enter Grand Haven harbour. Stuck on a sand bar, she was dashed to pieces. The *Detroit* was reduced to a schooner barge by Campbell, Owens and Company (April 1870) then to a steam barge (May 1871), using the engine from *Hunter*. On September 29, 1872, the *Detroit* was lost off Harrisville, Michigan, in Lake Huron.
Incidents (*Milwaukee*):	In early June of 1862, the *Milwaukee* struck the north pier coming into Grand Haven harbour, tearing away two of the guard knees of her larboard wheelhouse. She required a brief lay-up for repairs. On November 23, 1866, the *Milwaukee* collided with the propeller *Lac La Belle* in the St. Clair River, five miles above the flats. *Lac La Belle* sunk within a matter of minutes with two lives lost. Repairs to the *Milwaukee* cost $3,000. Captain J.F. Trowell of the *Milwaukee* was found to be at fault for the collision. On October 9, 1868, while trying to enter Grand Haven harbour during a gale, *Milwaukee* struck a sandbar, becoming unmanageable, and was forced toward the beach where she grounded. She split first amidships, then broke up into pieces.
Owners	**Dates**
Detroit and Milwaukee Railroad/ Railway	1859–68

Incidents (*Detroit*):	On September 29, 1872, the steam barge *Detroit* sprang a leak off Harrisville (Lake Huron) during a gale, with the schooner *Hunter* in tow. The fires in the boilers were extinguished and both vessels drifted offshore, becoming total losses. Both had been bound from Saginaw, Michigan, to Chicago with lumber. Both hulls were released by the tugs *Rescue* and *Kate Moffet* during the week of October 14, 1872, but chains parted on the *Detroit*. Enrollment was surrendered at Detroit on March 8, 1873. However, her original beam engine removed in 1869–70 eventually served in three vessels (*Planet*, *Northwest*, and *Greyhound* [2]) until 1936!
Owners	**Dates**
Detroit and Milwaukee Railroad/ Railway	1859–69
Campbell, Owens and Company	1870–72

Historical Collections of the Great Lakes
Bowling Green State University

Sidewheeler *Milwaukee*.

Alpena Public Library, Alpena, Michigan.

Sidewheeler *Detroit*.

CHAPTER 6

ACCIDENTS!

The Great Western Railway, despite its short lifespan of thirty years as an independent railway (1853–82), had the dubious distinction of being associated with three of Canada's worst railway disasters: at Baptiste Creek in 1854, at the Desjardins Canal near Dundas in 1857, and at Komoka in 1874. Numerous less newsworthy accidents leading to loss of life and limb and property damage occurred as well. In fact, the accident rate on the Great Western led to a Parliamentary inquiry in 1857.

As related elsewhere, construction on the main line of the Great Western did not begin until 1852 but, once started, it proceeded at breakneck speed until the final segment (London-Windsor) was completed and opened on January 27, 1854.

After several unmet promises, Charles John Brydges promised that the Great Western Railway would be open for business by the end of 1854. The circumstances surrounding this decision illustrate the authoritarian arrogance and abysmal disregard for human safety on the part of Brydges.

Chief engineer of the Great Western, John T. Clark, wrote a stunning letter to Managing Director Brydges dated October 17, 1854. After noting his understanding that Brydges intended to "run a train of passenger cars over the Eastern Division … on the first of November next," Clark continued:

> And now for the purpose of relieving myself from all responsibility in a transaction I deem so imprudent and unwise, I desire to inform you in my official capacity, that I do not consider the grading or the superstructure, so far as it is laid down, in a safe condition to be used for public purposes.

This was the one man who, above all, was charged with assessing the condition of the railway, stating in no uncertain terms that the railway was unsafe. Brydges' response was no less stunning. He upbraided the engineer for prejudging the results of the official inspection that, Brydges argued, could only be conducted after the contractor had declared the work complete. Since Brydges had announced his intention to open the railway on a specific date, he also prejudged the results of the official inspection. Then he tried to argue that his actions were driven by a balanced and carefully-thought process.

> It appears to me that a very grave responsibility rests upon any Board of Directors in neglecting to use a line of railway that is ready for use.... The public have a right to demand, that the earliest possible opportunity be afforded them of availing of a means of communication so essential as the Great Western Railway to the prosperity of the country at large.

What hogwash! This individual was not going to brook delay, not by reasonable argument and certainly not by that of an underling. He concluded his response to Clark as follows:

> I extremely regret that you should have so hastily pronounced an opinion upon a question which is not yet ripe for discussion, and the more so, that the course you have taken will appear to place your views and my own at variance.

What was Clark to do? Although the "train of passenger cars" had still not run by the third week of November, he felt that he had no choice but to go over Brydges's head and approach the board directly, complaining about the assumption of the chief engineer's responsibilities by the managing director and offering his resignation "in case of further palpable interference." Fortunately for him, just two weeks later Clark obtained a superior position as state engineer and surveyor for New York State, at which time he tendered his resignation. He received a vote of confidence from the board when it was communicated to him that the board regretted "that circumstances have compelled him [*sic*] to relinquish so soon the active duties of an office which you had filled with so much credit."

Why was the chief engineer so concerned about the condition of the railway in late 1853? Why would there be such a series of horrendous accidents on the railway over the next year and beyond? To obtain as low a gradient as possible to maximize the efficiency and minimize the fuel costs of locomotive operation, higher outcroppings of land are excavated as "cuttings" and lowlands are bridged or filled in as embankments (the latter often being built using the waste of the former). The sides of cuttings must be sloped, but not too steep and too close to the roadbed. Latter conditions may lead to obstruction due to falling materials, leading to derailments. The tops of embankments must be sufficiently wide that they will not be undermined, and the sides must be sloped so as to avoid collapse. Embankments must also have culverts at the bases to allow free movement of water, which otherwise might accumulate and eventually wash out the embankment from extreme built-up pressure.

North American roadbeds are almost universally composed of metal rails spiked to wooden crossties embedded in stone ballast. The stone ballast plays a vital role in maximizing the longevity of the structures that it supports and the locomotives and rolling stock that ride above it. The give provided by ballast allows minor deflection of the rails under load, which prevents the fracturing that would occur otherwise under the pounding of a heavy train. This give allows enough spring to occur so as to absorb some of this impact without so much deflection that the rails break. Ballast also facilitates drainage, especially important in cold climates such as Canada where a roadbed frozen solid into one slab would have virtually no give. Drainage also prolongs the lifespan of wooden ties, especially those not preserved with creosote. Ties were non-preserved in the pioneer era of the railways. Firmly packed ballast also holds ties in place to strengthen the roadbed as a whole.

On the Great Western, only a few miles of line were adequately ballasted when it was opened in January 1854. Three of the deepest cuttings were little more than trenches, with steep sides and grades from five to twelve feet above the intended level. John Clark was not alone among the railway staff in his opinions about the dangerous condition of the railway when opened. During the Parliamentary inquiry that would occur a year later, after a spate of accidents causing death and disfigurement to employees and the public, William Bowman, Great Western mechanical superintendent, would testify that the cuttings were in "a most dangerous state, that there was no proper drainage, and the mud accumulated on the track in such a way as to make it hazardous to run trains." Some cuttings had mud three feet deep! Trains, on occasion, had to be divided because the slime was too heavy for the underpowered locomotives of the era to pull them out intact.

Other glaring defects included unmarked and unguarded grade crossings and incomplete fencing along the right-of-way (ROW). The latter invited livestock to stray onto the ROW and led to train-livestock collisions, which had adverse consequences for both participants. When faced with horses or cattle on the ROW, engineers usually chose to run them down rather than stop and drive them away. The end result of dead animals and irate owners would lead to a public relations nightmare. In some cases derailments would occur, with loss of life and serious injury resulting. In fact, over an approximate seven-month period (December 12, 1853–July 6, 1854), three such derailments occurred, leading to a total of fourteen fatalities (one employee, thirteen passengers) and twenty-eight injuries. These will be covered in this chapter.

Just two months before opening, the crossing at Twelve Mile Creek at St. Catharines broke when the embankment slumped five and a half feet through the crude foundation on which it had been built over soft clay. The base had been formed as a crude concrete pad placed directly over the clay bed. On top of this, wooden planks had been laid and then the twenty-five-foot-high embankment piled on top. This poorly built structure had taken two years to build but only minutes to self-destruct. A nine hundred-foot trestle had to be rushed to completion as a temporary measure around the failed structure.

When the line opened, locomotives and cars were taxed with stressors beyond their limits, "injured and wrenched and twisted and disabled by the roughness

Niagara Falls (Ontario) Public Library.

The remains of the emergency replacement trestle across 12 Mile Creek, just outside of Hamilton, are clearly visible from the final trestle. Just two months before the line's opening in 1853, the whole structure of the first trestle (no remains are visible) began to slowly submerge into the poorly supported soil, providing ample evidence of the shoddy and makeshift methods of Zimmerman's construction company.

of the track." Locomotives were constantly in the shop for repairs. Parts like springs were so strained that they often fractured unexpectedly. The rudimentary condition of the shops made it difficult to effect repairs, taxing the ability of staff to keep the trains running.

Ready or not, C.J. Brydges had decided that the Great Western must open. Barely a month later, on December 12, the first fatalities (of many) occurred. Within one mile of Hamilton, a westbound train collided with three cows that had strayed onto the track due to inadequate fencing. The locomotive, tender, baggage car, and three passenger cars derailed. The fireman suffered severe crush injuries and died the following day. By that curious irony that seemed to haunt the Great Western, C.J. Brydges saw for himself the consequences of operating a dangerous railway — he was riding in the locomotive cab at the time. In another quirk of fate, the star-crossed locomotive that was to be involved in several other fatal accidents was the one involved in this first fatality — the *Oxford.*

Nor would all of the accidents be due to poor construction alone. A spate of accidents during the first few months of operation demonstrated that railway staff were ill-disciplined and unsuited to the responsibilities of running a railway.

Despite company regulations prescribing summary dismissal for any employee caught intoxicated on the job, drinking was a significant problem. In March 1854, near Chatham, a handcar transporting four drunken employees collided with a train, killing one and severely injuring two others. Several cases were reported of drunken individuals (employees and the public) who had passed out on the tracks and been run over and killed.

Other accidents, while not resulting in great loss of life, disfigurement, or disability, were more ominous because they demonstrated multiple breakdowns in the basic tenets underlying safe railway operations. At the end of February 1854 the *Oxford* was again featured in an accident. This one was just west of Hamilton, not far beyond the site of the horrendous Desjardins Canal bridge accident, which would occur in March 1857. A westbound train was ordered out of Hamilton without proper clearance and collided with the eastbound train headed by the *Oxford* on the Dundas trestle. Earlier in the same month, a freight train had collided with a gravel (ballast) train within a mile or two of the same location. That April a large boulder became dislodged from the steep side of a cutting near Niagara Falls, causing considerable damage to the locomotive and cars colliding with it.

Since all victims to date had been employees or trespassers, the railway was able to proudly proclaim that, after six months of operation, it had achieved commercial success without the loss of life of a single passenger. This claim would not last for long.

In the summer months, possibly due in part to the employment of higher speeds, the death toll began to rise. In June six passengers were killed in an accident that clearly illustrated the cavalier attitude of staff to operating rules and care of their passengers. This was the first accident to stimulate widespread alarm, and ultimately led to an official inquiry into the abysmal safety record of the railway.

With a huge wave of European immigration making for the American west, the railways were competing for this lucrative cargo. Many lines, including the Great Western, employed agents to recruit passengers. A party of Norwegians had contracted with such an agent in Quebec for transport through to Chicago. In early June 1854 the group was herded into a Great Western freight car (this is NOT a misprint) attached to a westbound train. Eventually, the train reached Chatham, where an Irishman confined to the same freight car complained that he had been taken beyond his stop in London. With a callous, unbelievable disregard for the other occupants in the car, the stationmaster ordered the car to be attached to the next eastbound train. The Norwegians were obviously confused by their passage back over ground that they had already crossed.

At Lobo, a town eleven and a half miles west of London, the train approached a high embankment. Like much of the railway's infrastructure, it was incomplete. There were no fences on either side of the approaches and the top of the embankment was narrow, barely wider than the roadbed it supported. Two cows had wandered out onto the tracks on top of the embankment. Obviously, there was no hope of escape from an oncoming train. Despite evidence that the cows were visible for a long way off, the engineer decided not to stop the train. He decided upon the easier course of action: to drive them off the track.

As might well be imagined, with so little of the line being fenced, there were multiple train-livestock "accidents" every week. Understandably, the farmers complained about the loss of livestock. Engineers intimated that some animals were driven onto the tracks so that compensation could be demanded when they were killed. A number of engineers made no effort to avoid livestock on the line. Many believed that if the animals were not deflected completely to one side or the other, the superior weight of the locomotive made it unlikely that it would derail — even if the cars following it would. This was, indeed, what happened at Lobo.

The locomotive *Reindeer* and tender remained on the track after the collision. The following first- and second-class cars, along with the freight car carrying the immigrants, were not so lucky. The first car teetered on the top of the embankment. The second car landed on its side halfway down the embankment. The freight car somersaulted and landed upside down at the foot of the embankment, broken into splinters. Five Norwegians and an American were killed. Fourteen other passengers were injured.

At the coroner's inquest, the railway, through its spokesman C. J. Brydges, defended the practice of transporting immigrants in freight cars, despite charging them second-class fares! In language that today would spark vehement protests, if not riots, Brydges claimed that immigrants preferred to travel in freight cars so they could stay close to their belongings, spreading out their bedding and consuming their own food. Such hypocrisy! If this wasn't bad enough, he went on to argue that the immigrants would have been no safer in the second-class coach since:

> The seats in the second class cars were very cumbersome, and had many nails and sharp points; in this case, they were all torn up, and together with the passengers [had fallen] to the further end of the car.

He argued that the poorly secured seats and exposed nails would have been as likely to cause injury to persons as loose baggage. One can only imagine what the patrons in the second-class coach were thinking when they heard this.

Over the next few months several additional incidents occurred. Later in June a maintenance-of-way employee removed a rail thirty minutes before an express was due and failed to even place warning flags up the line. Two passengers were killed in the subsequent derailment.

In July 1854 seven immigrant passengers were killed when a train collided with two horses on a level crossing at night. Brydges tried to defend the outcome by stating that at night it was impossible to avoid such events. The Commission of Inquiry ruled otherwise. They believed that the night was clear and the line of sight unobstructed. They harboured a strong suspicion that Great Western engineers continued to believe that the most expeditious manner to handle horses or livestock on the track was to drive them off with speed and momentum.

The commission unearthed several incidents that demonstrated an almost unimaginable degree of heartlessness permeating throughout Great Western management.

While conducting the inquiry into the collision with the horses, commissioners visited Thorold, where the incident had occurred. To their amazement and disbelief, the commissioners were told the lurid details of an incident that happened the day before their arrival. On December 7, repairs were still underway on the massive embankment collapse at St. Catharines that had occurred prior to opening of the railway (see previous text). The temporary trestle over Twelve Mile Creek was still in place and being used. On that day, John Donally, a twelve-year old boy, was being employed providing water to the workmen. Being summoned by workmen on the western end of the structure, he left the eastern end of the structure with a bucket of water. As it was a cold day, he had the flaps of his hat tied down to keep his ears warm. He obviously did not hear the sound of the approaching train as it rounded a sharp curve. Whether he saw the youngster or not, the engineer certainly did not blow the whistle. The boy was struck by the locomotive and badly injured, being thrown down the embankment where he was found half-frozen forty-five minutes later by a passerby. The commissioners concluded that the engineer had behaved with an unimaginably callous degree of inhumanity, neither stopping to tender assistance nor alerting the workers on the western end of the structure. The commissioners reluctantly accepted the claim of the engineer that he did not see the boy, nor realize that he had hit him. If that was truly the case, the engineer's ignorance could only be classified as reflecting gross negligence of duty, since at that location he should have been especially attentive to his surroundings.

Around this time, cholera was prevalent among immigrants due, at least in part, to the cramped conditions in steerage (third class) in ships engaged in trans-Atlantic commerce. There is little doubt that cholera was already present among a party of Norwegian immigrants who boarded a Great Western train in early July 1854. They had no idea of how horrendous their trip would become.

Within the first few minutes they experienced their first delay, this one due to the deplorable state of infrastructure on the railway. The footings of the embankment at the site of the Desjardins Canal had slipped, causing a serious collapse, which forced the railway to ferry passengers and goods around the break. On the other side of the break, the Norwegians were herded, like cattle, into freight cars, and set off. In the area of Chatham near Baptiste Creek, the extreme heat had caused a rail to buckle, leading to derailment of a gravel (ballast) train. With eastbound and westbound trains trapped on opposite sides of the blockage, the solution was obvious. The passengers of each train were exchanged and their trains were reversed. As there were no second-class cars on the originally eastbound, now westbound train, the immigrant cars were run into a siding and for all practical purposes, abandoned.

In the extreme heat and with little or no command of the English language, the now-sickly immigrants had to fend for themselves, with only swamp water to quench their thirst. When the blockage was relieved, the immigrant cars were pulled the remaining miles to Windsor some thirty hours later.

Imagine the conditions in those cars during this time. The only remotely equivalent conditions would have to be those experienced by victims of the Holocaust in the trains that carried them to the six extermination camps in Poland. Four of the Norwegians died on the day of arrival in Windsor and many more over the next two or three weeks. The final tally was thought to be as high as seventy, and included some Windsorites as well. Cramming up to forty or fifty persons, with their baggage, into one freight car in stifling heat facilitated transmission of the disease and did nothing to ease the suffering. The Commission of Inquiry ruled that the inexcusable insensitivity of the railway directly contributed to the death toll.

Before leaving this tragedy, it might be insightful to briefly review some of the testimony from various witnesses. The first of these will come from the trainman left in charge of the afflicted passengers:

> The emigrants were lying on the floor so closely packed together that witness could hardly get through. Thinks there were altogether about one hundred and fifty of them. Did not repeat his visit to the car. Did not consider it his duty to make any further enquiry about them. Did not think that they could understand him. Cannot say how many children there were in the car, but there were many.
>
> One died in the night, and was buried in the morning. Two men in the morning were taken out of the cars, and laid on some planks under

the shed; they appeared to be very sick. One, who spoke a little English, told witness that they had the cramps of the cholera. Witness did not approach them nor give them assistance; there was nothing that could be done for them.

A farmer living some kilometres from Baptiste Creek reported the following at the inquest:

> Remembers the occasion of certain Norwegian emigrants having been left in car on the railway track at Baptiste Creek. It occurred early in July, on a Sunday. The weather was very hot. Some of the French people living about there called in the morning to say that foreigners were in car on the track, and that they had sickness among them. Did not go down to the Creek to see, having a large and young family of his own, and not choosing to run risk of infection. Several of the people — the passengers in the cars — they were foreigners — believes them to have been Dutch or Norwegians — came to this deponent's house seeking for food or milk. They spoke just enough English to make their wants understood. They demanded "pred, pred." Furnished them with all they had. They appeared to be ravenous, eating voraciously. This was about nine o'clock in the morning of Sunday. Some of them eat the food up at once; others went down with it to the car, deponent supposes, to their families. They could have had no other water while at the Creek than swamp water or creek water, which deponent considers to be most unwholesome drink.

An eyewitness described the arrival of the Sunday afternoon train containing the immigrants:

> I recollect the arrival of a train of cars from the east on Sunday, the second day of July last; it was the only train of cars that arrived at Windsor on that day; it consisted of nine freight cars and two second-class passenger cars, and two or three first-class passengers. They arrived at the Windsor Station at about half-past four in the afternoon. Six of the freight cars contained Norwegian emigrants; another of the freight cars contained emigrants and baggage; the two second-class cars also contained emigrants; the two other freight cars contained baggage … there were about 600 passengers in all arrived by this train.… There was one person dead in the first of the freight cars containing emigrants in the train when it reached Windsor, and there were thirty-three of the emigrants fell upon the platform of the Station just after they got out of the cars, having been attacked with cholera.

Lastly, Dr. Alfred E. Dewson, the only physician in the village of Windsor, describes what he saw when he was called to the station to attend to the sick:

> On repairing to the Station House I found three or more cars standing there; I cannot say precisely how many cars, but the passengers had been disembarked and were scattered about; they were about 200 in number; they were all foreigners; emigrants; Norwegians, as I was told; I could not

> understand their language nor could they make themselves understood; my attention was first drawn to body of a man lying dead in one of the freight cars; he had died of cholera; I was informed that he had died that day on his way down from Baptiste Creek from whence I was told those emigrants had been brought; I forthwith gave all the attention in my power to the remainder of the emigrants; I found several of them sick in various stages of cholera....
>
> My impression is that there were no cases of cholera out of the second-class cars; those persons who fell upon the platform, after the arrival of the cars, came out of the freight cars. The freight cars are twenty-nine feet by eight feet and a half inside measure. I am quite satisfied that the emigrants who died of cholera were all, or nearly all, among those that were detained at Baptiste Creek.

The Great Western Railway attempted to remedy the poor state of ballasting by hiring private contractors. The railway would provide locomotives, gravel (ballast) cars, and train crews, but the operating costs (including crew salaries) would be provided by the contractors. Great Western employees found themselves in a strange position, caught between the railway company on the one hand and the contractors on the other. Were these individuals to think of themselves as railway or contractor employees?

The root of the problem lay in the differences in the interests of the railway and the contractors. The former, with profit in mind, had to have gravel trains operating as frequently as possible to remedy the ballast situation. However, such trains disrupted and endangered regularly scheduled rail traffic. The situation was aggravated by the absence of telegraph lines along the ROW. There was no way to communicate train movements, delays, and revised orders. The only means of communication was by use of locomotive whistles (bells were in use in this era of railway travel but not required on the Great Western Railway for reasons that will be detailed later in this chapter). This was unfortunate because ringing a bell for extended periods was the best signal to use when a crew thought that there might be a hazard but were uncertain where it was located. In contrast, blowing a whistle was usually considered a signal of imminent danger, by which time it might be too late to respond with corrective action.

The next incident to be described cannot be ascribed to fate or ill fortune. There are no lessons to be learned, no safeguards to be devised and installed. This is because this accident that took fifty-two lives was the result of an incredible degree of ignorance and arrogance on the part of Great Western employees and management.

BAPTISTE CREEK (1854)

Baptiste Creek, fifteen miles west of Chatham, was close to a gravel pit being used as a source of ballast by the local contractor G.F. Harris. Most gravel trains running from this pit were supervised by conductor D.W. Twitchell, who tended to order trains out early in the morning, even when it was still dark, in his effort to complete the work before winter. He trusted that through traffic would be passing fairly close to their scheduled times.

At 1400 hours, October 26, 1854, an express train left the Suspension Bridge on a westbound run. The train included a combination express/mail car, a baggage car, two second-class coaches, and four first-class coaches (eight cars in total). The train was scheduled to pass Baptiste Creek at about 2200 hours that night.

Unfortunately, this train suffered one delay after another. Near St. George (north of Brantford), it was caught behind a slow gravel train. Later, it was delayed by a slow freight. A locomotive breakdown occurred soon after departing London, leading to another delay while awaiting a replacement locomotive. One can only imagine the complaints amongst the passengers!

At 0510 hours, October 27, 1854 (seven hours late), the express was rumbling along at approximately twenty-five miles per hour, approaching the bridge over Baptiste Creek. It was dark and quite foggy due to the nearby presence of marshland. Suddenly, engineer Thomas Smith saw an obstruction on the tracks ahead. There was inadequate time to sound the whistle or apply the brakes in emergency mode. The express train was about to "head on" into the rear of a fully-loaded fifteen-car gravel train that had been backing toward the express train.

Conductor Twitchell, holding a red lantern (to signify potential danger and to stop), had been standing at the rear of the gravel train when he saw the express train bearing down. He jumped before the crash and survived, but a young African-Canadian helper with him died. One brakeman aboard the gravel train died when he was crushed between two gravel cars jammed together. These were the only casualties aboard the work train. Those in the express train would not fare so well.

The entire accident occurred over less than five seconds. A better result might have occurred had the express locomotive and tender remained on the tracks, such that they could absorb more of the kinetic energy of the impact. Instead, the locomotive and tender left the tracks, allowing fully loaded gravel cars to crash through, one after another, pulverizing the express-mail and baggage cars and then carrying on into the second- and first-class coaches. Only the last coach escaped major damage. As the roaring screech of tearing metal and snapping wood died down, moaning and screaming human voices began to be heard.

The crash had occurred in an almost uninhabited area. The nearest station was five miles away. Thus, initial rescue efforts would be in the hands of dazed passengers and crewmen, toiling in pitch-dark conditions without proper tools or first-aid supplies. Dawn would aid the work, but also reveal the full extent of the calamity. Men, women, and children had been horribly mangled, the details of which would be described in all its gory, ghoulish detail by contemporary newspapers, as was the practice of the era. The author will spare you from these.

Fires were lit trackside to provide light and warmth while those alive and dead were freed from their wooden prisons. Boards laid in the last two coaches provided shelter and comfort for the injured. As seen in all human tragedies, pathos, heroism, and grim humor mingled with the carnage. The November 2, 1854, edition of the *Hamilton Spectator* reported:

> A young man from the East, whose leg was terribly broken, never uttered a sigh while waiting his turn at rescue and moaned but once when being

> removed. "Must I lose it?" said he in a subdued voice, as he gazed on the shattered limb, and that was all. An elderly lady of great size, crushed beyond hope of recovery, wished not to be taken into the cars, but calmly awaited her death where she was. "Gentlemen," she said, expostulating mildly, "you will find it very difficult. I weigh two hundred and forty pounds." Her perfect coolness in such an awful moment was not surpassed on the field of Alma or in the dark of the Arctic.
>
> (Author Note: The last sentence refers to recent contemporary events — the Crimean War and the search for the lost Arctic expedition of Sir John Franklin)

The *Lambton Observer* and *Western Advertiser*, in their November 2, 1854, editions, reported on the dignified death of brakeman John Martin. With skull fractures and all four limbs broken, he refused removal from the rubble. "Never mind me," he ordered, "help those who are living, for I am done for." His only request was that he be turned on his side, so that he might die more quietly.

At least four hours passed before help arrived and the movement of victims to Chatham could begin. Forty-seven people had been killed immediately or had died during the subsequent hours while awaiting help. Another died on route to Chatham following a hurried leg amputation. At least four of the injured died in the hospital. The minimum toll was fifty-two dead. It is likely an underestimate, though, since authorities may not have pursued their tasks too rigorously, due to language barriers, official indifference to the plight of immigrants, and the race of survivors to continue westward and leave such a scene of suffering behind. Crash investigations centred upon Twitchell, the gravel train conductor, and its engineer, John Kettlewell. Why had they allowed the gravel train to proceed onto the main line at such an early hour? Were they unaware that the express train had not passed Baptiste Creek when they brought the gravel train onto the main line?

There seem to have been few rules/regulations established by the railway to avoid such accidents. In March 1854 an order with a few general rules had been issued. Gravel trains were not to venture upon the main line within twenty minutes of a scheduled train's arrival. If a scheduled train was more than twenty minutes late, guards with red flags and lanterns were to be posted six hundred yards down the track before the gravel train was moved out to the main line. Such guards were to remain on duty as long as the gravel train was on the main line.

Unfortunately, these rules were defeated by several factors working concurrently. One was the concern of the contractors that winter weather would curtail their work. Gravel trains had been ordered out at 0500 hours in the summer months. This practice continued even as the daylight hours shrank in the fall. Concerns by some railroaders that the early working hours endangered trains were brushed aside. Indeed, almost two weeks before the tragedy, a gravel train had operated on the main line almost up to the minute that a scheduled train was due. When the engineer protested, he was told to mind his own business (i.e., that the conductor was the person responsible for scheduling the train). The introduction of a new schedule on October 23, 1854, may have also led to confusion as to exactly when the express train was due.

The most serious problem at Baptiste Creek, however, was the lack of any precautions being instituted to warn of approaching trains on that particular morning. At 0400 hours on October 27 engineer Kettlewell had asked Patrick Price, an engine wiper (cleaner), if the scheduled express train had passed the switch near the gravel pit spur. Price claimed that he had heard an eastbound express pass about midnight (if so, it would have been a train that was scheduled to pass at 2100 hours). This appears to have been the only inquiry made about traffic conditions. The next eastbound train was not due until 2230 hours, while the next scheduled westbound train was not expected before 0800 hours.

Investigations and legal proceedings were swiftly initiated and promptly completed affairs in the mid-1800s. A coroner's inquest was convened in Chatham on the day following the accident. Company solicitors (lawyers) grilled witnesses incessantly. The coroner's jury withdrew to deliberate on November 2, but, after a day's deliberations, they were unable to agree on their report. Most jurors favoured placing blame on conductor Twitchell and on the management of the Great Western. In the absence of unanimity, however, the jury was dismissed and a new one was empanelled with twenty-two jurors in total. This jury reported back on November 4, recommending that the gravel train conductor and engineer be charged with manslaughter for having taken their train out in dense fog and having failed to satisfactorily inform themselves about the passage of scheduled trains. The company was merely censured for not keeping watchmen at switches and crossings. A grand jury promptly returned a "true bill" against the two men, who were incarcerated pending trial. The outcome of these proceedings is unknown.

(Author Note: Until the 1960s, grand juries were common in Canada. Cases were reviewed prior to going to trial to determine whether or not there was sufficient evidence to prosecute. A "true bill" indicated that a case would go to trial. "No bill" indicated that a case would be dropped. Grand jury hearings were finally abolished as being unnecessary given that preliminary inquiries [e.g., coroner inquests] performed essentially the same tasks. Another task of grand juries was the inspection of prisons, being supplanted in the twentieth century by Crown boards and agencies. The U.S. continues to rely on grand juries.)

This had been the final straw. The public became so indignant and strident in their disapproval of the safety record of the Great Western Railway Company that the government was forced to act. A Legislative Assembly inquiry was organized and Governor General Lord Elgin appointed M.C. Cameron and William E. Coffin as commissioners. The latter visited the sites of accidents as well as the states of Michigan and New York. They found that between November 10, 1853, (date of opening of the line) and November 1, 1854, seventeen serious accidents had occurred, all but one resulting in fatalities. In nine cases, death resulted from the carelessness or rashness of the victims, and in another no blame was attached to the company or its employees, leaving seven serious accidents being due, in some manner, to the company and/or its employees.

Their final report discussed the accident occurring at Princeton on June 24, 1854, which resulted in two fatalities and six being injured. The cause of the accident was removal of the rails for repairs, by a maintenance-of-way worker named Beemer, without display of the usual protective signals. When brought to trial, he was acquitted. The commissioners usually recommended a change of venue of a trial when local prejudice was likely to adversely affect the outcome of the trial. Unfortunately, that did not happen in this case.

The report described three other accidents that occurred due to a lack of fencing. These were the accidents on December 12, 1853, near Hamilton, in which a fireman was killed; on June 2, 1854, near Lobo, in which six were killed and fourteen injured; and on July 6, 1854, near Thorold, in which seven were killed and fourteen injured. The non-fatal accident involving the youngster on December 7, 1853, near Thorold was also reviewed. In all four cases, the commissioners remarked upon the necessity to use engine bells as a warning signal, as required under the Railway Clauses Consolidation Act of Canada. Of interest, the Great Western Railway was excluded from this act and did not have to equip locomotives with bells (to be discussed later). They also emphasized the need to sound bells at all stations/depots, bridges, and level crossings. The commissioners also stressed the need for "sign-boards of warning" at all level crossings with roads, another safety feature which the Great Western did not need to comply with for the reason previously cited.

The report then reviewed three cases, without fatal consequences, which demonstrated the dangers of operating on an unfinished line. It then finished with a review of the Baptiste Creek disaster, which left at least fifty-two dead and forty-six injured. This latter accident was also, indirectly, the result of opening an unfinished line. They felt that Twitchell's guilt was incontrovertible. In addition, the absence of a switchman at the junction of the siding and main line was negligence on the part of the company. The company was also at fault when it did not dismiss Twitchell upon hearing from Kettlewell of the unsafe conditions engendered by the previous behaviour of the conductor.

After recounting the unbelievable incident involving the Norwegian party in early July, the commissioners clearly stated that the punishment doled out to the unfeeling conductor and stationmaster was too lenient, being "little more than nominal." The commissioners also singled out the "conduct in vogue" among engineers, that is, running at and over horses and livestock on the track, for condemnation.

In summary, the report comprehensively detailed the failings of the company to complete the basic engineering responsibilities essential to safe operations before opening the line, such as stabilizing structures, establishing appropriate grades and construction gauges, providing fencing, and installing adequate warning devices. To prevent further recurrences, the commissioners recommended the establishment of a public railway inspectorate with powers to require compliance with all safety standards before granting permission to open new lines. This latter recommendation would stand as the greatest achievement of the report when, after a period of time, it was fully implemented.

In fact, once provincial and Dominion governments began providing financial support to railways in the form of grants-in-aid to the tune of up to $6,400 per mile, such payments would not be made until a government inspector ruled the road safe to open.

Although highly critical of the decision to open the railway in an unfinished state, the tone of the criticism levelled at the company was politically circumspect. The commissioners were not so polite in their condemnation of management and employees of the road. In censuring Brydges for his role in premature opening of the line, they stated:

> From information received from C.J. Brydges, Esq., the Managing Director of the Great Western Railway Company, it appears that the system of management in force at the Great Western Railway Company is unknown to those familiar with the administration of Railroads in America. The whole machinery of a complicated enterprise is not only superintended or directed, but is actually and practically worked out, or attempted to be worked out by one man. The Managing Director is not only the head but the hand to which every important duty is confided. That officer, whose natural talents, industry and zeal are universally admitted, has assumed or has had imposed on him more duties than one man can possibly accomplish.

Though the language is deliberately guarded, there is no doubt that this was a severe condemnation of the arrogance and dictatorial management style of Brydges. However, in the eyes of his absentee landlords (i.e., board of directors in England), his "natural talents, industry, and zeal," plus his ability to make the railway pay handsome annual dividends to stockholders, made the man untouchable. Far from being forced to resign after the embarrassing scandal, Brydges maintained his position until 1862 when, despite the history of his management of the Great Western, he took over as general manager of an even larger railway, the Grand Trunk.

Even after publication of the report, Brydges was vehemently non-repentant and continued to say that his hand was forced:

> I should have much preferred delaying the opening of any part of the line until the spring … that the public was most clamorous for it … that it would be hopeless to delay the opening after the track was actually completed … I conceived it better for both the public and the company that the line should be opened.

Despite the findings of the commission and its recommendations, fate, as well as the conduct of the company and its employees, would result in further carnage on the rails of the Great Western.

DESJARDINS CANAL (1857)

The Desjardins Canal was named for Peter Desjardins (1775–1827), the promoter who was practically bankrupted by its construction. The canal had been dug between 1827 and 1837 to connect Dundas with Burlington Bay, in a vain attempt to keep Dundas as a major shipping port. It proved a miserable failure, being used only sporadically until it was eventually filled in. It was still in use in 1857, spanned by a wooden bridge built in 1853 to carry the Great Western Railway tracks between Hamilton and Toronto.

A double line merged at a switch some 130 feet north of the canal. The single line then ran down a gentle slope across the seventy-two-foot-wide bridge, fifty feet above the canal.

On the afternoon of March 12, 1857, a short train comprised of a locomotive (*Oxford*) and its tender, a baggage car, and two first-class coaches was running from Toronto toward Hamilton. Crewmembers included the engineer (Alex Barnfield), fireman (George Knight), conductor (Edward Burratt), and at least five brakemen and express personnel. About ninety-five passengers were aboard the two coaches.

At 1610 hours, as the train approached the canal, it was waved through via a green flag. David Crombie, one of several railway employees standing at the switch, jumped aboard the last coach, intending to ride it to Hamilton. Despite later assertions that the train was proceeding too fast, the ease with which Crombie jumped aboard and subsequently jumped off the coach indicated that the train was only moving at about six miles per hour, a reasonable speed. This would also mean that about one and a half seconds would have elapsed from the locomotive's passage over the switch until it started over the bridge itself.

Later testimony revealed that several witnesses felt a distinct "shock" as the train ran over the switch. This was followed by severe bumping, indicative of one or more cars being derailed. A few passengers and crewmen leaped clear before their cars reached the bridge. Two survivors claimed that the conductor tried to uncouple the last coach from the consist, but Burratt denied doing this, as did the surviving brakeman. This story is one among several where recollections differed among witnesses.

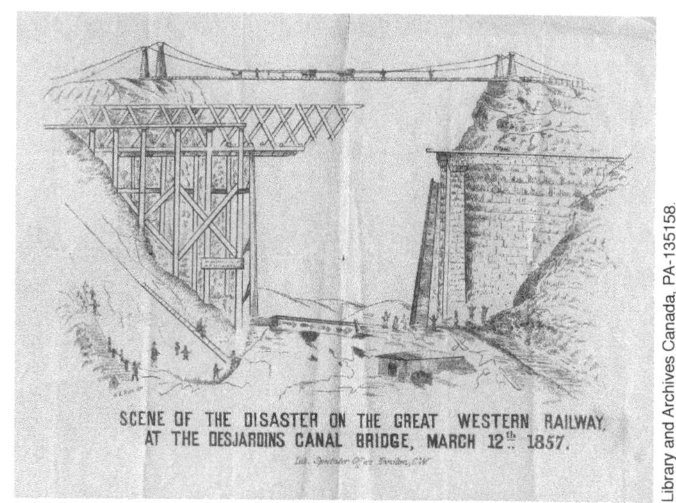

SCENE OF THE DISASTER ON THE GREAT WESTERN RAILWAY,
AT THE DESJARDINS CANAL BRIDGE, MARCH 12th 1857.

A saltwater paper print of the accident scene at the canal.

Library and Archives Canada, PA-135158.

A photograph of the accident scene at the Desjardins Canal on March 12, 1857.

Archives of Ontario, I0006719.

What is evident is that by the time *Oxford* was on the bridge its pilot wheels, and probably driving wheels, were off the rails, chewing through the wooden superstructure of the bridge. The engineer applied the whistle one time, probably for brakes, before the locomotive descended through the bottom of the bridge and plummeted into the frozen twelve-foot-deep canal. During its plunge, the locomotive rolled 180 degrees, its light, smokestack, whistle, steam and sand domes, and cab roof entering the water first. The tender and cars followed the locomotive in its deadly plunge.

Richard Jessup, a passenger in the last coach, jumped while it was still on the stone abutment. He saw the front truck and forward portion of the coach hanging over the abyss for but a moment before it descended to the canal.

Survivors told similar stories of jerks, whistles, and coaches crashing downward. Some kept to their seats while others were hurled to the front of the coaches. Most victims were likely killed by the impact, but a few drowned as icy waters rushed in. Edwin Richardson, an off-duty employee who had been sleeping in the baggage car, was awakened by the sensation of freefall then felt icy water around himself. His immediate fear was being crushed by the following car. A postal clerk intent on salvaging the postal bags was convinced by Richardson to exit the car.

Either fifty-nine or sixty people were killed in this accident. Almost all of the survivors were injured. Although most victims were just ordinary Canadians, one was a major public figure. Samuel Zimmerman, forty-two years old, had been a prominent businessman and railway promoter, with the Great Western Railway itself being one of his major "employers." His activities with regard to the Great Western Railway have been detailed previously in the introduction and chapter 2.

A coroner's inquest was convened in Hamilton and met until April 7. Jurors examined the damaged bridge, a scale model of the structure, a similar bridge over the Welland Canal, and witnessed the raising of the locomotive. Testimony was received from many witnesses. As expected, provincial newspapers sniped at each other, based on their railway loyalties. The Toronto *Leader* (a supporter of the Grand Trunk) was highly critical of the Great Western, suggesting negligence in bridge building and maintenance of locomotives and rolling stock. The *Hamilton Daily Spectator* and *Semi-Weekly Spectator* (supporters of the Great Western) staunchly defended the Great Western against its commercial rivals.

Two subjects were uppermost in the minds of investigators and jurors: the locomotive and the bridge. All parties agreed upon the sequence of events and causation. Wherever the axle was created (Great Western's Hamilton shops or Schenectady, New York, location of the locomotive's builder), deep inside the metal, invisible to the naked eye, there was a flaw. This was always a potential danger in primitive iron castings. This flaw was not revealed in the "hammer test," wherein a dull sound from a hammer tap connotes fracture or other flaw while a high, bright sound connotes sound metal. Somewhere between Waterdown and the switch near the bridge the axle cracked clear through. However, the flanges on the rails supported the axle in its proper orientation until close to the end. At times, the two axles did not rotate in unison, wearing the edges down and burnishing them, producing the specimen seen during the inquest. Somewhere just before the switch, the right-hand wheel, close to the break in the axle, would have begun taking on an independent momentum — probably tilting outward under the weight of the pilot truck while constrained by the inside flange. The pilot truck was still supported by three wheels and might not have produced any signs of instability. However, the free end of the axle would have begun to drop down into the right-of-way between the rails. The left-hand leading pilot wheel at this point would have left the rail, dropping onto the ties. What fouled the switch is unknown — wheels or free end of the axle. In any case, one connecting rod was severed and another lower one was gouged. At this point, there may still have been no obvious sign(s) of a problem, considering that the driving wheels were still on the rails and the sounds of the pilot wheel antics were probably drowned out by the usual cacophony of sounds emanating from the drivetrain.

The stone abutment of the bridge stood a few inches higher between the rails than the preceding ties. This was likely the point at which the train's fate was sealed. As the derailed left pilot wheel contacted the limestone surface, it would have heaved the weight of the locomotive upward, pushing the driving wheels off the rails. At this point, the pilot truck skewed right, just as the engine moved onto the bridge. The cowcatcher snagged the second tie, the engine pushing further to the right, pushing and crushing ties before it. The right buffer beam then tore out the lattice structure joining the top and bottom chords of the bridge. The bridge now began to collapse, followed by the locomotive, which continued twisting to the right. It ended up upside down, partially buried in the mud at the bottom of the canal.

The baggage car was whipsawed in the opposite direction, down the embankment and across the ice toward the bay. The first passenger car, in which virtually everyone perished, ran into the open gap, momentum carrying it outward and gravity carrying it downward. When the leading edge hit the ice, the forward impetus made its bulk rise vertically and then, somersaulting, it smacked the ice roof first. The second car, moving a bit slower, tipped over the edge and landed solidly on its leading face, wedged more or less vertically against the bridge pier. The front of the car pierced the ice at the relatively shallow edge of the canal and nearly all the fittings in the car, plus all of the human occupants, ended up jammed at the end of the car in a half-submerged mass.

In terms of the locomotive, the *Oxford* was only eighteen months old. It had been overhauled in the Hamilton shops between January 20 and March 6, 1857. Between March 6 and March 12, it had run only 147 miles. On the morning of the accident, it had been checked in Toronto, albeit by a rather crude test for the soundness of metal, i.e., "by eye and hammer." This, however, was the available contemporary method for assessing metal fatigue. It was clear that the fracture had been abrupt, since no rust was found at the break. At what point the right pilot wheel fell off was undetermined.

Discussions regarding the bridge were more contentious. Although not a very old bridge, the bolted wooden beams had been strengthened in August 1856. On February 14, 1857, a freight car had derailed on the bridge, causing minor superficial damage, which had been repaired. However, the visual remnants of this damage made it difficult to reconstruct the March 12 tragedy and decide exactly where the *Oxford* had begun to derail. One bit of irony was the fact that the carpenter doing the repairs after the February accident was a passenger in the first coach of the ill-fated train on March 12 and lived to talk about it!

Although the majority of experts considered the bridge to be of adequate strength (i.e., it could carry up to four times the weight of the usual train of 125 tons or less), one expert dissented. Frederick P. Rubridge, Department of Public Works, claimed that the bridge had inherent weak spots and was built using poor materials. He produced samples of wood rot that all of the other engineers had seemed to have overlooked. He testified that the bridge was a virtual "catastrophe-in-waiting" before March 12. However, by April 4, he had moderated his views, declaring "I consider the bridge safe, but only barely so."

Here is the tombstone of the engineer (Alexander Burnfield) and fireman (George Knight) of the Great Western 4-4-0 *Oxford*, killed on the late afternoon of March 12, 1857. The brass locomotive sculpture would remain on the monument until stolen in the 1930s.

Library and Archives Canada, PA-189177.

In the final report, jurors found little fault with the technical maintenance of the *Oxford*. The *Oxford* had been maintained properly and the fractured axle could not have been foreseen. With regard to the bridge, comments were a compromise between the unhappy Rubridge and the other more optimistic members of his profession. The bridge was felt to be

> of sufficient strength for the conveyance of the traffic of the line safely and securely over the said bridge ... provided that the locomotive ... and cars remain on the railway track but ... was not built of sufficient strength to sustain engine and a train in case they should run off the track while passing over the said bridge.

In their conclusion, jurors recommended construction of a "permanent" (i.e., iron or steel) bridge over the canal capable of carrying a double line, this latter aspect to eliminate the need for a switch, which some felt was a dangerous device so near a bridge. They also called on the Great Western to obey a law that it technically did not have to obey, i.e., the law mandating that all trains come to a complete stop before crossing a drawbridge. Had the locomotive come to a complete stop on March 12, 1857, the break in the axle likely would have declared itself and the tragedy may have been prevented. It is more than a bit ironic that the individual who lobbied for the exclusion of the Great Western Railway from the act promoting safe railway operation (including stopping before a drawbridge) would die as a result of his lobbying efforts.

One may ask how the Great Western Railway was able to circumvent the requirements of the Railways Protection Act and Railway Clauses Consolidation Act federal dictates. Simply stated, it obtained an extension to its charter that allowed it to do so. The 1855 act amending the company's charter contained the fateful section XXIV, quoted in full:

> And whereas it is doubtful whether the sixth section of the Statute passed in the sixteenth year of Her Majesty's Reign, instituted, an act in addition to the general Railway Clauses Consolidation Act, was intended to apply to the Great Western Railway; And whereas the only draw-bridges on the line of the said Railway are so situated in regard to their proximity to Stations, and other circumstances, that it is not considered necessary that the said sixth section of the said act should apply to the said Railway: Be it therefore enacted and declared, that the said sixth section of the said last mentioned act was not intended to apply, nor shall the same apply or be in force in regard to the said Great Western Railway, in so far as respects to the Bridge over the Desjardins Canal, nor to any swing-bridge whilst the navigation is closed; any thing in the said Act contained to the contrary notwithstanding.

Astounding! Not only does an act of Parliament absolve one single company from a law applied to all similar companies, but it is worded to suggest that the original legislation had never been intended to apply to that company and, above all, not to that company's bridge over the Desjardins Canal.

How did this legislation come about? The Great Western was seeking legislative authority to double-track its single-track main line. The company turned to Samuel Zimmerman to use his skills of persuasion to secure legislative approval. For his services, Zimmerman demanded and received the first right of refusal on the double-tracking construction contract. As an additional favour, he lobbied for the inclusion of the infamous Section XXIV into the act. The double-tracking did not take place for a number of years, so he would never profit from his lobbying efforts. The act stood, the accident was not averted, and Samuel Zimmerman died.

In the case of the Great Western, this bridge would be rebuilt as a standard iron bridge that did not need to move to allow ships to pass due to its higher elevation over the water. Despite this, for a few months, passenger trains proceeding over the new Desjardins Canal bridge would stop to allow nervous passengers to cross it on foot. Few took advantage of this opportunity.

The Desjardins Canal wreck was only slightly worse than that at Baptiste Creek, in terms of absolute number killed. However, in terms of proportions involved, it was much worse (Desjardins Canal about 60 percent, Baptiste Creek about 14 percent). Only one other accident was worse in Canadian railway history. It would occur eight years later (1864) along the Grand Trunk Railway. It, too, would involve a bridge — Beloeil, Quebec, June 29, 1864 — and ninety-nine souls.

As an aside, the disaster at Desjardins Canal on March 12, 1857, began a new era in documentation. For the first time in history, photography was used to document a terrible accident. Photographs would be published in newspapers for consumption by the public. In addition, photographs served as the basis for many engravings illustrating the disaster. Under orders of a Mr. Richards (a barrister acting on behalf of the Crown under orders from the Board of Works), photographs were taken of every fracture in the timbers of the bridge. This marked the first time that photography was used as a forensic tool in a coroner's inquest and in an accident investigation by a department of the Dominion government. Photographs were also taken of the faces of the "unclaimed dead," to be used in facilitating their identification and return to their loved ones. The effectiveness of this process for victim identification was never really tested here, since all but one of the victims had been identified and "claimed" for burial. However, a precedent had been set. Photography, with dissemination to the public by a number of ways, had begun to be used in victim identification. Photography came of age during documentation of the Desjardins Canal disaster in March 1857.

KOMOKA (1874)

During the nineteenth century some railway practices were considered downright dangerous. On the evening of February 28, 1874, the consequence of one of these practices would be experienced on a Great Western Railway train running west out of London, near the village of Komoka.

A frequently used railway practice at that time was the "accommodation train," made up by stringing together cars and coaches differing greatly in function and construction. In western Ontario, the most common of these so-called "mixed trains" comprised several oil tank cars coupled to a baggage car and one or two passenger coaches. With oil wells near Petrolia and Wyoming and refining facilities in London, it is no wonder that such mixed trains were seen so frequently on the Great Western.

Dominion law stipulated that on passenger trains there should be a device to allow conductors to transmit emergency signals from the end of the train to the engine crew. This meant running a bell rope the entire length of the train. On freight and "accommodation" trains this proved to be troublesome indeed. Crews complained about ropes snagged or severed on tank cars and sometimes whipping under the train while in motion, fouling the axles. In fact, a Great Western brakeman had fallen under a moving train and lost both legs while trying to free a tangled bell cord. The railway formally recognized this problem in 1870 when it published a regulation allowing crews of long freight trains to dispense with bell cords. Bell cords were still mandatory on Great Western passenger trains.

"Accommodation" or mixed passenger-freight trains were neither pure passenger nor pure freight trains. Theoretically, because passengers were carried on these trains, bell cord devices should have been mandated, no matter the type(s) of freight car(s) in the consist. However, Great Western crews adopted the procedure of disconnecting the bell cord while tank cars were in the consist, reconnecting it once the tank cars had been dropped off.

This procedure was never approved by any company official, but stationmasters were aware that it was being used routinely. It does not seem that knowledge of the problem and its risky solution ever made its way to middle and senior levels of management, at least not before March 1874.

The train dramatizing this problem and its dangerous solution comprised a locomotive with tender, three oil tank cars, one baggage car, one second-class smoker, and one first-class coach (six cars in total). It departed from London for Sarnia at 1828 hours on February 28, 1874. About sixty passengers were aboard, most sitting in the rear coach. The train ascended a long grade then began a descent toward Komoka station. Speed estimates vary widely, from twenty-five to forty miles per hour. The most likely speed appears to have been about twenty-five miles per hour, judging from survival rates amongst those injured who jumped off.

At this time, trains were lit with kerosene lamps, some being secured to the walls with a spring clamp. One such lamp was in the bathroom of the first-class coach. As the train proceeded westward, this lamp exploded or fell, starting a fierce fire in the tiny compartment.

Accounts of discovery of the fire vary. Conductor John Mitchell stated later that he saw a disturbance among passengers, which he took to be a fight. Instead, they were milling about the open door of the burning bathroom compartment. Attempts to smother the blaze using cushions had no effect. Mitchell closed the door and shouted that everything was under control. This, of course, was NOT true. Nobody was quite sure what to do. Panic was overcoming everyone. Had two doors been kept closed (i.e., the front door of the coach and the bathroom door), the fire may have remained confined to a small space. However, passengers repeatedly opened the bathroom door to combat the fire unsuccessfully. A strong draft whipped up the flames and the blaze spread down the coach. Few tried to break through the flames and escape to the smoker ahead of them. Most crawled to the rear, jamming the platform and clinging to railings until smoke, desperation, or the crush of other passengers drove them to drop or jump off.

A major problem was the lack of a bell cord with which to signal the engine crew to stop the train. An attempt by a brakeman to uncouple the burning car failed. Conductor Mitchell was nearly frantic since one of his daughters was among the passengers. He ordered brakeman William Burke to climb car-by-car to the locomotive. Burke ventured out, but turned back, fearful of falling beneath the train to certain death.

Mitchell took charge at this point. Climbing aboard the smoker, he made his way to the baggage car and then leaped upon an oil tank car. He scrambled along the tank car until he could leap upon the next tank car. He repeated this process until he could shout into the engine cab. Engineer George Williams immediately brought the train to a complete stop. It was estimated that it took Mitchell two minutes to clamber along the train to the locomotive and another minute to bring the train to a stop.

Once the train was completely stopped, brakeman Burke seized a lantern and started running down the track, ready to flag down the following Windsor-bound train. Mitchell, unaware of Burke's actions, also raced down the line with the same purpose in mind. Fortunately, although not far behind, the Windsor-bound train was stopped some forty car lengths from the burning coach.

By all estimates, the fire had begun when the train was about four miles from Komoka and the train was halted approximately two and a half miles from Komoka. Dozens of people lay along the line, bruised and battered from their escape. Seven bodies, including those of a mother and her three-month-old infant, were taken from the burned-out coach. London newspapers described the charred remains in graphic detail. Over the next two weeks, three more passengers succumbed to their injuries, providing a final death toll of ten individuals.

An inquest was opened on March 2, 1874. Considerable attention was paid to the lamp starting the fire. Less concern was given to the car coupling. Some witnesses said that it should have been easy to release the burning coach from the train. Obviously, it was not simple that night and there was no probing of the coupler's mechanics.

Understandably, the bell rope issue most occupied the jury. The problem of snagging/severed bell cords on tank cars was explained, but was not allowed to stand as an excuse. Obviously, the practice of disconnecting bell cords on mixed trains with tank cars was widespread. In the Windsor-bound train immediately following the Sarnia-bound train, the consist also contained tank cars and the bell cord was similarly disconnected that evening.

Jurors were scathing in their indictment of those involved. They urged that the government pass a law to ban the use of kerosene lamps on trains. They censured the Great Western Railway management for not inquiring about the degree to which employees were following rules/regulations. It was recommended that Mitchell, Williams, and Burke be charged with manslaughter for what was considered to be criminal negligence in not having a functioning bell rope connected the full length of the train. This last point aroused response by several newspaper editors. The *Sarnia Canadian* declared that the three men were being used as scapegoats, while the *London Advertiser* agreed that the trio were fit subjects for trial but suggested that the inquest jury had been unduly harsh on the railway company.

The Middlesex Assizes met in London on May 5, 1874, with Mr. Justice Joseph C. Morrison presiding. His presence on the bench brought about questions of potential conflicts of interest. Until his appointment to the judiciary in 1862, Morrison had been a solicitor and politician with close links to railway companies, including the Great Western. The case list before him included several civil suits arising out the Komoka tragedy, as well as the manslaughter charges laid against the trio of Mitchell, Williams and Burke.

In spite of his railway links in the past, Morrison's address to the grand jury was a scrupulous description of the law. He cited statutes mandating the carriage of communication devices in all passenger trains to allow conductors to contact engineers. He quoted other laws outlining the responsibilities of train crews. A close reading of his remarks suggests that he was clearly steering the grand jury toward bringing in a "true bill" of indictment, which would have let the criminal cases proceed to trial. However, on May 8, 1874, the grand jury returned a conclusion of "no bill," thus derailing the criminal cases.

Accidents, of course, were not limited to Great Western rails and happened on both sides of the U.S.-Canada border. Presented herein are details of two accidents occurring on the Detroit and Milwaukee in 1873.

Michigan's first serious train wreck occurred on the Detroit and Milwaukee line on Friday, August 29, 1873. Before dawn, the westbound night express stopped about a mile east of Muir after the loss of a driving wheel. The flagman proceeded to the rear of the train to protect it from a following freight train. He went back the required eight hundred yards and stopped, although he knew that the train was on a downgrade and would likely need more room to stop. The freight train engine personnel saw him. Despite reversing the locomotive and having hand brakes set, the crew could not stop the freight train in time and it ploughed into the rear of the passenger train. Two mothers and two children, all Icelandic immigrants, perished. Fourteen others (eleven from Iceland) were injured. A coroner's jury determined that eight hundred yards was not sufficient to protect trains on a downgrade and found the flagman criminally liable for not proceeding further down the line. In addition, all of the crew of the freight train were found to be negligent to some degree.

Only two weeks later (Monday, September 15, 1873) another wreck on the Detroit and Milwaukee ended in death for four passengers (two, instantly; two, weeks later) and injuries for fourteen passengers. Similar to the many incidents first recorded almost twenty years earlier on the Great Western, a cow, coming through a broken fence, was struck by the westbound Detroit and Milwaukee day train two miles west of Lowell. The locomotive remained on the rails, but several cars derailed leading to the fatalities. Fortunately, this was the end of serious wrecks on the Detroit and Milwaukee and its successor, the Detroit, Grand Haven, and Milwaukee.

It is interesting to note the rapidity with which civil court cases were conducted in this bygone era, when several could be handled in a single day. In Hooper versus the Great Western Railway, Ebenezer Hooper was awarded $250 for minor injuries suffered at Komoka. The case of Munro versus the Great Western Railway was more complex. Hugh Munro, a store clerk, suffered severe, crippling injuries as a result of the Komoka incident. He sought damages of $10,000. The Great Western offered him $450. The civil jury awarded him $1,450, a considerable sum in those days (more than two years' wages).

Dunne versus the Great Western Railway involved W. Dunne, whose seventeen-year-old daughter, Harriet, had died in the fire at Komoka. The father sought $1,000 in damages on the basis that he had lost the services that his daughter would have rendered him up to her twenty-first birthday. After considerable legal argument, the jury concluded that the Great Western did not owe anything to Mr. Dunne.

The last civil case related to the Komoka tragedy was that of Ryan versus the Great Western Railway, heard on May 8. Mrs. T. Ryan had sustained injuries to her head and hips. These had healed, although she still suffered from headaches. The company offered $300 in damages, which the civil jury increased to $600.

Table 6-1 illustrates a compilation of newspaper reports mentioning Great Western locomotives involved in accidents between 1854 and 1882. There were thirteen accidents involving thirteen Great Western and one foreign (Erie and Ontario) locomotives, with two Great Western locomotives each being involved in two separate accidents (#205 and #73/#30 *Medusa*). The number of events of Great Western locomotive damage/destruction in these thirteen accidents totalled seventeen. The accidents could be classified as locomotive wrecked (N=4), locomotive involved in a collision (N=7), locomotive destroyed by fire (N=5), and equipment failure (N=1 [firebox]).

Accidents on the Great Western Railway did not end with these incidents. Certainly they did become less frequent and less associated with death, injury, and disability. They were also less frequently associated with misbehaviours of railway employees and/or problems with railway infrastructure. But they still happened. Table 6-2 illustrates newspaper accounts of accidents on the Great Western, those reviewed in this chapter and additional accidents that could not be reviewed due to space considerations.

The Great Western had the dubious distinction of being the first Canadian railway to be victimized by train robbers on November 14, 1874, when five armed men stole approximately $45,000 from the Hamilton-to-Toronto afternoon passenger train. At about 1700 hours, shortly after departing from the Port Credit depot, an armed man entered the rear (train-side) door of the baggage-express car. Simultaneously, four armed men burst through the front (tender-side) door. The bell rope to the locomotive had been cut to prevent signalling the engineer to stop the train. All five men were disguised, with masks covering their faces and beards and white smocks similar to Ku Klux Klan robes covering their clothing. The baggageman (Montgomery) and American Express messenger (Dundon) were subsequently bound and gagged. Finding the key to the strongbox, seven valuable packages were quickly confiscated. When the train slowed at the junction of the Great Western and Toronto, Grey, and Bruce Railways, the robbers made their escape. The theft was not discovered until the train had stopped at the Queen's Wharf in Toronto. Collusion with Great Western employees had not been ruled out (*Globe and Mail*, November 14, 1874). In December 1874 American Express provided a $20,000 reward for information leading to the arrest and conviction of the five robbers.

TABLE 6-1. SUMMARY OF MEDIA REPORTS OF GWR LOCOMOTIVES DAMAGED/DESTROYED IN ACCIDENTS (IN CHRONOLOGICAL ORDER BY ASCENDING DATE)

Locomotive (#, name, wheel arrangement)	**Date (month/year)**	**Comments**
#38, *Jupiter*, 4-4-0	8/1854	Destroyed in a fire at St. George station
#27, *Reindeer*, 4-4-0	10/54	Collided with work train headed by #26, *St. Lawrence*
#5, *Hamilton*, 4-4-0	9/1855	Wrecked at Ingersoll
#7, *Middlesex*, 4-4-0	12/1855	Collided with Erie & Ontario locomotive *Niagara*
#42, *Firebrand*, 2-4-0	2/1857	Wrecked at Jordan
#s 72 (*Medea*, 2-2-2), 73 (*Medusa*, 2-2-2), 79 (*Erebus*, 0-6-0), unidentified Norris product	4/1859	Burned in fire in Windsor engine house
#20, *Wentworth*, 4-4-0	8/1860	Blew off firebox on Desjardins Bridge
#30, *Medusa*, 4-4-0	8/1870	Wrecked at Baptiste Creek
#78, *Pollux*, 0-6-0	9/1872	Wrecked in Toronto
#205, 4-4-0	12/76	Collided with #118 (4-4-0) at Paris
#205, 4-4-0	12/78	Collided with #199 (4-4-0) at Winona
Dummy #1, 0-4-0	1/1882	Wrecked in collision at Humber R., Toronto

TABLE 6-2. NEWSPAPER ACCOUNTS OF ACCIDENTS ON THE GREAT WESTERN RAILWAY[a]

Covered in text	Additional accounts
1853 December 7, Thorold	
1853 December 12, Hamilton	
	1854 February 5, Junction Cut
1854 March, Desjardins Canal	
1854 June 6, Thorold	
1854 June 24, Princeton	
1854 June, Komoka	
1854 July, Thorold	
1854 July, Baptiste Creek (Immigrants)	
1854 October 27, Baptiste Creek	
1854 December 7, 12-Mile Creek	
	1855 September 3, Ingersoll
	1855 December 16, Niagara Falls
	1856 June 30, Galt
	1856 October 10, London
	1856 October 17, London
	1856 October 22, Ingersoll
	1857 January 8, Junction Cut
	1857 January 15, Dorchester
1857 March 12, Desjardins Canal	
	1857 September 8, Beachville
	1859 March 19, Dundas
	1864 January 12, Port Stanley
	1866 December 31, Komoka
	1867 March 28, Woodstock
	1870 October 19, Newbury
	1871 January 21, Hamilton
	1871 January 23, Oakville
	1871 October 2, Ingersoll
	1872 April 10, Hamilton Junction
	1872 April 25, St. Davids
	1872 June 30, London
	1872 August 24, Copetown
	1872 October 30, Beamsville
1873 January 3, Windsor	
1873 May 30, Belle River	
	1873 June 3, Copetown
1873 August 15, Belle River	
	1873 August 21, Welland Canal
1873 August 29, Windsor	
1873 August 29, Muir, MI (D&M)	
	1873 August 30, Thamesville
1873 September 15, Lowell, MI (D&M)	
	1873 September 17, Stoney Creek
1874 February 28, Komoka	
	1875 August 30, Baptiste Creek
	1876 May 19, Hyde Park
	1876 August 14, Woodstock

	1876 October 6, Paris
	1877 March 30, St. George
1877 October 11, Windsor	
	1878 November 24, Winona
1879 December 18, Belle River	
	1882 June 22, Hamilton

[a]Only date and location are provided.
D&M = Detroit and Milwaukee Railway
With thanks to Mr. Carl Riff for providing the additional accounts (written communication by Don McQueen, March 2014).

EPILOGUE

The business/financial failure of the Great Western Railway came about because the directors had committed eight grave errors:

- Committed short-term to a disastrous Lake Ontario steamship service, which was not integrated into or complementary to the primary purpose of the company (i.e., providing east-west transportation of passengers and freight within Canada). Indirectly, was committed long-term to the disastrous Lake Michigan break-bulk steamship service of its U.S. subsidiary.
- Provided high-level ongoing financial support to a weak foreign (U.S.) railway without having in place a plan to fully integrate the two lines, such that the Detroit and Milwaukee/Detroit, Grand Haven, and Milwaukee could become an effective alternative to the Michigan Central.
- Engaged in an offensive stance against the Canada Southern Railway from the very inception of the latter road, rather than attempting to seek common ground through diplomacy.
- Invested in atrociously expensive and unremunerative branch lines, which did not contribute to the major east-west business of the parent line. These branches (Wellington, Grey, and Bruce; London, Huron, and Bruce; etc.) appeared to be intended more to injure rival lines (especially the Grand Trunk) than to complement and assist the parent line.
- Appeared to refuse to work with other railways that were not already controlled by the Great Western, resorting to either amalgamation or lease.

- Engaged in a "battle to the death" with parallel lines (e.g., Grand Trunk and Canada Southern).
- Virtually neglected local or Canadian interests through the domineering effect of the London (U.K.) board of directors.
- Attempted futilely to secure through traffic without considering alternative strategies. Through rate wars and strategic alliances, the American lines in Michigan and New York, as time progressed, were able to slowly reduce the Great Western's penetration into the through traffic market.

What was the chronological sequence of events that led to this disastrous result? Great Western traffic receipts had grown steadily from the early 1860s to 1873. For a few years beginning in 1868 they were enriched by the southwestern Ontario oil boom after the profitable extension to Petrolia was completed in 1867. However, working expenses grew even faster. In 1863 it had cost about 43 cents to earn revenue of $1.00. Ten years later, it cost almost 67 cents. With the onset of the recession in 1874, traffic receipts fell off dramatically and continued to fall for several years. Working expenses continued to rise in the first years of the recession and never returned to the levels seen in the mid-1860s.

For the first three years of the recession, the operating ratio (calculated here as working expenses divided by traffic receipts) exceeded 70 cents on the dollar, peaking at 76 cents in 1875. From 1865 to 1873 traffic was expanding but at the expense of increasing costs. After 1873 traffic receipts nosedived while expenses remained high. The Great Western operating ratio exceeded 60 cents on the dollar for every year from 1874 onward.

The greatly increased operating ratio in the 1870s and early 1880s is not explained by increases in payroll or fuel costs, although both did rise in the first half of the 1870s. This can be illustrated by examining fuel and wage costs and traffic receipts per engine-mile.

Receipts were quite high during the first few years after the opening of the road due to the lack of competition and lucrative passenger receipts due to the novelty of this transportation mode. They then fell precipitously in the recession of the late 1850s. Traffic receipts per engine-mile peaked in 1865 at $1.79 then declined steadily until 1875, plateauing at approximately $1.00. Aggregate wages were highest in 1857, at 44 cents per engine-mile. Although they fluctuated through the 1860s and 1870s, the clear trend was a decline in wages per engine-mile to a plateau after 1874 of approximately 28 cents.

Early in the railway's history, strenuous efforts by the locomotive department to cut fuel costs saw a reduction from 10 cents per engine-mile in 1856 to 5 cents per engine-mile in 1861. Fuel costs remained stable until 1867, when wood shortages began to escalate costs. By 1873 costs had returned to 10 cents per engine-mile. This resulted in reorganization of the fuel department managerial staff and a shift to coal as the fuel-of-first-choice. One of the reasons to concentrate fuel department staff at London in the 1870s was the availability of U.S. coal via the London and Port Stanley Railway, which had been leased to the Great Western. Except during the 1873 financial panic, fuel costs hovered between 7 and 8 cents per engine-mile from 1868 to 1881. In summary, declining wage costs and relatively steady fuel costs cannot explain the rapid increase in operating ratio after 1865.

The only explanation for this result is the precipitous decline in Great Western traffic receipts in relation to volume: earnings per car-mile fell from 27 cents in 1856 to 7 cents in 1877–79 and 8 cents in 1880–81. Increased competition resulted in declines in passenger fares and, especially, through freight rates. In the late 1870s the Great Western had to run four miles to earn as much as it did running one mile in the middle 1850s. This decline, beginning in 1866, reflected the growing importance of/dependence on through American freight traffic to corporate revenues and strategy. The decline in receipts per car-mile could only be partially offset by increases in train size. From 1866 to 1879 receipts per engine-mile (interpreted here as train-mile) fell by over 50 percent, although at that time trains were one and a half times as long. In other words, no more than about half of the decline in revenue per car-mile was offset by technological or manpower changes related to longer trains. The remainder was due to rate competition.

The twin evils of collapsing rate structure and crippling debt acquired to fight off its competitors left the Great Western with only one way to survive: allow a takeover by one of its competitors.

Carlos and Lewis (1992) calculated the private (i.e., shareholder) and social annualized rates of return for the Grand Trunk and Great Western Railways. Results are presented in table 7-1. In all comparisons, the Great Western produced superior rates of return to shareholders and society. It also produced a superior rate in the unaided private return compared with that of the Canadian Pacific calculated in the same manner. In contrast, the Canadian Pacific produced a superior rate in the aided private return. Six percent is felt to represent desirable private and social rates of return. It might be concluded that the Great Western provided more desirable returns for shareholders and society than did the Grand Trunk. However, there is more to return on investment than can be calculated in this fine piece of forensic accounting.

It has been said that it is characteristic of early Canadian railways that their value or success can seldom be measured in financial terms (i.e., dividends paid or profits made). Although stockholders of the Great Western Railway may disagree, historians readily recognize the value of the railway in the growth and development of southern Ontario.

Existing towns and villages were energized, and new towns and villages were created as industries gravitated toward the hinterland of the railway. Once isolated, towns and villages reaped the reward of rapid communication with the outside world and became hubs of transshipment for the rural districts around them. These rural districts began to fill up with the tide of immigrants following the railway.

The railway had benefits not just for urban areas. Growing colonial population and wealth increased the demand for and price paid for the farmers' produce. The livestock industry benefitted especially from the improvement in transportation.

As important as the economic impact of the Great Western was to Canada, one cannot deny its profound psychological effects. Districts, once considered backwoods because of their distance from navigable waters or passable roads, suddenly found their isolation at an end. Farmers could receive merchandise or news from urban centres in a matter of days instead of weeks. Businessmen, now assured of markets and of the stability of communities, created enterprises that formerly they would not have dared to undertake.

The effect of the railway on the city of Hamilton was profound. Before the existence of the railway most of the produce of the district was sent to Dundas and, via the Desjardins Canal, to Burlington Bay. With the arrival of the railway, trade was carried past Dundas to Hamilton, leading to a decline in the commercial importance of Dundas (one of the few examples of communities adversely affected by the railway). In contrast, Hamilton rose to prominence as a great commercial centre. Another important aspect of its development was its development of an industrial base, with mills, grain elevators, foundries, and machine shops rapidly emerging. The population surged, from 10,248 in 1850 to 21,855 in 1856 to over 28,000 in 1859. During the 1850s and 1860s the Great Western became a significant employer due to its locomotive and car shops and rail re-rolling mill (the latter being a predecessor of the Steel Company of Canada or STELCO, a prominent, long-term employer in the region).

In their monograph on the Great Western, the authors of the City of Hamilton Directory (1858) might be excused for their effusive civic pride.

> The Great Western Railway has done more for Hamilton than any other one enterprise could possibly have done; and, in fact, more than all other circumstances combined, if we accept the natural advantages of her position. It is a source of prosperity which can never run dry. It is a great vein which is constantly pouring a current of life into the heart from all parts of the system. Its impulses to [*sic*] over trade are sound and healthy. Hamilton is destined to be the most important city of Canada West.

Although the tincture of time was to prove the fallacies of some of the predictions made by these authors, it cannot be denied that Hamilton was one of the greatest beneficiaries of the Great Western.

In some ways, the effects on London were even more substantial. Hamilton before the railway had enjoyed some commercial importance. London before the railway was a backwoods community, inadequately served by Simcoe's Dundas road and too far from Great Lakes commerce. Aware of its admirable location in the heart of the rich Ontario "peninsula," it was unable to overcome its relative isolation. With the arrival of the Great Western everything changed virtually overnight, with new businesses springing up and a wave of optimism for the future setting in. Population of the town soared, from 5,000 in 1848 to 16,000 in 1855. As per the *London Times* of June 23, 1854: "Wherever you go in London, the masons appear to be busy, new houses springing up in all quarters, and all rented before they are finished."

In its early planning, directors of the Great Western had debated whether to terminate the line on the Detroit River at Amherstburg, Sandwich, or Windsor. The significance of the choice of terminus is clearly illustrated by the population growth in these three communities between 1846 and 1866. Respective values for Amherstburg,

Sandwich, and Windsor were 985 to 2,500, 450 to 1,000, and 300 to 4,500. The change in municipal status of Windsor over a four-year period, being a village in 1854 and a town in 1858, indicates the rapidity of its growth. The effect of the arrival of the Great Western at Windsor was immediately evident.

> Daily trains brought in immigrants who often stayed overnight in the numerous hotels and purchased commodities from local merchants. Fortunately, there were many places to stay. The railway brought in labourers to build new homes and ambitious businessmen to invest capital. Indeed, the pattern remained similar to other countless small communities suddenly startled from lethargy by intimate connection with the east.

Many other communities considered the arrival of the Great Western to be a great turning point in their histories (e.g., Chatham, Sarnia, Paris) and its influence was widened by the later construction of various branch (feeder) lines.

The most optimistic of dreamers could scarcely have forseen the impact of the Great Western on southwestern Ontario.

> The whole district, animated by a new spirit, saw beyond the narrow limits imposed by nature, made far-flung communities more suburban neighbors, ridiculed old problems and set out hopefully to conquer the impossible. The railway, at once the symbol and the medium of that spirit, helped to break the shell of isolation and inferiority, and, more than all the turnpikes [roads] and canals combined, made Western Canada an extroverted and expanding society in the heart of North America.
>
> — C.M. Johnson, *The Head of the Lake*, 1958

Perhaps a financial failure, the Great Western was always a public asset. Although eventually succumbing to its chief competitor, during its lifetime the Great Western Railway made a significant contribution to the economic development of the Provinces of Canada (1841–67) and Ontario (1867–present).

TABLE 7-1. PRIVATE AND SOCIAL RATES OF RETURN FOR THE GRAND TRUNK AND GREAT WESTERN RAILWAYS (IN PERCENTAGES)

	Grand Trunk		**Great Western**
Private rate of return	Actual Starting Date	Jan. 1 1861	Actual Starting Date
Unaided*	1.71	2.25	4.06
Aided**	3.00	4.79	5.20
Social rate of return	2.77	3.57	6.10

Unaided = non-subsidized (i.e. in the absence of loans, subsidies, land grants, aid to construction, debentures).

*Comparable percentage for Canadian Pacific was 2.4.

**Comparable percentage for Canadian Pacific was 8.4.

APPENDIX

EXTANT GREAT WESTERN STATIONS IN ONTARIO AND DETROIT AND MILWAUKEE/DETROIT, GRAND HAVEN AND MILWAUKEE STATIONS IN MICHIGAN

Station	Railway	Current Location	Current Use	Date Built	Bldg. Material	Condition/Notes
Brucefield	LH&B	Moved to Albert St. in Clinton	Murphy Orange meeting hall	1876	Frame	Fair, retains shape
Centralia	LH&B	In situ within community	Lumber mill storage bldg.	1875	Frame	Poor (exterior sagging, falling apart), front covered by addition
Chatham	GWR	In situ (360 Queen St.)	VIA Rail station	1879	Brick	Excellent, retains many original features
Sarnia	GWR	In situ (125 Green St.)	VIA Rail station	1890	Brick	Excellent, exterior fully restored
Denfield	LH&B	Relocated to nearby Allen farm property	Storage shed	1875	Frame	Details unknown

Grimsby	GWR	Relocated to property off Ontario St. (close to original location)	Pottery/antique store	1855	Frame	Good, retains many original features, portions have been restored
Niagara Falls	GWR	In situ (4267 Bridge St.)	VIA Rail station and leased commercial space	1879	Brick	Excellent, exterior restored, RSR-designated in 1994
Tillsonburg	GWR (CAL)	In situ (125 Bidwell St. at Hale St.)	Part of Tillsonburg Station Arts Centre complex	1879	Brick	Excellent, fully restored
Woodstock	GWR	In situ (100 Victoria St.)	VIA Rail station	1880	Brick	Excellent, exterior fully restored, RSR-198 (1993)
Palmerston	WG&B	In situ (William St.)	Palmerston Railway Heritage Museum	1872	Frame	Excellent, exterior fully restored, RSR-075

Abbreviations: GWR = Great Western Railway; LH&B = London, Huron & Bruce Railway; CAL = Canada Air Line; WG&B = Wellington, Grey & Bruce Railway

RSR refers to the designation issued by the Canadian federal government under the provisions of the Heritage Railway Stations Protection Act.

Station	Railway	Current Location	Current Use	Date Built	Building Materials	Condition/Notes
Gaines	DGH&M	In situ (103 W. Walker Street)	Branch library	1884	Brick	Excellent condition, lovingly restored
Holly	D&M/F&PM	In situ (223 South Broad St.)	None	1886	Brick	Poor condition, awaiting restoration, was a joint station

Abbreviations: DGH&M = Detroit, Grand Haven and Milwaukee Railway; D&M = Detroit & Milwaukee Railway; F&PM = Flint and Pere Marquette Railroad (a Pere Marquette predecessor)

SOURCES

Angus, F. "The 'Great Western' Debentures of the County of Oxford." *Canadian Rail*, 1982; 364:147–152.

Anonymous. *Scientific American*, 1851; 7(10):74 (November 22).

Anonymous. "Steel for Locomotive Boilers." *Scientific American*, 1862; 1006(23):362 (June 7).

Arbaugh, T.A. "John S. Newberry and James H. McMillan: Leaders of Industry and Commerce." Arthur M. Woodford, ed. *Tonnancour: Life in Grosse Pointe and Along the Shores of Lake St. Clair*, Volume 2. Detroit: Omnigraphics, 1996.

Ashdown, D.W. *Iron & Steam. A History of the Locomotive and Railway Car Builders of Toronto.* Toronto: Robin Brass Studio, 1999.

Barger, R.L. *A Century of Pullman Cars.* Volume One, Alphabetical List. Sykesville, MD: Greenberg Publishing Company, 1988.

———. *A Century of Pullman Cars: The Palace Cars.* Volume 2. Sykesville, MD: Greenberg Publishing, 1990.

Baskerville, P. "Americans in Britain's Backyard: The Railway Era in Upper Canada, 1850–1880." *Business History Review*, 1981; 55:314–36.

Brown, R.R. "The Battle of Gauges in Canada." *Railway and Locomotive Historical Society Bulletin*, 1934; No. 34:36–39.

Carlos, A.M., and F. Lewis. "The Profitability of Early Canadian Railroads: Evidence from the Grand Trunk and Great Western Railway Companies." C. Goldin, and H. Rockof, eds. *Strategic Factors in Nineteenth Century American Economic History: A Volume to Honour Robert W. Fogel.* Chicago: University of Chicago Press, 1992.

Cobban, T. *Cities of Oil: Municipalities and Petroleum Manufacturing in Southern Ontario, 1860-1960.* Toronto: University of Toronto Press, 2013.

Corley, R.F. "The Grand Trunk Railway: Motive Power Acquisitions." *Railroad History*, 1982; 147:31–41.

Craven P. *Labouring Lives: Work and Workers in Nineteenth-Century Ontario.* Toronto: University of Toronto Press, 1995.

Dakin, T. *For the Directors of the Great Western Railway of Canada. Reply of the Directors to the Report of the Committee of Investigation Appointed 30th October, 1873.* Charleston, SC: Bibliolife, 2012 (reprint).

Easterbrook, W.T., and H.G.T. Aitken. *Canadian Economic History.* Toronto: University of Toronto Press, 1958.

Edson W.D., and R.F. Corley. "Locomotives of the Grand Trunk Railway." *Railroad History,* 1982; 147:42–183.

Halliday, H.A. *Wreck! Canada's Worst Railway Accidents.* Toronto: Robin Brass Studio, 1997.

Hilton, G.W. *The Great Lakes Car Ferries.* Berkeley, CA: Howell-North, 1962.

Hodges, M.H. *Michigan's Historic Railroad Stations.* Detroit: Wayne State University Press, 2012.

The International Railway and Steam Navigation Guide. No. 13, August 1875. C.R. Chisholm & Bros., Railway General News Agents.

Johnson, J.K. "'One Bold Operator': Samuel Zimmerman, Niagara Entrepreneur, 1843–1857." *Ontario History*, 1982; 74:26–44.

Keefer, S. *Report of Samuel Keefer, Esq., Inspector of Railways, For the Years 1859 and 1860.* Toronto: Board of Railway Commissioners, 1861.

Keefer, T.C. *Philosophy of Railroads and Other Essays.* Montreal: John Lovell, 1850.

Lavallee O., and R.F. Corley. "The Grand Trunk Railway: A Look at the Principal Components." *Railroad History*, 1982; 147:19–30.

Lehmann, F. "A Thorough Man of Business: Daniel C. Gunn, Pioneer Canadian Locomotive Builder." *Railroad History*, 1987; 156:30–53.

Lepkey, G., and B. West. *Canadian National Railways: An Annotated Historical Roster of Passenger Equipment 1867–1992.* Ottawa: Bytown Railway Society, 1995.

Magee, J. *A Scandinavian Heritage. 200 Years of Scandinavian Presence in the Windsor-Detroit Border Region.* Toronto: Dundurn, 1985.

McQuade, R., and A. Merrilees. *From Wood to Steel: Classic Canadian Railway Passenger Cars from 1860 to 1920.* Toronto: Martin Grove Press, 2003.

McQueen, D.R. *Canadian National Steam! A Locomotive History of the People's Railway.* Montreal: Railfare DC Books, 2013.

Mitchie, R.C. "The Canadian Securities Market, 1850–1914." *Business History Review*, 1988; 62(1):40 (Spring).

Nicholls, R.V.V. "The Erie and Ontario Rail Road." CRHA News Report, 1961; No. 118: 3–7.

Porter, H. "Railway Passenger Travel." *Scribner's Magazine*, 1888; 4(3):305 (September).

Rafuse, T. *Wooden Cars on Steel Rails. A History of the Crossen Car Companies, Cobourg, Ontario.* Port Hope, ON: Steampower Publications, 2004.

Redfield, W.B. "The New Fuel." *Putnam's Monthly Magazine of American Literature, Science, and Art*, 1869; 14(23):583–88.

Schwartz, J.M. "Studies in Documents. Documenting Disaster: Photography at the Desjardins Canal, 1857." *Archiveria*, 1987–88; 25:147–54 (Winter).

Siddall, William R. "Railroad Gauges and Spatial Interaction." *Geographical Review* 1969, 59(1): 29–57.

Smith, R.D. "The Early Years of the Great Western Railway 1833–1857." *Ontario History*, 1968; 60:205–27.

Spriggs, W.M. "Great Western Railway of Canada. Some Particulars of the History of the Road and its Locomotives from its Commencement to its Amalgamation with the Grand Trunk Railway." *Railroad History*, 1940; 51:6–59.

Taylor, G.R., and I.D. Neu. *The American Railroad Network: 1861–1890*. Cambridge, MA: Harvard University Press, 1956.

Thomas, G.F. *Appleton's Illustrated Railway and Steam Navigation Guide*. September 1859. Appleton and Company, New York.

Torrens, L.J. *The London and Port Stanley Railway*, Volume 1, Book 1. Self-published. 1984.

Trap, P. "The Weakest Link: The Detroit & Michigan Railroad's Lake Michigan Ferry." V. Brehm, ed. *A Fully Accredited Ocean: Essays on the Great Lakes*. Ann Arbor, MI: University of Michigan Press, 1998.

Traves, T., and P. Craven. *Labour and Management in Canadian Railway Operations: The First Decade*. Toronto: York University Press, 1981.

Trostel, S.D. *The Barney & Smith Car Company: Car Builders, Dayton, Ohio*. Fletcher, OH: Cam-Tech Publishing, 1993.

Underwood, J. "Fruit of a Poisoned Tree: The Stephensons and the Standard Gauge." *Canadian Rail*, 2002; No. 489:123–43.

White, J.H. Jr. *The American Railroad Passenger Car*, Parts I & II. Baltimore: Johns Hopkins University Press, 1978.

———. *The American Railroad Freight Car: From the Wood-Car Era to the Coming of Steel*. Baltimore: Johns Hopkins University Press, 1993.

Yates, H. "Great Western Railway of Canada." *Scientific American*, 1855; 11(5):33 (October 13).

TRADE JOURNALS, PERIODICALS, ETC.

American Railroad Guide
Appletons' Illustrated Railway and Steam Navigation Guide
Herapath's Railway Journal
International Railway and Steam Navigation Guide
Lovell's Canada Directory
The Official Railway Equipment Register
Railroad Age Gazette
Railroad Gazette
Railway Age
Railway Locomotives and Cars
The Railway Times
Scobie's Canadian Almanac
Travelers' Official Railway Guide

NEWSPAPERS

Acton Free Press
The Canadian Illustrated News
The Comber Herald
Detroit Free Press
Detroit Tribune
The Dundas Warden
Essex Record
The Globe
Globe and Mail
Hamilton Spectator
The Kingsville Reporter
The Lambton Observer
The Leamington Post
London Advertiser
The Marine Record/Review
Montreal Gazette
The Newmarket Courier/Era
The Provincial Freeman
The Sarnia Canadian
Stouffville Sun-Tribune
Toronto Leader
Western Advertiser
The Windsor Evening Record (*The Windsor Herald*)

GOVERNMENTAL CITATIONS

An Act to Incorporate Certain Persons, Under the Style and Title of the London & Gore Railroad Company. Chapter 29. Assented to March 6, 1834. Acts of the Legislature of Upper Canada.

An Act to Incorporate Certain Persons Therein Mentioned Under the Name and Style of the Erie and Ontario Rail Road Company. Chapter 19. Assented to April 16, 1835. Acts of the Legislature of Upper Canada.

An Act to Authorize the Construction of a Rail-Way from Galt to Guelph. Chapter 42. Assented to November 10, 1852. Province of Canada Statutes.

An Act to Amend the Charter of the Erie and Ontario Railroad Company. Chapter 50. Assented to November 10, 1852. Province of Canada Statutes.

An Act to Increase the Capital Stock of the Great Western Rail Road Company, and to Alter the Name of the Said Company. Chapter 99. Assented to April 22, 1853. Province of Canada Statutes.

An Act to Incorporate the Port Dalhousie and Thorold Railway Company. Chapter 136. Assented to May 23, 1853. Province of Canada Statutes.

An Act to Invest Certain Portions of East York Street, East Bathurst Street, and Wellington Street in the Town of London, in the Great Western Railway Company. Chapter 229. Assented to June 14, 1853. Province of Canada Statutes.

An Act to Amend the Act to Authorize the Construction of a Railway from Galt to Guelph. Chapter 70. Assented to April 3, 1855. Province of Canada Statutes.

An Act to Extend the Line of the Port Dalhousie and Thorold Railway Company. Chapter 23. Assented to May 16, 1856. Province of Canada Statutes.

An Act to Increase the Capital Stock of the Port Dalhousie and Thorold Railway Company, and to

Change the Name of the Company. Chapter 141. Assented to May 27, 1857. Province of Canada Statutes.

An Act to Incorporate the Fort Erie Railway Company. Chapter 151. Assented to June 10, 1857. Province of Canada Statutes.

An Act to Amend the Acts of Incorporation of the Great Western Railway Company. Chapter 116. Assented to August 16, 1858. Province of Canada Statutes.

An Act to Enable the Great Western Railway Company to Connect the Oil Springs in the Township of Enniskillen by a Branch Railway, and further to amend their Acts of Incorporation. Chapter 15. Assented to May 5, 1863. Province of Canada Statutes.

An Act to Amend the Act Incorporating the Fort Erie Railway Company, and to Change the Name of Said Company to the Erie and Niagara Railway Company. Chapter 59. Assented to October 15, 1863. Provincial Statutes of Canada.

An Act to Incorporate the Wellington, Grey, and Bruce Railway Company. Chapter 93. Assented to June 30, 1864. Province of Canada Statutes.

An Act to Amend the Acts Relating to the Welland Railway Company. Chapter 89. Assented to June 30, 1864. Province of Canada Statutes.

An Act to Incorporate the Norfolk Railway Company. Chapter 58. Assented to January 23, 1869. Provincial Statutes of Ontario.

An Act Respecting the Norfolk Railway Company. Chapter 52. Assented to February 15, 1871. Provincial Statutes of Ontario.

An Act to Legalize Certain Bylaws Passed by the Corporation of the Town of Brantford, and Certain Agreements Made Between the Said Corporation and the Great Western Railway Company of Canada and the Grand Trunk Railway Company of Canada, Respectively. Chapter 55. Assented to February 15, 1871. Provincial Statutes of Ontario (including Schedules A, B, and C).

An Act to Incorporate the London, Huron, and Bruce Railway Company. Chapter 42. Assented to February 15, 1871. Provincial Statutes of Ontario.

An Act to Revive and Amend the Act Incorporating the Norfolk Railway Company. Chapter 52. Assented to March 2, 1872. Provincial Statutes of Ontario.

An Act Further to Amend the Act Incorporating the Norfolk Railway Company. Chapter 92. Assented to March 29, 1873. Provincial Statutes of Ontario.

An Act to Amend the Acts Incorporating the Wellington, Grey, and Bruce Railway Company. Chapter 82. Assented to March 29, 1873. Provincial Statutes of Ontario.

An Act to Correct an Error in the Act of the Present Session, Intituled "An Act to Amend the Acts Incorporating the Wellington, Grey, and Bruce Railway Company." Chapter 83. Assented to March 29, 1873. Provincial Statutes of Ontario.

An Act to Amend an Indenture Made Between the London and Port Stanley Railway Company and the Great Western Railway Company. Chapter 51. Assented to March 24, 1874. Provincial Statutes of Ontario.

An Act to Amend the Several Acts Relating to the Norfolk Railway Company, and to Change the Corporate

Name Thereof to the Brantford, Norfolk, and Port Burwell Railway Company. Chapter 53. Assented to March 24, 1874. Provincial Statutes of Ontario.

An Act to Amend the Acts Relating to the London, Huron, and Bruce Railway Company. Chapter 77. Assented to February 10, 1876. Provincial Statutes of Ontario.

An Act Respecting Aid to Certain Railways, and for Other Purposes. Chapter 22. Assented to February 10, 1876. Provincial Statutes of Ontario.

An Act Respecting the Galt and Guelph Railway Company. Chapter 46. Assented to March 7, 1878. Provincial Statutes of Ontario.

An Act to Amend the Acts of Incorporation of the Great Western Railway. Chapter 50. Assented to May 12, 1870. Acts of the Dominion of Canada.

Bylaws: Collection of Various County and Municipal Bylaws in Ontario Relating to the Stock and Debentures in aid of the Wellington, Grey, and Bruce Railway Company. Ontario. s.n. 1867–70.

Sessional Papers of the Legislative Assembly of the Province of Ontario. No. 15. 1875–76.

Spencer, J.W. *Elevations in the Dominion of Canada*. U.S. Geological Survey. Washington, D.C.: Government Printing Office, 1884.

INDEX